House of
MUSIC

House of
MUSIC

Raising the
Kanneh-Masons

Kadiatu Kanneh-Mason

ONEWORLD

A Oneworld Book

First published in Great Britain and the Republic of Ireland
by Oneworld Publications, 2020
This paperback edition published in 2021

ISBN 978-0-86154-029-7
eISBN 978-178607-845-2

Typeset by Fakenham Prepress Solutions, Fakenham, Norfolk NR21 8NL

Printed and bound in Great Britain by Clays Ltd, Elcograf S.p.A.

The Royal Variety Performance, London Palladium, UK
© Matt Frost/ITV/Shutterstock
In the Garden, Nottingham 2016 © Decca

Oneworld Publications
10 Bloomsbury Street
London WC1B 3SR
United Kingdom

MIX
Paper from
responsible sources
FSC® C018072

Contents

For my mother, Megan Kanneh, and for my father,
A.B. Kanneh. For my sister, Isata, and my brothers, Steven and
James. Also for Stuart, and of course Isata, Braimah, Sheku,
Konya, Jeneba, Aminata and Mariatu.

Into the World

I T WAS BRIGHT and warm, with nowhere to hide. I swallowed the impulse to cower inside, willing the hours to pass. We were at the precipice and there was no turning back. The 15th May 2016 was a day that the whole family had worked towards for longer than we could remember. All of us were implicated in the collective drama, reaching its final act on a day stark with light. I wanted to pull away from the glare and tuck my children in behind me. I wanted to wear a black jumper and creep inside, somewhere out of view. My third child, Sheku, had worked unrelentingly for this moment. We as a family had listened to him, watched him play, commented on every note, every expression, every intonation of each bar, each piece. We watched him become a cellist, guided and honed by his teacher, and helped him to grow into this boy who had to fill a London concert hall with sound and meaning.

Today was the Final of BBC Young Musician. At sixteen, Sheku had gone through nine months of gruelling work to make his way through each round of the competition. Now he had turned seventeen. I thought about how and why we had started on this long road, with all the demands of daily practice and hours of unremitting focus. I remembered the six-year-old boy with the quarter-size cello and how he transformed when he touched it. The wild, active, naughty boy with a love of gymnastics, football and secret jokes with his brother would become still and almost reverential, listening to the sound that came from bow and string and hearing nothing else. The sudden concentration on his face as he touched the cello, the flow of feeling that came from boy and instrument, seemed to change both and to create something entirely new. We had no choice.

We arrived early. Sheku was already backstage at the Barbican, having stayed nearby and rehearsed for a few days. He had shared a hotel room with his Dad, Stuart, the perfect companion. Stuart was utterly involved, intensely committed, but he was also the one who could give Sheku those relaxed evenings, watching football on the TV and talking sport. Had I been Sheku's companion, I would have been a wound spring and comprehensively got on his nerves.

We all entered the cool building and there, coming out of the backstage door, was Sheku. I paused, knowing that the full wave of my unruly emotions had no place here. Braimah, his brother, went straight to him and I was grateful for that easy, big-brother companionship. My role was different, and I needed to stand back and let Sheku breathe. But he was too compassionate for that and came for a sympathetic hug. I burst into tears.

I wiped my face as Sheku disappeared backstage, aching with the effort to let him go, and we all entered the main foyer. It was crammed, loud with speculation and curiosity.

The BBC Young Musician Final is an event heady with precedent. Many major British classical musicians have emerged from past Finals, and the fact that it has been televised since 1978 has pushed it to almost mythic status. My son had made it to this legendary Final, and here we all were – Sheku's six siblings, my husband and myself – unimaginably entering the Barbican for the last concerto round.

There had been an article in *The Times* the day before by Julian Lloyd Webber, which finally asked the question that the media had not dared name. It brought to the fore what everyone had been thinking. How did a young Black boy from a state-funded school in Nottingham get to this prestigious Final? And why was he the only one – ever?

Suddenly, we were surrounded by representatives from Trinity School, not only Sheku's music teachers but also his head teacher, former head teacher and other subject teachers, all coming as a surprise to support their pupil. I was overwhelmed by this swell of belief and celebration. They had travelled all the way from Nottingham to London to gather around Sheku and cheer him on. Then Sheku's grandmother, aunties and cousin arrived. Sheku's cello teacher and some of the children's instrument teachers also came, as well as a host of friends. The luthier who had made the cello Sheku played before and during the earlier rounds was there with his wife, and other parents of musical children. This sense of companionship made me melt with gratitude.

The crowd started entering the concert hall, impressive in its width with tiered theatrical semi-circular seating and a long stage ready with the orchestra's chairs. Most of us had never before set foot in a major London concert hall. Now, we were taking our seats to see Sheku play Shostakovich's 'Cello Concerto No. 1' with the BBC Symphony Orchestra on the most important day of his life.

But this was a competition. Two other soloists were to take their turn on the stage, and they were formidable competitors. Ben Goldscheider would play the French horn and Jess Gillam the saxophone. All three were friends, and all bright with concentration.

We watched the television cameras around the hall and close to the stage with mounting anxiety as the hall filled to capacity. I looked at the faces of the six of my children who were in the audience. Mariatu, aged six, was sitting bolt upright with her braids falling like corkscrews around her face. She was wearing her favourite going-out dress and couldn't wait to see Sheku walk out with his cello. Her quarter-size cello was waiting at home, wrapped up in its dusty canvas case. It had been Sheku's and Jeneba's first cello, but Mariatu had not yet started playing it. For now, she was continuing with violin, but turning her attention all the time to the cello. Whenever Sheku played, Mariatu would move closer and sit on the floor in front of him, transfixed by the sound.

Aminata, aged ten, was sitting nervously with her big dark eyes darting round the crowds, not missing a thing. Konya and Jeneba sat next to each other, bound by anticipation. I looked along all their black-braided heads to Braimah, who was also thinking only of his brother, and Isata – sitting further along with her fellow Royal Academy of Music students. Stuart, my husband, fidgeted beside me while I sat rigid.

There is something mesmerising when a moment long dreamed of begins to unfold. We sat, our whole family, in the hushed shadows of the audience, all faces turned to my son on stage, in the centre of a fierce and magical concentration. I knew every note of the concerto. Every phrase of music had been practised, discussed at length, experimented with for months before. There had been in-depth lessons at the Junior Royal Academy. Sheku had worked carefully through the score with the composition teacher. He'd had run-in performances and consultations. Braimah had sat with Sheku for hours, focusing on the bowing, the tone, the meaning of each note and passage.

There was nothing rushed about this moment, and yet it was intensely spontaneous. Something new and unrepeatable happens in live performance and Sheku can create a new and bold alchemy every time he walks on stage. Even though I had heard every note before, I found the performance a revelation.

The conductor, Mark Wigglesworth, looked at Sheku and the sudden sound of the cello gave me a visceral shock. Sheku played the first determined bow strokes before my mind had settled. I was dazzled by the sudden fact that we were *here* and it was *now*. The unified sound of the BBC Symphony Orchestra was incredible. It was as though Sheku were leading everyone on an extraordinary journey into an expression of anguish, despair and passion. How could a boy, just turned seventeen, feel all of this and communicate it so powerfully through a cello?

Where did that knowledge come from? What was the experience that informed it? How did he know what he was playing?

Sheku turned his head to hear the clarinet and usher the sounds into the foreground. Then the horn, an alarm heavy with portent, was signalled by a tilt of his body. The power of the string section swelled through him as he leaned his head back and allowed the cello to join forces. I was held breathless with attention. I didn't dare move. I had to hold every bow stroke, feel the indent of the strings in the flesh of my fingers, hear every signal from the orchestra. If I flinched or missed a beat, the threads that held Sheku in alliance with the orchestra might loosen. It all depended on me, his mother, to carry him through.

In the interval before Sheku played, I had rushed Mariatu into a toilet cubicle. She was inconsolable, tears racing down her cheeks. 'But Mum, what if Sheku doesn't win? What will he do? I can't stand it'. At the age of six it was unbearable to her that Sheku might not achieve the prize for which he had worked so hard. What if all our careful listening, all our love, did not carry him through? I bent down to her and put my hands on her trembling shoulders. 'Sheku will play other concerts and enter other competitions', I replied. 'Playing music doesn't have an end. And we'll look after him'.

I emerged from the cubicle into the crowds of excited people who were high on delight and expectation, and smiled. I wondered if I had done enough. I had bought Sheku's clothes, polished his shoes, taken his bow to be rehaired, cooked his food, listened to him play. But the loneliness of the soloist hit me hard. On stage, bow in hand, there was only him. During the quiet movement, full of ethereal harmonics on the cello, high as whispers, and the answering notes of the celeste, I realised that it was the moments where Sheku was *not* playing that haunted me. I watched his face as he listened to the orchestra, his attention utterly absorbed. He had the gift of drawing all the separate instruments, performance personalities and phrases into one centre. By watching his face, I could see into the heart of the music.

The orchestra was coming to its biggest crescendo and the raging focus in Sheku's face and body lifted him out of his seat for the final flourishes. Then it was over. A roar filled the concert hall. Sheku was bowing, embracing the conductor. People were getting to their feet, and Stuart and I were dazed, elated, our hearts full.

Sheku walked onstage three times to bow again to the audience, carrying his cello like a talisman before him. He was the humble seventeen-year-old boy again, smiling pleasantly and without show at everyone, the dark forces of the concerto gone from his face. I was exhausted, as though I had trekked through a dense forest in the dark, alert to every threatening sound. Even though I had listened with the nervous energy of a parent who had followed each note and shift in practice, I had been transported into a new space that existed only here and now, driven into being by the energy of the live concert. It was thrilling.

In the Beginning

I WAS BORN in Magburaka, Sierra Leone, the second child of four. Although I was born in Temne country, my father was Mende, and when I was two years old we moved to Bo, where most people spoke Mende. My Welsh mother had met my father in Birmingham while she was at an all-female teaching college in Hereford and he at an all-male teaching college in Birmingham, studying to teach carpentry. Mum's subject was English and she wanted to be a primary school teacher. A dance was arranged between the two colleges and my Dad came on the bus from Birmingham to Hereford. Mum was nineteen and danced with my Dad, who had no shyness and loved to be laughing and dancing. No one would ask the stern-faced principal of my mother's college to dance, so my Dad did and she was flustered with delight. He had the gift of joining people together, of starting a party.

When he walked Mum to the bus that night, he had already made up his mind and sent Mum a letter the next day, telling her he had fallen in love. She thought this young-faced boy was a dreamer, living in a world that didn't exist and wasn't possible, but he persisted. They used to walk together through the streets of Birmingham, vilified by many. Mum told me these stories as though describing a world that was separate and skewed but which she simply ignored. They both ignored it and I marvelled at the lack of inner pain and damage, as though they had blazed through it all in a bubble of their own. But that can't have been true.

When Mum defied everyone to sail on a ship to Sierra Leone to marry my Dad, her father was convinced that she would die of fever in the tropics. She was twenty-two, defiant and in love. Grandpa was heartbroken and didn't want her to go. He could only see death like a shadow over the future. Mum had found out this young African was actually ten years older than her – he'd just *looked* young and unknowing. He knew, with utter conviction, what he wanted. And it was her. He was one of forty-five children from twenty-one wives, the eldest son of the favoured wife, and it was shocking to marry a foreign White woman. But they were young and determined and brave.

My mother sailed for nine days on the Elder Dempster Line from Liverpool docks, a line that used to voyage regularly to West Africa. The ship was full of African students returning after years away studying in the UK. There were also some expatriate British diplomats from the High Commission and one who ran the Paramount Hotel in Freetown. The ship stopped at La Palma, Canary Islands, and then Sierra Leone, before continuing to Ghana and Nigeria. The students were excited to be going home after years away, having been unable to afford return passage any sooner. A one-way ticket cost several months' salary for a primary school teacher. Mum was going to see Dad for the first time after a year apart. (He had gone to secure a job and a home for them both, communicating only by letters which took weeks to arrive.)

While on the ship, she spent time with a student who was returning to Ghana, full of joy at the thought of seeing his family again after so long apart. The day before the ship pulled into Freetown harbour, Mum went to get her hair done in the onboard hairdressers, agreeing to look after the student's camera while he joined in the friendly diving competition at the pool. Each had to dive in and see who could stay down the longest. The one who held his or her breath under the water's surface for the longest time was the winner. They all resurfaced one by one, but he never did – and would never see his home shore again.

The mixture of grief, excitement, wonder and love in my twenty-two-year-old mother's head as the ship pulled into the astonishingly beautiful harbour in July 1963 is hard to imagine. The white sands and palm trees, the density of green vegetation and the red earth rising into the hills around the coast took her breath away. Dad appeared at the harbour with his brother, S.B., and a radical new haircut ready for their wedding. Mum spent time that evening on a deserted Freetown beach with her husband-to-be, watching with wonder how quickly the huge sun went down below the line of the shining sea. They were married the next day, surrounded by my father's family, in a Freetown church, and climbed aboard a train for the interior that cut slowly through the dense forest upcountry and took them further into Sierra Leone. There were no phones and Mum was cut off from everything she knew.

After a long train journey through forests and villages, where women sold sweet-tasting fruit from the trees, she woke up the next morning in my father's village, in a small house with a tin roof and a crowd of children peering through the window at the first White woman in the family. She found out she was pregnant three months later when a woman in Grima looked her in the face and told her the news. Some of the women asked if White women were able to breastfeed like they did.

My brother Steven was the first to be born, in a local hospital in the country where my Mum gave birth with no modern amenities. The midwives went to bed at night and my mother had to stumble and crawl along the corridor to find and wake them up when she thought the baby was coming. When Steven was born, my parents proudly marvelled at how healthy, bright and happy this baby was, with the face of his father.

When Steven was a year old they took the plane from Lungi Airport to Heathrow and visited my Nanna and Grandpa, who were in Essex at the time and adored their new grandson. Grandpa phoned his sister, Annie, and suggested a visit. She announced she was far too embarrassed for them to visit in case the neighbours saw. Grandpa was furious. His other sisters, Elsie and Rosie, were warm and welcoming. (As a young man in his twenties, my Dad had collapsed on the football field in Sierra Leone, and because he knew something was wrong with his heart, he visited a doctor while in England. But he was told that he was healthy and strong – because that's how he *looked*.)

I was born eighteen months after Steven. We then moved to Bo, and my sister, Isata, and then my brother, James, were born after a gap of two and a half years and nineteen months, respectively. We were now a family of four children, aged five years and under, and my father was proud of us. He was the first educated son from a big extended family and so we had relatives living with us, including his little sister, Miniatu.

My father was a dreamer. He loved music and played the guitar by ear. All the Mende family would sing and harmonise naturally, as though it were as regular as breathing. My father chided my mother for the piano lessons she'd had as a child and didn't value now, because he longed to play the piano and couldn't understand her indifference. He talked about it with such sincere desperation that she was stunned. No one in his family played, and most of them had never even seen a piano. One time, he was sitting in a chair, eyes closed, with a look of sublime joy on his face. Mum disturbed his reverie, asking what on earth he was dreaming about now. 'I was dreaming that I was conducting an orchestra', he said.

Mum's experience of piano lessons had been with a friend of her parents from chapel, who taught her the mechanics of playing. It was piano teaching informed by accompanying Baptist hymns on a Sunday, and playing for the choirs. As Mum played the rigid chords, she gained no insight into self-expression and the meaning of music. The teacher demanded that she, at age six, practise for one hour a day. Piano practice was, for my grandparents, part of the aspiration of education. Mum was put in the cold 'front room', which was set aside for visitors and outside the warmth of the lived-in house. If she stopped to stretch her aching back, there would be a shout from another part of the house that the piano playing had stopped. She liked the piano but not the cold separation, the sore back and the sense of punishment it entailed. My father, meanwhile, a culture away from ever learning to play, framed the piano and classical music as the centre of his desires.

While my father grew up with an extended family and village of singers and dancers, my mother lived in a silent house where the piano was shut into the front room. No music records were allowed to be played and no radio music. My Grandpa was tone deaf, loving only the 'Chorus of the Hebrew Slaves' from Verdi's *Nabucco.* It was music he understood and he would listen with eyes closed. He was convinced that his ancestry was the Jewish diaspora, and equally convinced that music was a mysterious realm beyond his reach. We would all laugh when he would lustily break into song – either 'Happy Birthday', a Welsh Baptist hymn or 'On Ilkley Moor Baht At' – with no attempt at a recognisable tune. My Nanna had grown up with her father singing in Welsh all the time, and their lives were centred around the Baptist chapel choirs and Welsh songs. Every year after she was married, for her birthday, my Nanna's father would come from

Beaufort, Ebbw Vale, and collect his daughter from Newport, South Wales, to take her to the opera in Cardiff.

My parents went to dances and collected records. Mende music, Nigerian Highlife, Caribbean Calypso and Jim Reeves were all hugely popular in Sierra Leone at the time. My father bought me the single 'Fatty, Fatty' by Clancy Eccles, because I would dance wherever I heard it and he loved to see me dance.

One evening, my father came home to find my brother, Steven, missing from the house. He hadn't made it back from school and it was getting late. Being near the equator, the sun set suddenly in the early evening all year round and there were no street lights so far from Freetown. My father searched for a long time, looking for his son, getting more tired and worried as the night grew darker. Steven came home of his own accord, not realising at age five how long the extra time with his friend after school had been. When my father came home, frantic and full of panic, the relief at seeing Steven was the only thing in his heart. A few months later, his heart began to fail and it was him we began to lose. The condition was never fully diagnosed – perhaps West African hypertension – and he descended into illness, dying within a few short months.

My father had always been a focal point for me, the timeless loss that I couldn't step beyond. It seemed to me that, as a child, I was blissfully whole until he died. I have a vivid memory of seeing him in the doorway just outside, and not being able to get to him. He was dropping me off at nursery in Bo and the nuns who took me wouldn't let me escape from between their flowing skirts. He stood in the doorway, hesitating and smiling uncertainly, not wanting to leave as I screamed for him, 'Don't leave me, Daddy!' I remember having a bath with my brother and Daddy was laughing. The whole room met in his face.

Another time, Dad was asking me to scratch his back with a comb outside on the porch. The night was big and black, and I could hear the cicadas in the grass. The mosquitoes were dancing in the light of the oil lamps and he was singing. Another time, we had the white nets draped over the doorway. There was lots of shouting, and coming towards the light were the termites, big and swarming. They were trapped in the nets, a forest of brown legs and feelers. I caught some from the air to eat. When they came off the grill, they were warm and crunchy, full of protein like Marmite. But I hadn't tasted Marmite yet.

The last time I saw my father alive, he was sitting up in white hospital sheets with his wide smile. When my mother told us he was dead, the oil lamps were yellow and the smell was hot and damp. In Freetown the rains were heavy, but in Grima, for the funeral, it was hot and dry. From the time that he died and we left Sierra Leone, two months before I was five, he continued to be the most important thing in my life.

2

Departures and Arrivals

MY MOTHER CAME back from Sierra Leone with her four children, aged six and under, into a freezing November day at Heathrow, grey with fog. We lived with my Nanna and Grandpa in their home in Chipping Ongar, Essex, for four years, the five of us sleeping in one bedroom. Then we moved to South Wales, the country of my mother's childhood, and lived in Caldicot, a steel-working community where we could walk or cycle out to the hills of Wentwood, or take a short drive to beautiful Tintern.

The shock of that arrival in England at the end of 1970 never left me. On Christmas Day, our first Christmas in Britain, it snowed wonderful, impossible puffs of white that spangled into patterns in my hand. It was beautiful but so cold I couldn't believe it. We had hot-water bottles for our feet in the freezing bed, and I got chilblains all over my toes which hurt, hot and red and itching. The food tasted of nothing at all and all colour had gone from the world.

Britain in the 1970s was a cruel place to be Black and mixed race. I had arrived with my whole vision taken up with my father's face, and come up short against an idea of me which hadn't been there before. When I was in Sierra Leone, I was at the centre of the world, with no colour to my body and no shape, and I was afraid of nothing. Here, children laughed and shouted at us in the street, words I came to understand meant *us*, words I couldn't repeat because they were like broken glass in my mouth: nigger, half-caste, wog, sambo. We went to the sweet shop every week with two pence from Mum and two pence from Nanna and Grandpa. It was a treat to see the glass jars full of shiny sweets and watch as the nice old sisters who owned the shop would unscrew the lids and show the lollies with layered colours. The kind old ladies would smile indulgently at us as we chose what we would buy with our lavish four pence. One day, they began praising my mother for her charity in adopting these little Black children from Africa. Mum explained that we were her own biological offspring. They stopped smiling after that and they were no longer nice.

The lemon sherbets cut the inside of our mouths and my teeth hurt. Steven came home from school and said that we could no longer speak any Mende or Krio to each other because the children were different here. We tried to pack ourselves up and start again, keeping our father as secret as we could.

When I walked into school on my fifth birthday the class froze into silence. I stood centre stage, freakishly brown, and learned to be afraid of the mirror. We read classroom books about golliwogs and Sambo – stupid and Afro-haired and laughable. Peter and Jane had no place for me and I didn't fit into any story. When I joined the Brownies at age five I was immediately cast as Mowgli from *The Jungle Book* for the Chipping Ongar carnival, even though I was a girl and 'Mowgli's' girlfriend was a tall, blonde eleven-year-old. I was stripped to the waist and wore a snake around my neck, paraded conspicuously brown and confused through the streets. I always disliked *The Jungle Book* after that.

At home, we had our own world, our own imaginary games

and secret life. There was country cloth on our beds, raffia baskets and books, some written in Mende, which still smelled of tropical damp. I always felt that I was hiding in a secret world, with a home that was always there, warm, unreachable and separate. I loved my father with the ferocious passion of a five-year-old girl, and all my memories of him and of Sierra Leone were drenched with happiness and light and rage. I could smell the oil lamps the night my mother told me that he had died, and I never stopped waiting for him to come back.

Leaving Sierra Leone and my father was a loss that formed my childhood and from which I would never grow up. When the racism of the 1970s and 1980s were at their height, I felt as though I were inhabiting a body that was rudely in the wrong place, screaming its presence when I was trying to hide. I was like a ghost walking beside a monster. I spent my childhood in a reality that was constantly split in two. There was a real world to which I was always returning, that hot path of white stones bordered by the deep red earth that led to my father's carpentry shed. I was also constantly in the doorway of the nuns' nursery, trapped behind the flowing black skirts, trying to get to my Daddy who was smiling uncertainly outside. England was the 'playroom' extension built for us by Grandpa, with the garden outside, soaked with dew or hazy with the sunshine of the early 1970s. It was our own private world where we huddled together playing our magical games and waiting for Daddy to walk in.

The landscape beyond these two secret worlds was fraught with danger. From the age of five I began to have recurring dreams of walking along the road just outside the house. I was separated from my body, watching myself walk and screaming with horror, no sound at all coming through the silence. I would regularly wake up sick with terror. The experience of actually walking along the road became one of trying to control the outrageousness of my own appearance, of my own body. I would try to make myself invisible, to push myself into smaller and smaller spaces, inhabiting the margins. But I was loudly and insolently visible, no matter how polite I was.

The mirror became a site of confrontation. I would take deep breaths before looking but could never fully anticipate the wave of shock that would hit me when faced with my reflection. I was an alien, landed from another planet, and I couldn't assimilate. I learned to feel shame. I was taking up too much space and, like a one-man band, I was making too much noise. Heads turned and people whispered, laughed or shouted when I approached. I learned that my hair was the wrong texture, my skin was too brown and my nose too wide. My sister, Isata, and I spent our time in the house with tea towels on our heads, turning our necks to swish the long 'hair' from side to side. At last we were beautiful. I agonised over Rapunzel's long straight hair. Even Minnehaha and Shanti (Mowgli's girlfriend) had long, heavy braids that didn't stick up or float softly around their heads. I was the brutish frog that no one would kiss.

Being racially set apart somehow stripped me of femininity as well. 'Kiss Chase' at school would involve all the boys chasing the girls and catching them to steal a kiss. I would long to be one of those giggling girls with straight hair who, when caught, could delightedly be the flurried object of desire. No boy caught me, and if they did out of a momentary lack of attention, they would relinquish me at once, embarrassed.

Only at home with the doors shut, my face reflected in the eyes of my brothers and sister, could I be natural. It was as though I divested myself of my gorilla costume and monster feet at the door in order to walk easily into the family.

School, church and Brownies were the world outside. Grandpa would put on his Baptist minister dog collar in front of the hallway mirror every Sunday morning and we would walk to the Congregational church for the family service led by him.

He was an excellent public speaker with a booming Welsh voice that filled the room. Even at a young age I understood that his sermons were beautifully structured, full of enlightened research and actually interesting. When I was a teenager, Nanna brought down some old diaries from the attic. One had been written by Grandpa during the Second World War amid the Cardiff bombing raids. There were some lovely entries describing the experience of being a new father to my mother, and how he had been up all night with the baby and then had to rush off to preach or to visit his parishioners the next morning. The recounting of waking up one morning covered in black soot from the bomb that had hit next door was written as eloquently and as acceptingly as that of the long night trying to get baby Megan to suck from the bottle.

My great-grandfather's diaries, also discovered in Nanna's attic, were more poetic, telling all the time about spring, nature and the beauty of the Welsh hills. This was all the more moving to read as I knew that he spent most of his life down the coal mines with black coal dust permanently engrained in the cuts and lines of his skin. He'd had a mining injury that gave him a limp and fascinated my mother because Grandpa told her he now 'had no bone in his leg'. He had studied his Greek and Latin in the darkness of the mines, lit only by an oil lamp, determined to qualify as a Baptist minister, a position of the utmost respect and status. Both of Grandpa's parents were from West Wales and Welsh speaking, but Welsh was discouraged in the schools and actively attacked. They understood Welsh to be a marker of lower status and a barrier to education, so Grandpa and his three sisters were banished from Welsh, seeing only English as a language of worth.

All the diaries disappeared before my Nanna died. We don't know why. Perhaps Nanna was embarrassed by the deeply personal memories in these diaries from her husband and his father. Emotion, sorrow, pain and love were not things to communicate from one generation to the next. The vulnerability of being young or of feeling too much could not be discussed. The Welsh language that had been driven deep into the memories of my grandparents still structured and formed much of their speech. It would form the grammar of their sentences, the rhythm of their words and the sound of their vowels. There were also lots of Welsh words that would bubble into their sentences and had become part of the English that they spoke. On the record player we would listen to *Under Milk Wood* by Dylan Thomas, narrated by Richard Burton, with Welsh actors speaking the characters' voices. This recording still sounds like home to me. When my mother began learning Welsh when I was a teenager, with the renaissance of the Welsh language, I found the pronunciation simple and obvious, the rhythms natural.

Very soon, Grandpa was the person I wanted to please the most. His presence helped me to survive not having the Daddy I still loved with absolute passion – a need that had stuck at five years old and remained untamed by age or maturity. It was a passion caught in its own eternity, without irony or relativity or balance. A part of me was forever consumed in a little girl's tantrum at being left at nursery school. I would open doors and search rooms every day to find Daddy. When the doorbell rang and I heard a man's voice, I would wonder, gripped with joy, if it was him. But so unrestrained and complete was this ancient grief that I never spoke a word of it. Thankfully, in the dizzying landscape of this loss, I had Grandpa.

He had a huge personality, full of irreverent jokes and irony, always ready to laugh or shout, and ready with demonstrative affection. From him we got tickles and teasing. He would lie on the floor and we would jump all over him and expect a mock wrestle, like cubs with an indolent lion. Up on the pulpit, he was clear, precise and interesting, gifted at meeting and greeting, full of laughter or sympathy. At home, he would often describe people in exaggerated caricatures and 'almost swear' in ways that would make Nanna tut and hush. His rise through education from his poor background in Ceri, Mid Wales, was an example of defiance against the forces of money, snobbery and class, and he always retained that sense of fighting against the powers that be and having to use all his wit and will to succeed.

Grandpa used to tell the story of his school years. He was clever but poor and had to stand up for himself. There was a bully in the playground who constantly made a beeline for him. Grandpa had been brought up tough. As the only boy of the four siblings, he had grown up digging potatoes and getting as much food as he could out of the land through hard physical labour. Even as an old man, he had a vice-like grip and a strong handshake. One day, pushed to anger by the relentless bully, Grandpa thumped him with his hardened fist and laid the tormentor out cold. No one in that school ever bothered him again.

He went on to take two degrees at Cardiff University, the first in his family to enter higher education, leaving with a Bachelor of Arts and a Bachelor of Divinity. As well as serving as a Baptist minister throughout his working life, living in Cardiff, Newport, Birmingham and Lancashire, he also became Head of Religious Education at Harlow Comprehensive School before he retired. He loved teaching these cheeky Essex boys, many of them from families moved out of London's poor East End and getting by on their wits. He recognised the sharp intelligence in a lot of them and revelled in their sense of humour, even when it was directed at *him*. He would disarm them by suddenly roaring with laughter at a subtle insult because it was witty, but quelling them with the unshakeable power of his voice and personality.

I loved him. I loved the smell of toffee-scented tobacco on his old tank tops when I would sit with him in his armchair. I loved his dark cups of tea and the way he laughed from his belly up. He puffed his pipe with complete satisfaction and dug at it with pipe cleaners, and I could listen to his stories for hours.

But for a long time after we came to Britain, there was a blank space where my mother used to be. It had started on the night she told Steven and me that Daddy was dead. We were sleeping in the room in Freetown. I remember the dim yellow light from the oil lamp and the mosquito nets around the beds. We were staying with Uncle S.B., one of my father's brothers, because Daddy was in hospital in Freetown. We had travelled from Bo to this house in Freetown and it was different. In our own house, we had Bill and Ben, the yard dogs, and they would eat the leftover rice thrown out for them. We had the path of hot stones that led to my Daddy's carpentry shed. We had the deep black nights on the porch where he was always laughing or singing. When Mummy came into the room that night with the yellow light, there was a big group of women with her and the air was heavy. There was no expression on her face and her words made no sense. 'Daddy's dead', she said, and then she put her head in her hands and turned away. I grinned and giggled because something important was happening and it made no sense. Steven stood still and straight next to me.

But we had seen him every day. Sitting up in the white hospital bed, with the white sheets, he was laughing, and he was so happy to see us. He wouldn't have wanted to leave. It was 1st September and the rainy season had not ended. The hot rain was on the back windscreen as we drove through Freetown and I saw the bright lights through the lines of running water. We bounced on the back seats and looked out at the hot night, teeming with noise. He wouldn't have wanted to leave.

It was a long journey to Grima village, Pujehun District. We had to cross the big river on a raft and there were a lot of people talking. But it was very quiet under the elders' shaded place in the middle of the village. We used to visit here with Daddy when the devils danced, wild and loud with drumming. I used to hide behind my mother in the hut for the uninitiated because these were the women's devils and Mummy was not in the women's society and not initiated. My grandfather, Pa Braima, head of the village, was blind by this time. He had been handsome, and the photo of him with my grandmother, his beautiful, favourite wife, was still hanging in the main village hut, serious-faced and stern. He had cataracts as an old man and refused colonial hospital treatment, insisting instead on the herbal and supernatural services of the medicine man, which blinded him. He was led around the village by a boy, one of my cousins, and so dread and powerful was his presence that I remember cowering behind my mother while he held court, surrounded by my relatives.

As I said earlier, my father was one of forty-five children from twenty-one wives. His own mother, Haja, had ten of those children, and my father was the eldest. Almost everyone we met in the village was a relative, and around my father there was always noise and laughter. But today was different. There were no loud voices and I couldn't hear Daddy laughing. There were lots of people but everything was quiet. Until the singing started. He lay on his back in a dark suit and his feet were in shiny black shoes. They were at the same height as my face and they didn't move. If I reached out my hand I could touch his shoes and the dark material of his trousers. His face didn't move and his eyes were shut. The women were singing but Mummy was in a place far away and her face had closed. It wasn't raining and the air was white with the sun. He wouldn't have wanted to leave.

We were packing up to leave after having stayed with Uncle Paul near Pujehun, my grandmother's village. Country cloth, woven baskets, photographs and dresses were all bundled away.

There were books which smelled of hot damp, even in Britain. 'In England it rains every day', said my friend. I walked, looking at the dry white stones and the hot red earth, and thought it must be true.

We were at the airport and I was weaving in and out of the women's long skirts. Their legs were hung with Gara cloth and there was a lot of noise and a lot of crying. We were saying goodbye and I ducked under a rope and looked up at their faces. Then we were on the aeroplane and my little brother, James, who was a baby, was swinging from the baby hammock above my head and crying. We spread out on the seats to sleep, covered in blankets, and when I looked out of the window all I saw were clouds and the aeroplane wing. We were simply suspended in air, quite still, and Mummy's face had frozen in time.

In that cold grey November air of Heathrow, when we stepped out into a world with no colour at all, the sky was smaller and further away, and Mummy was a shocked wall of silence. We arrived in this bleached world and I believed that I was the only one who remembered what had come before. It was my secret, too scorching hot to touch and indecent in daylight.

Nanna and Grandpa moved out of the biggest bedroom and Mum shared the room with her four children. James was in the cot, Isata and Steven had single beds and I was in the double bed with Mummy. She came to bed very late and I loved the warmth of her next to me. I would try to get close but she was silent. Later, after we had moved to Wales and I was in a different bedroom, I would lie in bed taut with fury. Daddy was there with her and I was left out. I couldn't get past the nuns' legs and long robes blocking the doorway, and Mummy had Daddy all to herself. But he was mine, there in my dreams, throwing armies over walls; there, in the white hospital sheets, happy to see me; there, face unmoving, under the elders' shaded canopy. In her face of no expression and in her silence, Mummy kept him away from me. I would imagine walking into the room where Mummy lay in her single bed, climbing in to cuddle her warm body, and finding my Daddy there.

At age twenty-one, the second time I went back to Sierra Leone, with my Mum and brother Steven, my grandmother Haja (known before as Mama Kaata, or Kadiatu) was there to welcome us. She told my Auntie Mini the dream she had after the first night that my mother slept in the house in Kenema. She spoke only Mende (although she could speak good Krio) and my Auntie translated for me. The dream, which for Grandmother Haja was real, was that my father arrived at the house and entered swiftly. He looked for my mother and sought no one else, and with hurried determination he walked straight to her room, longing to see only her. I was hot with rage and jealousy. Why hadn't he wanted to see *me*?

But sometimes he would come to my room, sit at the foot of my bed and sigh. I would feel the bed sag softly beneath his weight and wait, still as a stone. In my dreams I would walk to his carpentry shed, which smelled of sawn wood. It was my brother Steven's place, where he learned to use the tools. And I was whole and complete and neutral.

When we arrived in Essex, Mum immediately went to work as a primary school teacher and was almost immediately ill. She disappeared into bed, unable to speak, and left me at a great distance. Her chest seized up, tightened by severe bronchitis, and it was as though her body gave way and she sank out of sight. When she was better, a long time later, she went out of the front door. Her hair, long and beautiful, was always swept up in a loose bun at the back. I loved her hair and thought that she was the most beautiful woman in the world. When she came back, all her hair was gone. It had been cut so short that I thought Mummy had left and not come home. After my father, she never allowed herself to be with anyone else; no boyfriends or men at all. I asked her once and she said that she had given everything to Dad, and when he went there was really nothing left.

After we moved to Wales, Mum began to come back and became always present again. Her total dedication as a mother made home a safe place and made us children the most important thing in that world. She would tell us stories about Dad. When she spoke, the whole room would fall tense and silent, as though the air had changed. No one would breathe, and I would feel the hot rush of embarrassment in my face and body. We always looked at the floor, never at each other, and I longed for these moments to end. Later, alone in my head, I would tiptoe up to the facts and sift through the story she had told, carefully examining each detail as though it might ignite. She had told us that when Dad was in the colonial Bo school in Sierra Leone, no one was allowed to speak anything but English. If a teacher heard a word of Mende, the boy would be caned. She had told us about the jokes he told and how funny he was. But none of us had laughed.

As a primary school teacher, she shared our holidays and we would always drive or walk out to the countryside and spend time running, climbing trees and playing French cricket. The woods and hills were our total freedom, and Mum loved taking us to Wentwood, Tintern or Highmoor Hill. There was no fear there and no identity. Mum was strict but fair. She expected proper public behaviour, as did our grandparents, and we would sit still and quiet as mice during the long church services on Sundays. I am always perplexed when I see children who misbehave in church or at public concerts. My husband, Stuart, and I were both brought up to sit still and be quiet in public spaces, and if we didn't, we both had parents who would sort us out when we got back home. Boundaries always felt like safety fences, and routine allowed us space to be free without chaos.

In Essex, Steven went to school and I stayed at home with Isata, James and Nanna for the first two months. Grandpa told funny and irreverent stories, and time with him was a bold and brilliant adventure. Nanna was quiet. She moved neatly and took up little space, showing me how to make the perfect pot of tea. She would warm the pot with hot water first, pour the water out and put in a measuring of tea leaves. Then the tea had to brew for the right amount of time before pouring through a strainer into the china tea cup. Nanna was always cooking or looking after baby James while Mummy was at work. She was very strict about food and not wasting it. But to me, this food had no taste. I couldn't stomach the bland yellow custard or the hot creamy milk with skin on the top. The boiled vegetables with no pepper at all, and the soft white potatoes, were a mystery to me. Liver and onions were better because the onions tasted of something, and English mustard – especially when generously added to Grandpa's special Welsh rarebit – was good. I discovered Marmite in hospital (at five years of age while being surgically treated for a navel hernia, which is very common among West African children) and it was the only thing I would eat. Spread on toast with the strong savoury tang of salt, it was real food.

I was the elder girl and expected to be self-sufficient. Isata and James were the 'little ones', loved and petted and looked after. Isata was a pretty, soft-faced girl who was always giggling and acting, posing coquettishly for every camera shot and irresistibly endearing. James was the sweet baby, unable to say his letter 'r' when young. He was inseparable from his furry toy 'wabbit' and his best friend at infant school was 'Wobbie Woberts'. I loved them both and felt an overwhelming sense of responsibility for them. I panicked that I would lose them and had recurring dreams of fighting off the bad witch who tried to snatch Isata from her bed at night and take her away.

What would I do if the house caught on fire? Who would I save? I was constantly wracked with guilt that I had done something wrong, that I was bad and should be punished because I hadn't been kind enough or nurturing enough and I would lose my precious siblings one by one. I thought that it was all up to me now.

Once, the grown-ups took us to a funfair at Southend-on-Sea. I sat in the front carriage of the electric train, with a steering wheel and carriages hooked up behind me, full of my brothers and sister with other children. I was convinced that I was in charge of the train and that it would crash if I didn't steer well. Rigid with concentration and dread, I gripped the wheel and turned it with anguish at every bend in the track, tearful with relief when the train stopped and no one had died.

I looked at my little siblings, who were helped to get dressed and carried and petted. I looked at Steven, who the Kanneh family wanted to keep in Sierra Leone, his father's first son. I decided to stop brushing my teeth. I got attention. The Sunday School teacher, Mrs Edgeley, asked me in front of the class if I was brushing my teeth front and back. I said yes and relished the lie. My friends at school commented on my grey teeth and I enjoyed rubbing the classroom crayons in thick smudges on my front teeth and seeing their shock. Mummy would stand outside the bathroom every morning and waylay me with the question, 'Have you brushed your teeth?' I waited with delight for this direct interrogation and felt the warmth of the spotlight and the secret joy of the lies I told. At the same time, the guilt built up inside me and I had to pray harder every night. My sense of responsibility to my siblings – *it was me who kept them safe* – and my guilt that I wasn't the beautiful soul that Steven was – *it was my fault that they were not safe* – made me serious and quiet. This was mistaken for maturity and serenity, and I craved the special attention and solicitude that the others got. In the end, I was taken to the dentist, talked to with great urgency and intent by her, and found myself in the lounge at home, surrounded by the grown-ups who scrutinised every step of my teeth brushing. It was marvellous.

Steven was the oldest and 'the man of the house'. Grandpa had always wanted a son, and here was a strong boy who could be relied on and brought up to be responsible. I was especially close to Steven when we were young. To me, he was an angel, perfectly good, strong-hearted and loyal. He found it impossible not to tell the full truth and was utterly candid about everything – impatient and amused by any falsity in anyone else. When I had to go to hospital to have my 'dodo' (navel hernia) operated on, he rushed to me on my return to the house and wouldn't let me go. He was gentle and loving, and missed his father wordlessly. One day, when he was six, a workman came to the house to talk to Grandpa. Steven was in the playroom extension at the back of the house and heard the man's voice. He ran to the front door and leapt into the man's arms. Suddenly realising that it wasn't his Daddy, he ran back through the playroom and on to the bottom of the garden, where he hid himself away. In Sierra Leone, after Daddy died, relatives came to the house. One uncle slipped on the flip-flops that Daddy used to wear and Steven rushed to him and tore them off, cradling them in his arms. They belonged to Daddy.

In Bo, Steven had gone to school. Everyone around him spoke Mende and he was soon fluent. He was also a good reader and he could write well. When we came to Britain, he forgot how to read and write, and he had to start again. Everything confused him. I used to hide behind the settee with him before school to tie his shoelaces because he couldn't. He couldn't tell his left from his right and it became clear that he couldn't spell anything. But I knew that he was the cleverest person I had met. When he began reading again, he read everything and seemed to know everything. He would reason and analyse the biggest questions of science and philosophy and teach me as much as he could. His mind was creative and quick, and he thought about things in novel ways, always approaching them from a new perspective. If he told a story, it was fascinating and funny, but always brilliantly askew and upside down. He would turn fashion and culture on its head and expose why it distorted people's behaviour. For Steven, the world was a crazy place, people were deluded, and he could see through it all.

For a while he had been finding his feet in Britain and loved singing. He had a lovely voice, could sing beautifully in tune and enjoyed it. But one day it was noticed at school that he had stopped singing altogether. Eventually, Mum realised that it had happened when he had been moved from the front to the back of the class, and the words were on the blackboard at the front. She took Steven for an eye test and it was discovered that he was very short-sighted. When he put on the National Health glasses, the world was in such sharp focus that he was afraid to walk forwards. The pavement, in sharp distinction, came up at him, and it was clear that until then he had inhabited a hazy and blurred world, seen as though from a great distance.

Four years after we arrived in England, it was the day of moving to Wales, a place where I thought that women wore tall hats, aprons and shawls, and where my mother and grandparents were from. I woke up and felt myself completely paralysed. The adults told me, with irritation, to stop being so silly. This was a busy day – no time for childish dramatics. I tried to move my legs but they were frozen, and my whole body was full of pain. Sighing with exasperation, adults were forced to carry me, my teeth gritted, from one place to another, putting me on the floor to lie there while they got on with moving furniture or carrying boxes. I was paralysed from the waist down for a week. I didn't know why. A week later, when I could finally walk, I called out with surprised joy...and was completely ignored. It never happened again.

Grandpa wanted a conventionally strong grandson, ready to be practical. Steven was too dreamy and vulnerable, not yet ready to take up the reins of the man of the house. He was still looking for his Daddy. The week before they moved back to Wales, a year after we had arrived with me in paralysis and pain, we went to stay with them, back in the house in Chipping Ongar. I spent time with my best friend next door, Cathy Brick. Steven got up at dawn, desperate to please Grandpa the way he had pleased Daddy in the carpentry shed. He knew how to work with wood and he understood the tools. Grandpa had said that he wanted the shed dismantled for the journey. He meant that he wanted the shed separated into five parts – the walls and roof. Steven, zealously aiming to win Grandpa's approval, got up at first light and took apart every panel of wood, prising the nails out carefully and working obsessively until every separate plank was placed neatly on the grass. The work had been hard and long but done with great care. Grandpa got up, saw the minutely dismantled shed and shouted so loud and so long that I could hear every word from my bed. Steven was quiet for a long time.

In Caldicot, South Wales, Steven began to withdraw further into his creative world. He read books all the time, using the little hut of a library to borrow fantasy books, reading all of J.R.R. Tolkien, for example, and many books of history, science and science fiction. But at school he stayed at the back of the class. They thought that his inability to spell, or to write stories and essays in a linear way, meant that he was not bright. I knew that he was far cleverer than me, but while I got A in everything, he seemed to slip out of the classroom structure and was neglected. It was only when he made it to university, after applying when he was already in his twenties, that I felt able to intervene. He was getting into trouble with deadlines and essay writing, and I thought that I now understood. I was lecturing at Sussex University at the time, so I went to see his lecturer at what was then the Polytechnic of North London, soon to become the University of North London. He was quickly referred for tests and it was discovered that he had dyslexia and dysgraphia. It now made sense why he always drew maps back to front and could not organise things in a structural way – neither time, his bedroom and surroundings, nor his academic work. I felt sad for all the years where he had sat, neglected and ignored at the back of classrooms, sliding through the gaps. His energetic creativity, his restless, spontaneous and backwards approach to everything didn't need to be diagnosed. He was full of a brilliance that didn't fit into conventional ways of thinking. But I was uninterested in the labels. Steven was simply a genius.

And his story was more complicated. He often acted out just how I felt. He was incapable of cant or conformity. I approached the hostility of the world with smiles, eager to please and hiding behind politeness. If I felt the horror of the wide social landscape, I masked it by trying to hide myself in smaller and smaller spaces, invisible behind the smile that I had perfected, learning to look unthreatening. Steven had to endure the experience of approaching a bus stop and having all the elderly ladies back away from him and leave. He was stopped and searched by random policemen. He was the one beaten up badly, with his beloved bike smashed beyond repair. We didn't talk about it. He began leaving the hood of his coat firmly over his head and running with all his might out of the front door after leaving it wide open for a while. Steven perfected a run-up along the hallway first, as though preparing for the long jump. I understood this. I would stand, trying to steady my panicked breathing, looking in the mirror and looking away. I would approach the door and find spurious reasons to retreat. Then I would open the door just a crack and the blaze of daylight and sound would blare in, making me rock on my feet. Finally, outside the door, I would hear it click shut and the wide open spaces of outside made my legs feel weak and dazed with the danger I was in. When the shouts came and I heard the words I anticipated and dreaded, I would count and breathe, trying to keep my legs moving. Once, invited to a friend's house, I found myself in the centre of the living room with the whole family surrounding me and giggling that I was a 'wog' in their house. My friend laughed too.

As siblings we didn't exchange stories. We would wince if we witnessed it happening on the street to one of us, appalled and raging, but try to disassociate ourselves from the scene. Isata, more unaware for a while, her first memory that of coming off the aeroplane at the age of two and seeing a strange new world, finally realised that it was she who was the blot on the landscape, the thing that didn't fit. One day, walking to school through snow that had formed a layer of ice on the top, she was struck by a lump of jagged ice which hit her cheek, flung with the word 'nigger' in its wake. She was about twelve or thirteen and had to enter her needlework class with the hot sting of a livid bruise on her face. Teachers were not trained or told in any way to be anti-racist, and anyway, in a small White steel-working town, we were the only family to which it would have applied. The needlework teacher hated us with a focused passion that was more than the careless teenage attacks on street corners. This was deeply personal and I would stand shocked at the meaningful directness of her malice. Isata was yelled at and punished for having the punch and puncture mark of the ice wound on her face like a permanent and angry blush, and for being late as a consequence, her school uniform wet and untidy. She spent the lesson in deep and vocal disgrace.

But within the house, we were loved. The adults were not unaware of the world outside but discounted the psychological impact. I understood later that Mum suffered too, and that Grandpa had ugly fights with his sister, Auntie Annie, who was ashamed of us. But they valued education, and Grandpa was passionate about the education of girls, deeply proud of any of our academic achievements and giving me the A-Level Religious Education lessons that gained me the top marks. We were also very proud to be Welsh, brought up to love the language and the songs. The way that the Welsh are ironic and down to earth, and the sense of humour, are deeply embedded in us. My sister now lives in Mid Wales and is almost fluent in Welsh, and I take the children to Wales every year for our annual holiday. We have learned to live in a kind of split personality, but I'm coming to realise that it is needlessly divided. I inhabit two worlds at once, strangely blurred in the borderlines of each.

As a teenager, James decided that he was only Welsh, and he couldn't bear to hear about a Sierra Leone he couldn't remember. I was always protective of James and we were naturally close, our temperaments similar. James was very funny, hugely entertaining and very witty. We would seek out each other's company and he adored me as a little brother adores his big sister. He had febrile fever fits until the age of seven, which were diagnosed as epilepsy because the British doctors he saw did not know that West African children could fit two years longer than White children. James was put on tetracycline antibiotics, which blackened his milk teeth, and epilepsy drugs which were unnecessary. Eventually, his tonsils were taken out and he lay, miserable and lonely, in the dungeon-like ward for days before he was released from the vicious nurse who ruled the beds.

Before this, I remember entering the bedroom for years in the midst of the panic and shouting, and seeing James, mouth rigid and foaming while the adults tried to bring down his temperature. He had to have ice baths through which he suffered and cried, and once in Caldicot my mother had to carry him, shaking and frothing at the mouth, across the square to the car while I stood uselessly at the door. He loved his Nanna who looked after him from a baby, and Nanna and Grandpa spoiled him because of the illness. They would come with chocolates and sweets for him and enter the house looking only for him. In a home with strict rules on parity, everything was handed out in equal portions because there was no money for excess waste or second helpings. James's inequitable pile of sweets and unbalanced attention would make the rest of us seethe with jealousy.

When I went away to university, he was unsettled and missed me. I was trying very hard to act tough and independent, knowing that this was a trial of adulthood that I had to prove, fighting agoraphobia every time I left my room. After a few weeks he came to visit with Mum. He was fourteen and longing to see me. I decided that I had to put on a show of great success and practicality, talking about how wonderful life was away from home, an act I carried on when I came home at Christmas. He was quiet after that and kept his distance a little more, something I didn't understand until later and deeply regretted.

Suddenly, after refusing to talk about Steven's, Isata's and my visits back home to Sierra Leone, James decided that he would go. At Heathrow, Terminal 4, Mum and I waited with him, watching the screens. It was time for him to go through to the gate. He was the youngest to go back, and I wondered how he would cope with a world that he didn't remember and had no consciousness of leaving.

He was gone for six months and came back in love, having his beautiful son, Lahai, with Nancy less than a year later. His next child, the lovely-faced Nyanje, was also with a Mende woman, Jeneba. James went in the middle of the civil war and I knew that he had suffered. He spent time with his grandmother, aunties, uncles and cousins, and he was full of excitement and the surprise of an identity that simply walked up to claim him when he stepped off the plane. But he saw things that we never discussed and there was a sadness in the back of his eyes after that. James did tell us about the fear all around him when the armed rebels came closer and closer to Kenema, their guns growing louder by the hour. Groups of screaming people were running along Wamanabu Road outside Auntie Mini's house. In the opposite direction, in the middle of this fleeing crowd, he saw one young Kamajor (Mende huntsman), with one rifle, walking alone and calmly towards the guns. Two weeks after James left for Freetown, the rebels broke into Kenema and beheaded Auntie Mini's next-door neighbour. 'Were you frightened?' I asked. 'Remember', he answered, 'I didn't have three babies to carry and run with. How can I claim fear?'

James also told us all, acting it out with great hilarity like a slapstick comedy, the 'snake story'. A group of his little cousins spotted a snake just over the wall of the backyard, not too big but poisonous. James clowned around, pretending he would deal with it, leading the way, swaggering while wisely keeping a safe distance. While he gesticulated and joked he accidentally trod squarely on a King Snake, massive and deadly, and its fangs delivered a venomous bite to his leg. In an instant, little Memuna, a small girl, ran forward with a machete and hacked the snake to death. James glossed over the fever he'd had to endure for the sheer fun of the tale, reminding my mother of his Dad. Mum used to say it was uncanny how James' manners and walk were so like those of the father he couldn't remember.

I don't know how that feels, to feel the weight of a grief with only photos and stories behind it. But then the loss is somehow deeper still. Isata told me once that she felt doubly bereft that her father was not in her memory, only the walk from the aeroplane that brought her away from him. And Steven's clearest memory is of when he ate all the bananas that his father had brought for the family and was told off loudly. Steven told me this once with his characteristic but quiet humour and I haven't spoken with either of them about these things since.

I wanted a family to mirror my own, perhaps to make up for the loss at the centre of my childhood, and years later I was married with two boys and two girls. Stuart and I lived in Bahrain for three and a half years while he worked for Gulf Air, and I was afraid of coming back to Britain. We had arrived with two children and were returning with four. I was afraid that we wouldn't be able to protect the children from that onslaught on their confidence. Would they also feel that they couldn't be whole and claim their own space? As an immigrant to the UK I had always felt as though home was a place based on loss. The children would have to be better than everyone else in order to be deemed equal, and they would have to work twice as hard.

I try to shield the children from my own grief and the psychological damage that racism inflicts on a child. I never talk about my sorrow on 1st September, the anniversary of my father's death. I never describe the bleak, long aeroplane flight, landing in the freezing fog, or those names being shouted on every street corner. The children belong to a new generation, and this is their home. They will learn to confidently take up new space for themselves and be as loud as they like.

When my first daughter was born, I was astonished at the amazing completeness of this new person. She was all herself, immediately, and not me or Stuart. But she was the continuation of a story, in a different context. I knew we were responsible both for creating that context and for responding to it honestly. The most difficult task, it seemed to me, was understanding what that context was and how much was our creation. It was not the past and we were not in control of the world. But it was a world and a past of which she had to be a part, and our job was to make her interact with it, to impact upon it and to change it.

There is a piece of writing that I still have from when I was five. I wrote that: 'Today I made a new hairstyle. I showed my new hairstyle to Mummy and Nanna and Grandpa. They did not say anything'. I imagine that they didn't say anything because they were very busy with four children in the house, working as teachers and a Baptist minister, cooking, cleaning, dealing with toddlers younger than me, but for me, this was the only significant moment. Me, in the mirror, making sense of myself in the frame and wanting reassurance.

For my mother and grandparents, appearance was a frivolous preoccupation. Vanity was discouraged, and one never told a child they were pretty. But for us, against a world that was disgusted, shocked, alarmed by our sudden presence, how we appeared was central to our psychology. Would I misunderstand what was central to my daughter, Isata? Would I mistake the cultural landscape by mapping my own past on top? Or should I compensate by saying, all the time, what I saw and thought and believed. She was the most beautiful person I had ever seen and I was floored by her.

When I was eighteen, one of my close friends in the sixth form came back from his summer holiday with a swollen stomach. He was soon diagnosed with leukaemia. I went to visit him with another friend just before he died. He was seventeen. Nicky Jones had lost all his hair and could barely walk. He died three days later. The funeral was overflowing with his teenage friends and his family. I drove some friends there and came back late that afternoon. I lay on the settee. The funeral had put me into a state of shock that I didn't understand. I was crushed with grief and unable to speak. That evening my body collapsed. I lay on the floor in pain that was so complete that I couldn't stand. It was similar to the waist-down paralysis I had when I was eight, but this time the pain was internal and overwhelming. In hospital the doctors could not understand what had happened. I lay writhing on the bed and was repeatedly dosed up with painkillers. Eventually, the surgeons took me in and cut me from chest to pubis to see what had happened. Apparently, for no reason and with impressive suddenness, my intestines had twisted and exploded through the wall of my stomach.

I couldn't go back to school for weeks, and my A-Level teachers visited me at home. My world closed in again and I would wait eagerly for visits from friends who would tell me the gossip from school. I thought of Nicky, going between hospital and home, finally realising that there was no way out. I did my A-Level exams back in a school uniform which now hung, too big, from my waist. But Steven and I had planned to spend the summer in Sierra Leone, and I was determined to go.

I returned to Sierra Leone three times as a young adult: at eighteen, twenty-one and twenty-four. As soon as I stepped onto the ferry at Lungi Airport, I could smell home. The food tasted like food and the smell of the rain was the same as when I had left. I stayed with cousins, aunties, uncles and my grandmother, and we travelled to my father's and grandmother's villages, welcomed with love and recognition as though we had never gone away. The villages were full of our relatives and they sang and danced on our return.

Coming home was an onslaught to my senses. It were as though I had been in a strange coma for many years and here I was, awake again. Taste and smell were back to normal and the volume had been turned back up. I was overwhelmed to be recognised, remembered, welcomed back. What I had thought was a private dream, somewhere in a past I had imagined, had come true again and, unbearably, everyone talked about our

Dad. Steven and I had come together, alone, and suddenly, from an embarrassed silence and a hush that we had collectively imposed on the name that hurt too much to say out loud, everyone was speaking the unspeakable. We only got through the airport's maze of bribes and backhanders because an airport official recognised the name and had known our Dad. Suddenly, as his son and daughter, we were escorted, important, through the doors.

My father's brothers, Uncle Sheku and Uncle Moses, talked about how funny and impressive he was, Auntie Mini (his sister) talked about how kind he had been to her, and Auntie Angela (another sister) lit a candle on 1st September, a day we never addressed out loud, and cried openly. Steven and I didn't look at each other. Suddenly, through a wave of translation, Grandma Haja presented me with a tiny, two-year-old girl's faded shoe. It smelled of the hot damp I remembered. It was *my* shoe that she had kept for sixteen years. I sat in a deep trance, amazed by the wash of my emotion. She had kept something of me. She had thought about me. And that secret girl, with all those raging thoughts and all that need for love, really had existed.

When we arrived at Grima village, on the back of a truck filled with cousins, barrels of food and a goat which trod on everything, I stood surrounded by relatives singing, dancing and shouting out. A crowd of people wanted to see us and touch us. The translations told us that we were beautiful, that they had missed us, that they had been waiting for us to come home. The drums were loud and jubilant, and we found ourselves swept into Kanneh Street and 'Kanneh Lah' (Kanneh Place). We had followed another timeline and been swallowed into another dimension, but here, all along, was the world we had left, in parallel. We were familiar and strange, with our faltering baby steps back to languages we had forgotten, tottering like children along paths sunk into memory. Suddenly, we were in my grandfather's house, mud walled and tin roofed, and there was the big framed photo of our handsome grandfather, Pa Braima, and beautiful young Mama Kaata (Grandmother Haja). I gasped because there, in that photo, stood Steven, looking out of Pa Braima's face. They were exactly alike.

I felt a wave of shock. My brother's face, already mirrored in the cousins around us, was now in this big, sepia image of our grandfather, proof of my brother's connection to the past, framed and definite on the wall. The crowd pulled us in irresistible procession outside again and everyone stopped still. Before we had time to understand the stillness, as though a wind had dropped at full strength, there we were. Faces looked towards us, holding us up and sharing the moment. All together. A mound of earth. We stood, not knowing what to do with our hearts and minds, stripped bare at the edge of the world. This was our homage to the beginning of time. No one needed an explanation. No one was puzzled or surprised or disbelieving. We were held up by a whole village who shared the story, who already knew, and who felt the same. And here was Daddy. Where we had left him. All along.

Surrounded by cousins in Pa Braima's house, we were overwhelmed. The grief we had hidden through childhood in our own private corners was here, shining with understanding from every face. *Hosh ya* and *Benahway* (meaning 'sorry', 'sympathy' and 'condolences' in Krio and Mende, respectively) was muttered from every voice, witness to a shared reality that hadn't suddenly ended at the close of 1970. We felt hands on us, sad faces watching and reflecting our own. We sat like stones, too naked to breathe, white bones under the heavy sky. Later, walking unsteadily to the wash house with an oil lamp, and squatting to wash while the cockroaches rattled away from the light, I listened to the cicadas singing their raucous crowd songs in the night. We had come home. The night was huge and black, humid and hot, and the damp smell of the rains made the earth rich. The white sun of the day, bringing everything into sharp focus, making the colours so bright, had been swallowed into this magical, humming darkness, deep enough to lose anyone.

That, now, is in the past, before the civil war and the outbreak of ebola. I'm afraid to take the children to a country in which I am now a ghost, still in love with the country I left, and still grieving. But I have to remember that the past belongs to them too.

3

Growing Up

WHEN I ARRIVED in Southampton the next month, having chosen the university because the prospectus had a picture of the sea on the cover, I understood who I was. But now I was in an environment where no one else could see me at all. One of my new friends asked me about my summer, so I explained where I had been and what my family was. He got angry and accused me of making it all up for effect. I stopped telling people. The English Department consisted almost entirely of White middle-class and mostly private-school children. I had never met anyone from a private school before and I was simultaneously amazed by their advanced knowledge of literature, their superior education and their utter ignorance. I was so overjoyed that I blurted out to one student that my Auntie Gwyn, my Mum's sister in Florida, had just adopted a Black, mixed-race baby and showed them the photo. He asked, puzzled, where her baby-blue eyes were. I said that Black children were not born with blue eyes, and that I had been born with dark-brown eyes. He didn't believe me.

I didn't know how to speak in these tutorials where students talked about Evelyn Waugh and travelling abroad to places that I had never been. I tried to flatten the Welsh accent that would keep singing into my mouth, ringing oddly in the room when I tried to say something. My voice became a tight croak in my throat and I put it all into writing. When I wrote, I could sing as much as I wanted. One student who was studying a different subject tried to stretch out a hand of friendship to me over the perceived racial divide. He told me, with great politeness, that it was okay because when you shaved a monkey it was white underneath, so I was probably no closer to an ape than he was. Why he thought it necessary to tell me this was a mystery.

Going home, sinking back into the warm carpets and low ceilings with rice steaming again on the cooker, I had to learn to shed the armour that I had put on. My voice relaxed and flowed again. But I was so many identities that I was getting confused. Out in the pubs of Caldicot at night, I was now wearing student clothes and stood out even more. But I learned to be bilingual with accents and phrases. Home was changing. Grandpa moved into absence. His memory scrambled, breaking up into floating crumbs that attached to dreams, childhood and a half-remembered professional life. He would talk about countries he had travelled to in retirement, imagining that he'd had teaching jobs in each place. I had gone to university to make him proud and he hung on to that, waiting for me to graduate and telling everyone who passed the house just how proud he was. He knew who we all were, but not who anyone else was. From his days as a Baptist minister, he could talk charmingly to everyone and each person thought that he remembered them. He was warm and affectionate, but he was becoming less able to connect his past to the reality he was in.

He came to my graduation with Mum and Nanna, brimming over with pride, and he gave the blessing at my wedding, still able to speak beautifully. That was his last public speech as a Baptist minister. After that, he began to forget who everyone was, and his attachment to his grandchildren was as a gentle man who loved children but didn't know who they were. He began looking for his mother and thinking that he was in the Ceri countryside as a boy, keeping a pig in the garden. One time, looking happily out of the window, he told me, dreamily, how he had been high up in the nest on the tree outside that morning, helping the bird to feed her chicks. I missed him. But as his memory of us faded, he began talking all the time about a war he had hidden away. We heard of the jobs he'd had to do as a Baptist minister in bombed-out Cardiff, walking through a girls' school one morning to find the girls had been bombed to death in their dormitories. He talked about the loss of children, the bereaved families at the endless gravesides and the ministering to homes full of carnage. The tone was different to the diaries Nanna accidentally showed us, which were gentle, ironic and matter-of-fact. When he talked, the barriers lay fallen with his face young and open with bemused grief.

As Grandpa began fading, wandering into other, broken worlds that he could no longer connect, Nanna began to find her voice. Her personality grew into clearer focus every time I saw her, as though a space had opened up at last for her to step into and shine. She looked after Grandpa with fierce loyalty and became witty and sharp. She had always shone at the bedside of a sick person, and her warm and funny stories came out best at those times. When I was in hospital at eighteen, I would look forward, longingly, to her visits, when she would tell me about her experiences of giving birth during the war, of being stitched up hurriedly in candlelight because the bombs had knocked out the electricity and the air raid sirens were on. She talked about how she could barely get on a bus for months because they had stitched her up so badly. Then there were the hilarious accounts of Grandpa visiting her as she lay in her hospital bed, weak from the birth. On one visit he entered, full of anxiety and bombast, loud voice in evidence, and suddenly disappeared in one swoop under the bed. (He had been in such a hurry that he slipped and flew underneath on his back.) It was a revelation to have this new person with me, so clear and interesting and funny, who had emerged just as I began to lose my beloved Grandpa.

In my second year of university, I came home to a crisis. My sister, Isata, seventeen and in the lower sixth, studying for her A Levels, had got pregnant. The father, Kevin, was from a big Irish Catholic family of seven brothers and sisters, all clever and good-looking, and Isata decided to keep the baby. I was full of relief. I'd had a dream of a little girl, trying to get in, and I loved her. In my dream, she looked like me and I wanted her to come in.

While Isata was pregnant (and lonely), she came to stay in Southampton, and my dear friend, Gary Keeling, was kind to her. He invited her to come for a break to his home in Jersey whenever she needed it, and I loved him for his kind heart and the way he adored his sister and parents. Just after his Finals, celebrating after the last exam, he was killed by a taxi as he walked in the road. He was one of the kindest people I knew. I lay down for a day when I heard the news. I shut my door and stayed on the bed. I wouldn't talk to anyone and I couldn't move. I kept thinking how it must feel to lose a beloved child, one's own son, and thought about Grandmother Haja.

The night that Rhiannon Kadiatu – 'little Kadie' – was born, Isata suffered for hour upon hour and didn't utter a word. Mum and I stayed with her, amazed at her silent endurance. It became clear that the baby was stuck, facing upwards instead of down and now too wedged for a caesarean. I had never seen such suffering before and I couldn't bear it. Only Mum could stay for the forceps delivery; I had already broken down.

After the baby was born, deep gashes and dents in her temples, they took Isata away and put her under general anaesthetic to have the placenta removed, which had broken up inside her. After the operation, they wouldn't let me see her, assuring me that she was fine. I began raising my voice and I could feel the white flame inside me. The witch had come back to steal my sister. Had she died? I refused to leave until they gave her back to me. When the midwives and nurses had to give in, I stumbled to her bedside and leaned into her sleeping face to hear her warm breathing. She was rosy cheeked and alive. I cried with relief and kissed her.

'Little Kadie' belonged to all of us, our little baby, the brightest child in all the world and beautiful beyond words. We adored her. Isata would bring her to stay with me in Southampton and later in Brighton when I started studying and teaching at Sussex University. She was *our* child, the first one. I wondered how it would feel to have such a miracle grow inside and then be part of the family – of *two* families. It was wonderful.

I could see what motherhood meant. My own mother worked relentlessly and there was no get-out clause. She was always there and, wherever we might be, it was always a *home*. She worked full time and never missed a day, cooking for us when we were all home from school, washing all our clothes by hand, taking our work at school seriously and giving us routine. Whatever dizzying surveillance existed outdoors, we were cushioned and safe indoors, and her voice rooted us to the earth. She inherited a dry wit from Grandpa and we learned to laugh at ourselves and enjoy each other's idiosyncrasies. We were not encouraged to be self-indulgent or overly senti-mental, and we were expected to do regular chores. Collecting coal with the coal scuttle for the fire, hoovering and dusting our bedrooms, weeding and digging vegetables in the small back garden, cleaning the bathroom and washing up were all part of the daily routine. Every night, after reading our books, we would be tucked into bed individually and asked what we liked best that day. We would then each say a prayer and turn into our pillows, knowing what the next day would bring, and knowing that we would all be there.

We ate Mende cooking, which Mum had learned from my father and relatives in Sierra Leone, tempered by what ingredients were available. We couldn't get cassava, so we had potato. We couldn't get the African hot peppers, so we had curry powder and chilli. We couldn't get Bonga fish, so we had tinned sardines. All served with rice, which we ate with a spoon rather than our hands. Mum was a talented and versatile cook, and everything was full of flavour, but she didn't see that as part of her identity at all. She cooked like she gardened – generously, with contempt for rules or set texts of how to plan ingredients or landscape flowers. She liked colour, profusion, bursts of flavour and spices. She was clever, brilliant with words, intellectually incisive and ironic. I don't think she ever acknowledged just how kind she was, and how much sacrifice she made, every day, to put us first.

I only realised the loneliness of being a single mother when I watched Isata, brilliantly clever herself, taking her A Levels and going to Birmingham University as a teenage mother. She did it all with a steely defiance I admired. She said that pushing a pushchair was like sporting a beehive hairstyle out of doors – far too conspicuous – so she carried Rhiannon Kadie in a sling or on her hip for months. By the time Isata had her A Levels and was ready for university, Kadie at nearly three was as articulate and clever as her mother. They were like a force against the world.

With a toddler to care for at university, Isata couldn't join in the student parties and bars where her contemporaries were. I visited them in the Birmingham University 'family flat'. It was grim, in the outskirts of the city on an isolated plot – no washing machine and a miserable laundrette, the flat itself dim and cut off, and the loneliness palpable as I walked in. The weekends, with no lectures, seemed like a prison sentence, and Isata and Kadie clung together in an intensely creative existence, full of reading, writing and artwork. I could see the resilience that Isata had to show, and the pride she had, stubbornly in the face of each day's demands. For the last summer term of finals, at the end of the three-year degree course, Kadie spent the term in Caldicot with Mum at what was already her home. She went to Llanmartin Junior School where Mum taught, and she shone. Meanwhile, Isata took her finals and achieved the only first-class honours in the department.

I saw the way the two of them would sit side by side in the bed together and write their diaries and stories. I saw how Isata would sing Mende lullabies to get Kadie to sleep, and hand-wash her clothes in the sink at night when the trek to the laundrette was too bleak to contemplate. I saw from my sister and my mother that motherhood was a state of determination and constancy, and that love of one's children was the single urgent mission of life.

The First Piano

I WAS EIGHT when Mum collapsed with a severe attack of malaria. The first year we lived in Wales, Nanna and Grandpa stayed behind to pack up the house with the playroom, the 'quiet room' (living room) and the garden with the washing line and the holly bush. They were still there when Mum began vomiting uncontrollably at teatime and shaking with fever, so they travelled to Caldicot to look after her. We had sat and watched with alarmed interest – mostly distracted by the delay in our after-school meal – as Mum shook and gagged. The Blackaby family lived next to the Baptist church in Magor which we attended every Sunday, and they offered to have all four of us children stay. Magor was a small village four miles from Caldicot, and the little chapel was old and beautiful with wooden pews and an organ that covered the walls. The Blackabys, warm and generous, were already a family with six children, and they welcomed the four of us into their home for a week without hesitation. We played in their house and garden, and their youngest boy, Peter, who was slightly older than us, would tease us by pretending to be a 'Wirrn' from *Doctor Who*, slithering into our bedroom in his sleeping bag and making us scream. It was like being on an Enid Blyton adventure. Their house, bigger and older than ours, drew us into its magical world, and its centre was a room with the piano. I had never before encountered such a thing, and I was entranced. It was in the loud melee of overly excited children that Mrs Blackaby had to give us all timed turns on the keyboard, banging out our tuneless improvisations one after the other while she sat and winced bravely. From then on, I remained hooked, utterly in love with this thing called a piano, and my wildest dreams saw me sitting with a piano for hours in my very own home.

When we had moved to Caldicot we went to Llanmartin Primary School on the Underwood council estate. These were the days when the government believed that music should be part of everyone's education. There was a teacher, Mrs James, who put all her energy into engaging children in singing and playing, and she noticed how much I lit up when I heard music. She handed me a recorder which I learned quickly and easily, loving the harmonies and the musical layers we created in recorder groups. She taught me and another girl, Katie Hodges, music theory and decided I was musically gifted. I didn't really know what that meant, but music made sense to me and occupied a natural centre of school life, as vital as reading, writing and maths. I also received one-to-one clarinet lessons in school and played in the school band.

The school's old piano was about to be thrown out, so Mrs James suggested to my mother that she take it home for me to learn. That was when my dream came true and the old upright piano, with discoloured keys that smelled of warm wood and endless possibilities, now stood in the middle of our living room. The open fire was there that choked smoke from the cheap coke and newspaper it fed on, with the flickering black-and-white television in the corner. There always seemed to be colouring pencils and crayons slipping between the keys, and the room wasn't kept quiet and separate. It was Mum who taught us all in the beginning, sitting next to Steven or me first as the older ones. I loved the lessons with Mum, learning how to memorise the names of the notes and how the written music related to the keys that my fingers pressed. It was a kind of logical magic, ignited by the feeling of fingertips on keys and the sound, full and real, that rang or hummed or sang.

After the piano, old and uneven, appeared in our house, I rarely left it alone. Mum stretched her income to pay for all of us to have piano lessons, one at a time. Steven gave up quite soon, reading music a challenge he didn't want to fight with any longer. Isata and then James, after me, didn't stay for long, but I didn't want to give up, working diligently for all my grades with Llouvain, the piano teacher. I only stopped when hospital and A Levels collided, but it left me with the longing to know more than I did. I felt what I played deeply, but a gap opened between the technique I had learned and the feelings I wanted to express. I knew there were hidden secrets in the music that I couldn't access because I needed to know how to play them in the right way. (There was no YouTube then and we couldn't afford live concerts.) It was as though I had knocked at the door but couldn't get in. I learned enough to understand the vastness of what I didn't know and to long for more. We didn't live in a city and concert halls were places where we would have been uncomfortable. But I knew there was a beautiful mystery within those buildings, and one day I would, breath held, enter these enchanted spaces.

5

From the Margins

S TUART'S PARENTS CAME from Antigua to London
in 1958. His mother, Enid, left her job as a teacher to
catch a plane to England and work as a nurse. Stuart's
father, Arnold, a brilliant mathematician, followed her by ship,
determined not to lose her, and took a job as a bus conductor.
These were the jobs open to migrants from the Caribbean, and
the National Health Service and public transport in Britain
were desperate for such workers. For Stuart's father, the worst
aspect of the job came at the end of the shift when, in the days
when London buses had no doors, he had to jump off the
moving bus, which didn't slow down. Stuart's mother also found
bus journeys difficult because she couldn't understand what
they were saying when they said 'All fares please' in a London
accent. Stuart witnessed their courage as a child growing up in
the late 1960s and 1970s. He saw the humiliations they had to
endure: doors slammed in their faces when they went to view
houses to buy, neighbours turning their backs, subtle blocking
of their ambitions at work. But they had the gift of family and
community, and they stood together. One day, a boy at the
hospital where Enid worked told her to her face, 'Don't touch
me. My mother told me not to let any Black person touch me'.

She answered by giving him a slap and saying, 'Take that back to your mother'.

Britain was cold, and they lived in shared houses with others who came to London from Antigua. They lived in small, crowded rooms with cooking and washed clothes hanging, and they worked hard and long. Arnold began working for British Telecommunications and Enid started working in Barclays Bank. They had Rhonda and then Stuart four years later, and had the ambition to buy a house of their own. They were able to buy a very small house but kept saving for something better. Eventually, they had saved enough to plan moving again.

When they went to view houses to buy, they would go after dark so the neighbours wouldn't see Black people coming to look at the house. The estate agent made them an appointment to visit a house one evening in Catford, an address on Callander Road. When they arrived, the owners opened the door and blocked the way, determined not to let them inside. The next day, there was a phone call from the estate agent. The owners wouldn't sell to Stuart's parents and pretended they had suddenly sold the house overnight. Since then, Stuart has never forgotten that address. The inferior house they were forced to keep living in, with the bathroom built onto the kitchen as an afterthought, lingers in Stuart's mind as a personal affront to his mother, who felt the pain of that rejection every day she walked into the kitchen.

There had been classical music in Antigua when Stuart's parents were young. Arnold, one of seven children, used to wander over to where the rich, White people lived to hear the beautiful music coming from their open windows. He longed to play the violin, and the strains of music that hung in the air moved him, making him yearn to play the classical music he heard. He managed to have some lessons, loving the sound of the bow on the strings and how quickly he could learn, understanding the music he played. But he was left wanting more that he couldn't have, unable to access or afford the lessons he needed. Enid, in her home of twelve brothers and sisters, was able to learn the piano, and her youngest brother, Roland Prince, became a celebrated jazz guitarist who travelled to New York when he was young and who was known in Antigua as extraordinarily gifted. When I knew him, he was a reggae, jazz and calypso artist in Antigua, lean and full of a vibrant and energetic generosity to the children. He would teach them jazz chords on the piano and throw back his dreadlocks to look at them full in the eyes to see if they also heard and felt the wonder of the music.

Stuart and Rhonda grew up in a house saturated with classical music. Their parents subscribed to *Reader's Digest* and received lots of records in the post by Alfred Brendel, Ashkenazy, Rubinstein, Christina Ortiz and Marta Argerich, playing Beethoven, Chopin and Rachmaninov. Stuart and Rhonda loved the music and were brought up to respect and understand it, but they never believed that they could *be* one of those musicians. This was a world to admire and enjoy, but there was no one within it who looked like them, and they never imagined they could be one of these fabled people who played concerti to concert halls full of people.

When Rhonda was ten and Stuart six, their parents managed to buy an old upright piano to put in the London terrace in Hither Green, Lewisham. At first, they each had to practise for half an hour a day, with a clock on top of the piano to mark the time. Piano practice was disciplined, but it was also supported. Enid would accompany Rhonda for her viola exams, swallowing down the painful nerves and sense of unendurable responsibility every time. Arnold would come home from work and sit with each of them as they practised. He went with Stuart to Blackheath Conservatoire for his lessons, taking him on the bus as they couldn't afford a car. This gift of time and concentration continued with his grandchildren, and Arnold has sat for hours, listening as Isata, Braimah, Sheku, Konya and Jeneba played piano, violin, cello. The children's beloved grandparents moved back to Antigua when Aminata and Mariatu were still young, and all of them missed their grandfather's presence in the room.

Enid was determined and strong. Constant complaints from neighbours about the piano practice did not deter her for a moment. She simply ignored it all and ordered Stuart and Rhonda to continue. They were gifted and that was that. The clock would go on top of the piano during school holidays when she was at work at the bank, and Stuart did that daily half hour of practice. It never occurred to Stuart to cheat or disobey his mother. He would practise and stare at the clock's strict measuring of time. His parents knew there was negative reinforcement all around. When Stuart began school, the teachers told his mother that he had learning difficulties and could not get far. He should be sent to a specialist institution because he didn't have the academic ability to be in a mainstream school. He was a dreamer, but his mother knew how bright he was and her strength lay in not accepting someone else's truth as final. Enid simply didn't listen and stood her ground. Within a year, the teacher was forced to apologise and admit that Stuart was the brightest boy in her class.

They were able to excel on their instruments, having free one-to-one, hour-long lessons through the Inner London Education Authority (ILEA), opening school cupboards full of orchestral instruments and playing in the free Goldsmith's youth orchestra every Saturday. This was music accessible to everyone as part of state education, and Stuart and Rhonda's parents wanted them to value it. BBC1 and BBC2 television showed classical music regularly as part of prime-time output in a world of only three television channels, with ITV very much the third, more sparsely broadcast channel. It was on BBC television that Stuart and Rhonda watched the performance of Schubert's Trout Quintet in a documentary, with Jacqueline du Pré, Daniel Barenboim, Itzhak Perlman, Zubin Mehta and Pinchas Zukerman. They loved and revelled in this music which they intuitively understood, even though it was music played by people from a different world and a different culture.

Being able to access free piano lessons in London, with Stuart having free cello tuition and Rhonda free viola lessons, they learned easily. As astonishingly talented musicians, they were both playing beyond the standard of their Grade 8 successes from an early age. The music teacher at their school, Ennersdale Primary, a mixed city school, had encouraged Stuart to audition at Blackheath Conservatoire for scholarships from the ILEA in their last year there. When he won a full scholarship it opened up a world of exploration in the music he had been taught to love. For them both, it was the piano that allowed them to enter the intimate space where self-expression and creativity meet, but the cello and viola presented the chance to collaborate with others in the energetic social conversations of orchestra and ensembles.

Enid and Arnold received a letter in Stuart's final year at primary school, stating that Stuart was musically gifted and offering him a scholarship for Pimlico school full time and a specialist music education. They were delighted. For them, music was the world of Jacqueline du Pré and Daniel Barenboim, of Ashkenazy, Radu Lupu and Moura Lympany. But a specialist music education was outside their experience, so they consulted with Stuart. As an eleven-year-old boy, he wanted to play football outside in the park and stay with the friends he knew. He saw only the possibility of being denied the physical, 'normal' life he had, playing cricket and marbles on the street, instead of being isolated in an environment where they spoke a language he didn't quite understand. There was no roadmap and there were no role models, and none of the family understood what specialist music school would mean for Stuart. He refused to go and they accepted his decision.

Stuart's parents did insist that both of their children sit the exams and take the interviews for Roan Boys and Roan Girls grammar schools, even though there were only two or three other Black boys in Stuart's year. This was also horrifying to Stuart – leaving the local friends he knew and catching the bus to this very different territory in Blackheath – but his parents were determined. He still remembers the interview with the headmaster where he had to recount the geography of his route to school and was called by his surname, but the boys' and girls' schools allowed Stuart and Rhonda to continue playing the music that their Black friends thought alien. And Stuart was gifted at maths, languages and sport which helped him to win a place in the minds of the teachers and pupils.

The family went to see Daniel Barenboim playing the complete Chopin Preludes. At age eleven, this was Stuart's 'Eureka!' moment. After that, he began practising for at least an hour a day with no need of the clock on top of the piano. Stuart's parents took out a bank loan of seven hundred pounds to buy a better upright piano. This piano is now in his parents' home in Antigua, and the children play on it every time they return to the island.

Being in England was a daily struggle for education and aspiration, and it took daily determination for Enid and Arnold to believe in the gifts of their children. The family couldn't afford to visit Antigua together so, after saving money, Enid took Rhonda for the first trip in 1970, when she was ten, and Stuart went at the age of eight with his father. For them, it was simply a visit to see relatives, and Stuart's and Rhonda's impression, as children from London, was that the family was poor, and there were too many insects. Antiguans didn't spend their lives on the beach, except for maybe a picnic at Fort James, the beach at St John's at the weekend. Tourism was not established, and Rhonda's most vivid memories are of the lack of mesh over the windows and the mosquitoes and cockroaches that got in. Stuart remembers his grandmother, Mama, who spoiled him, and, when Rhonda went to Antigua, the mulligatawny soup his Dad gave him every day. For Stuart's children, Antigua is a place of wonderful discovery, where they are surrounded by relatives and by young people who want to hear their music. The carnival, the beaches and the landscape, the people they meet there who are generally so well educated and respectful, make them want to return every year. But Stuart and Rhonda could *not* return every year. Air travel was prohibitively expensive and people from Africa and the Caribbean could not go home. Consequently, a real connection with Antigua happened after Stuart's and Rhonda's childhood, when they were young adults, and now that their parents have gone back home to stay.

What Stuart and Rhonda's parents showed them was the value of a disciplined approach to learning, that working regularly at music would lead them to their own joyous engagement. The time Enid and Arnold spent listening, travelling on the bus to music lessons, going into debt to afford the instruments, ignoring those who said they shouldn't or couldn't was a long and powerful act of love. That final step of owning this music world and becoming an active figure in it, rather than only an enthusiastic audience member, that final step of being the person who *plays* the concerto, had to wait for another generation.

So many couples who formed in those early days of immigration couldn't survive the financial and emotional stress of moving to Britain. Many separated under the psychological strain of losing home, but Stuart's parents stayed together. His childhood memories are a contented blur of family – aunties, uncles, cousins and house parties. His parents worked hard but were always there. He remembers waking up as a child one school morning after a full night's sleep and seeing that his parents had entirely stripped the wallpaper off his bedroom walls as he slept. When Stuart practised the piano, it mattered to him that his father would come home from work and quietly sit in the room, listening. They expected brilliance and believed absolutely that it was there. In school holidays when his mother was at work, she would phone Stuart and remind him to put that clock on top of the piano. And he would do it. Enid and Arnold achieved the heroic feat of creating a world of calm possibility around their children, shielding them with the force of their supreme confidence.

When I entered Stuart's family home as a twenty-year-old student, it was full of humour and crammed with relatives. The music and the voices were loud, and there were tables piled high with Antiguan food. I felt easy and familiar. This is how it had been in Sierra Leone. A home full of cousins. And I fell in love with them all.

I think of Stuart's father standing in the street to listen to classical music coming out of the open windows of the expatriate homes as a boy in Antigua. I think of my father dreaming of the piano and of conducting an orchestra. I think of my Nanna spending her money to rent a piano so that my daughter Isata could practise her concerto while we were in Wales, and my grandfather finding five hundred pounds to buy me a better upright piano when I was a young teenager. It has taken generations of love and sacrifice to create the conditions and the confidence for our children to be classical performers.

6

The Magic of Time

S TUART AND I met at Southampton University, where I arrived to study English and Stuart was beginning the third year of his Physics degree. I loved Stuart's social curiosity, the way that events would coalesce around him and a party would start. He loved dancing and talking, and I craved his confidence. I desired his sense of place in the world and his right to it. We met in the coffee bar at Southampton University in 1984. I was an eighteen-year-old girl from the South Wales countryside, fresh from a steelworkers' village in the midst of strikes. I had made it to university from a patchy Welsh comprehensive school with some dedicated teachers and a family interested in education. I was lucky, excited and out of my depth. Stuart was a Londoner, full of the sense of centrality that Londoners have, and had come straight from his boys' grammar school.

We clashed immediately. I resented his utter lack of shyness and his need to be at the centre of the fashionable and exciting. At that time, the number of universities in the country were few and the Black students studying in them *very* few. So sparse were the numbers in Southampton that we all knew each other, and I couldn't avoid Stuart. We had mutual friends and ended up at the same social occasions. He irritated me, but I couldn't ignore him. He felt that I was beneath his notice but kept noticing me anyway. We kept finding ourselves in each other's paths, even though we tried to go in different directions. He thought of me as just a girl from the village, uninteresting but sweet enough. I thought of him as pompous and loud, but I was annoyed not to be in the centre of his vision.

In my first year, I was wilfully trying to remain at the margins. That was where I felt at home. I avoided lectures and missed classes. Everyone in the English department seemed to be comfortable there, overwhelmingly privately educated and all White. I felt like a visible fraud, with an Afro and a Welsh accent, ludicrous and silent. I grimly envied Stuart's refusal to lurk at the sidelines and wondered at it.

But I loved my subject. I read Virginia Woolf for hours in my room and swam through Tennyson. Critical Theory was a new and fascinating world, and I indulged secretly. In the last lecture of the first academic year, the sun unable to penetrate the big lecture theatre, I sat amidst the horde of students, small in my seat. The exam results had been decided. I felt vaguely bleak, tongue-tied and far too brown. There was a special prize, the Lyttel Prize, for the student with the most outstanding exam results in the year. A vision of White, private-school privilege loomed in my mind. If I could say a clipped and full sentence out loud in a tutorial about *Brideshead Revisited*, perhaps I could have been that person, I thought.

The winner's name was called, and it was me. The whole lecture hall turned as one to see me, standing, in a theatre of surprise, incongruous, the only Black student. And I had won.

Stuart thought it was very funny that I had been singled out in this way and viewed me as even more of an enigma. For him, the world seemed simple. The interesting people looked inter- esting, and I was a paradox. He said that I wasn't the sweetie he had thought I was, and we shared a wicked sense of humour. I also realised that this confident, good-looking, centre-of-the-room person was surprisingly gentle and sensitive. And I noticed him looking at me with studied interest. I began to find my feet in this new world and life was exciting. I changed how I dressed and how I cut my hair.

Briefly, we began finding ourselves together, seeking each other out at the end of evenings. But I wanted to stay friends and not be a formal couple. I felt I had too much freedom to lose when I was still unfurling.

He invited me to his family home for a party. I was very much a student, wearing black and skinny and at ease. Stuart's sister and cousin were ironing their outfits for the night and asked me if I wanted to borrow the iron. Stuart laughed. He knew I had no intention of dressing any other way for any occasion. I wondered then what an anomaly they thought me to be, this strange, mixed-race student from Wales who was not a Londoner and not from the Caribbean. Miraculously, his parents and sister liked me, and I adored them. They made me laugh, and I loved the chicken and patties and Antiguan food. I loved Stuart's family.

We returned to the chaos that all students lived in. We shared a big house with six students, all friends and cheap rent, managing somehow to survive the house parties, the staying up all night and still, in intense sleepless stints of work, getting our degrees. Stuart was like a constant, there in the network of my life but not in the centre of my conscious thought. When I saw him, it was like coming home, and I knew there was no need to put on an act or pretend to be cleverer or more interesting than I was because he would think that was ludicrous. He was annoyingly perceptive about who I was, eyebrow raised in comic question. We were not a couple and yet it seems now that he was always there.

One day, Stuart, serious and quiet, asked me to marry him.

I laughed. I was twenty at the time and I thought he was a dreamer. Perhaps his social gift, always the instigator of a party, had made life seem simpler than it was. He had told his friends that he would marry me, that he just knew that he would. They all laughed at him and told him that he was wrong, but nothing altered his conviction. He said it came to him while we were walking through the park in Southampton, beautiful with its big trees in early summer, and I was chatting away, letting my mind spark all sorts of idle thoughts. I saw him looking steadily at me, his face calm. He told me that was the moment that he knew he was in love – that he would marry me some day.

I had no intention at all of marrying Stuart. Life was long and I was going to fly so high and so far away that I would never stop. The world was full of so many possibilities and I was clever and free. Anyway, I was far too scattered and scared to be a person fit to marry. And I thought I knew everything. Then I kept getting tripped up by him. He ran deeper than I had first thought and was more powerful. When he looked at me there was nowhere to run.

Stuart finished his Masters in Maths (Operational Research) and left Southampton for a job with British Airways in London. I stayed with what was left of our group of friends, moving out of the student house we had all shared together and into a smaller house with two friends, Charlotte and Courtney.

I stayed at Southampton for a year to complete my Masters and then went to Sussex University to write my PhD. Stuart came to visit now and then, and we would walk together to the heady world of nighttime Brighton. I loved entering the clubs and bars with him. He was working in London and then the US, so he always had fashionable clothes. He was a dancer I could watch all night. His lack of shyness and his love of social occasions made him brilliant company, and I didn't realise how much I loved being with him because I knew him so well. We talked for hours and we always told each other everything. Nothing was off limits and everything was funny. We would go shopping together, spend days together, and then part as firm friends. He was always in my peripheral vision and in the blind spot I didn't always turn to.

After he left for London, I began to look for him and I missed him. We wrote letters for years, seeing each other intermittently and giving each other news of where we were and what we were doing.

With him, so much was already understood and didn't need to be said. We agreed about everything and saw the world through the same filter. If someone said something ridiculous in our presence, we would each know that the other thought the same. It was that ease and familiarity that had made me discount the excitement of marrying Stuart. Surely love should be more edgy and dangerous! I would fold into his body and relax, utterly at home, but I also wanted to sail out and find war zones I hadn't yet explored.

Then, at twenty-five, I began lecturing at Sussex University while I was still working on my PhD thesis. It was an extraordinary time of growth, having to present myself to students and lead tutorials and seminars when I was little older than them. I would give lectures to full theatres, pretending to be the real thing and sure that someone would find me out. I spent a year as sub dean of student affairs while lecturing, facing the young students who came into my office and hearing their problems and personal issues, their missed exams and loneliness. I felt overwhelming sympathy for these young people, dealing with the terrible onslaught of adult life while they were still teenagers away from home. There were accidental pregnancies, botched abortions, psychological breakdowns and innocent stumbles into plagiarism that were more mistake than malice.

As sub dean, I had to defend plagiarism cases on behalf of

any given individual student in a bizarre university court where I acted as defence advocate. I remember the first of these. The university was not used to academic women in positions of authority, and certainly not if they were part of an ethnic minority. I knew of one Black lecturer in another department at the time, but there were certainly no other Black lecturers in English when I started and few Black students studying English. I walked in with the male student. He had a very ordinary male English name on the papers in front of the panel, who were all White, middle-class older men. I sat down, introduced myself, and ushered the student to sit. Immediately, the academic leading the inquiry began addressing me with the outline of my transgressions and warning me that plagiarism was a serious crime. I was forced to interrupt, point out that my name was not the obviously male name on the 'legal' papers and that I was not an undergraduate. In the shocked and flustered moments that followed on the panel, while I sat icily angry, it was clear that I had turned the world upside down. The White, privately educated student, in his moment of vulnerability, was discouraged. Later that day, another White male lecturer was sent to my office to apologise on behalf of the man who had made the mistake. But I remained furious.

As the payback for the constant pressure of students coming to my office over the year for help, advice and internal legal defence, I was given a term's sabbatical to finish the PhD. This was wonderfully welcome and the reason I had taken the difficult position. It was also very pressurised. Now I had to confront the rotting remains of research, words and ideas that were blotched and botched over years of academic flashes of enlightenment, insecurities, changes of direction and bleary-eyed exhaustion from teaching. I had to prove that the overarching concept was there and I could write something worthy of the title 'Doctor'.

I knew I couldn't. After years of PhD study, it had all begun to feel like an insurmountable goal. It no longer felt like an academic project but a prolonged mental illness, and I began to feel, hysterically, that I could not be a person, I could not get on with my life, until it was finished. And it was impossible to finish something that had taken on a life of its own, panting maliciously in the corners of my mind at all hours, devouring every steady breath like a creature in the attic. I was a fraud. I certainly didn't look like an academic. I was a demonstrable charlatan, an imposter, and there was now so much sick emotion lodged around those combinations of letters, 'PhD' and 'DPhil', that I couldn't look them in the eye.

I spent the autumn term of 1994 in a state of trembling adrenalin and exhaustion, regularly up all night. The deadline was close and my term's sabbatical was coming to an end. There were always several books open on the table around me and the Amstrad with its winking green words would glare at me. The neighbour in the flat below me, always drunk, would keep up a monologue of night swearing directed at me, and then post invitations through my door in daylight inviting me to meet him for a drink.

I would try to manage the nervous fear of the man below, who would pace and roar with bitterness, and force the words in front of me into patterns of meaning and sense. (My daughter, Isata, now talks to me about Clara Schumann's battles to compose music against the demands of being a mother and wife to the manically disturbed Robert Schumann.) It was an effort of will keeping my focus on finishing the thesis.

There were so many connections, so many patterns to find. I was like a spider, joining the threads and re-reading history. Beneath each pattern was another, secreted behind a wall of rigid fact. All this writing – history, anthropology, literature – was informing itself, cross-referencing and creating ideas of

Africa and identity that knotted together whole continents. I was unthreading and re-weaving a narrative.

The next evening, my head swollen and fizzing with thought, I crossed the few streets, lit with lamplight, to see Stuart again. I hadn't seen him for a few years, but we had written letters to each other while he had been working as a consultant for American Airlines in Texas, and he was now staying with our friend Charlotte in Brighton. On that sabbatical, I was having a lonely time. It was difficult to see the world outside. I had a knight in shining armour in the form of Roland-François Lack, a colleague who helped me to wrestle with the fitful moods of the computer and type pages of scribbled paragraphs into the early hours.

Now I was out in the night streets of Brighton, calm with winter, taking a breath of sea air over the houses at the top of the hill. Charlotte's house was warm and bright, and there Stuart was. I swam up from my mind's preoccupation with words and sank into familiarity. I had forgotten how easy it all was, to stretch out my legs and to feel at home.

Stuart had been posted to Sardinia. When the aeroplane tickets to Sardinia arrived at my flat on Valentine's Day three months later, I was so wrung out with exhaustion that I accepted them in a kind of sleep. I had arrived at the binders in December with three books of typed pages on the day of the PhD deadline. The staff there, sympathetic in a flurry of military-style support, had marshalled a team of people to bind, glue, press and create three books out of the raging panic of my writing. Three hairdryers were blowing forcefully over the glued spines and I was hardly upright, sinking at the knees with the exertion.

After heaving the tomes onto the ledge at the university office, and dragging myself through a kind of post-traumatic term of intense lecturing and teaching, I arrived on the plane to Sardinia, barely sensate.

A Surprise Beginning

I LAY, SLIM, brown and light as air, in the living room of Stuart's flat in Sardinia, the sun coming through the waxy leaves of the lemon tree onto the cool floor tiles. Everything was clean, shining and clear. Stuart played chess with me on a thick wooden board hewn from a tree in Australia, outmanoeuvring me every time.

It felt like a bright new start, a chapter that had suddenly revealed itself under the weight of other histories. It had always been there, this new story, and I had always been in love. Stuart asked me to marry him again. It was nine years since the first time he had asked and everything looked different. I was now twenty-nine and I had been on a long journey to find what had been there all along, hiding just out of sight. It was like a shadow lifting from a garden and I was speechless with humility.

Stuart said that life was a question of timing, and he was someone who understood time like no one else I knew. It was an extraordinary sixth sense that I still can't explain. If we drive back from somewhere, no matter how far away, or take public transport, Stuart will state, to the minute, exactly what time we will turn into the house. I have never known him to be wrong.

We used to meet from other ends of the M25, fraught with the vagaries of rush-hour traffic, at the Excelsior Hotel near Heathrow, when he had weekends or a day over from the US. It was a time before widespread mobile phones and neither of us had one. I would arrive, at a completely random time, park the car, turn round and there he would be, strolling to the front door, knowing I would be there. He presented this kind of prescience as a matter of maths. Everything to Stuart was mathematical and he was astonishingly brilliant at maths. But to me, his understanding of time, of people, of the future, was more than maths. It was a kind of magic.

If someone loves you, unbidden and unsolicited, it can make you arrogant of its value. I was slow to see just how deep Stuart's intelligence was until it confronted and stunned me. He knew me too well and I longed to be someone else. As he was in the physics and maths departments, I decided that he must be a person without creativity and thus without depth. Then I heard him play the piano. He was an incredible pianist. When he played, I understood what he was saying, and it was full of meaning and beauty in a way I didn't expect. When we had met in the coffee bar when I was eighteen and he talked about playing the cello, I just thought that he was a Londoner and therefore conceited, and the cello was for people with pretensions. When I slipped out of his vision that day, beneath his notice, I thought he would never fully look my way and see who I was.

Stuart's sense of magical timing had caught me out again. He had known something all along that I had not known, that I hadn't even suspected. Those games of chess, where he seemed to have an uncanny understanding of several moves ahead, were a mystery to me. He would sit, maddeningly patient, seeming to help me with ideas, pointing out problems and patterns that I hadn't understood, and yet still sweep me off the board with a set-up that I could not possibly have foreseen. It was dizzying and glorious, and I laughed at the obviousness of it all.

Before the wedding I would stand in my rented flat, looking at the summer evening, and wonder what I was sleepwalking into. Then I dreamed about Stuart and I was filled with such an indescribable warmth and peace that I knew this was the right door to open.

I thought of my mother's courage: boarding the ship to West Africa at age twenty-two, sailing to meet my Dad again at Freetown harbour against everyone's warnings. They had been apart from each other a year and would marry the day after she landed. She had never been to West Africa, and when my father tried to push the too-small gold ring onto her finger she had no idea what was ahead.

We planned our wedding and lives together in a kind of outrageous innocence. Everything could be done: jobs and countries changed and ourselves intact and in love in the midst of it all. We married in Caldicot on 7th October 1995 and had our reception in Tintern, caught inside with the rain driving down outside the windows. My close friends, Denise DeCaires Narain and Ulele Burnham, both from Guyana, did the 'Best Woman' speech – a tour de force of funny assessments of my personality and past. Old friends from school, including Shournagh Rowe, were there. Shournagh laughed at the tale in the speech of me separating my eyelashes with a needle (entirely her fault). John Thomas played the harp throughout the service and reception, and in the morning we woke to a day so bright and beautiful and clear that it felt like a portent. My sister Isata had cried as she read the poem during the church service and I had cried as I explained to everyone at the reception why it had been my brother, Steven, instead of my father, who walked me down the aisle.

I think I surprised everyone. I was one person, then suddenly another. My work colleagues could not understand what was happening. I was young, ambitious and independent. Who was this bride?

Two days after our wedding, beginning our honeymoon in Sardinia before flying to St Lucia, I lay in the hotel bathroom unable to stop being sick. I couldn't lift my head or think. Something had taken over my body and all my senses. The two blue lines on the test proved I was in the early stages of pregnancy and the honeymoon lapsed into a dazed time of sick exhaustion. I was doubled over with severe pregnancy sickness and could barely walk at all. After our time away as a newly married couple, I stumbled out of my flat and tried to stride along the Brighton streets as I had done before but found that I could barely stand. One day, I leaned in a shop doorway, my legs shaking, and tried to remain upright. In the shop, standing in the queue, I collapsed and came round on the floor, faces peering down curiously. I had read that pregnancy was not an illness, that in this post-feminist world women could reclaim everything and not be limited by their bodies or their repro-duction, but I was physically floored. My body raged with hormones. I drowned in a swamp of violent smells and tastes. I couldn't eat, or think, or walk. Everything hurt and I felt deathly sick all the time. Perhaps this was how old age felt. At twenty-nine I was hobbling, crushed with nausea and pulsing with pain. It was better when I was immersed in a seminar. All my focus was directed at the teaching and the books. Then the students would leave and the fact of my disrupted biology would drown me again.

Stuart, living in Sardinia, asked to be posted to East Midlands Airport, the nearest he could get to me. I applied for the job of Lecturer in English at Birmingham University, the closest I could get to *him*. I prepared for the interview, pushing through each hour of my disabling pregnancy, and turned up as one of the handful of interviewees, wondering if everyone could see the war I was waging with my own body.

I got through the long day, all energy going into the questions, the dialogue, the lecture to the department. On show, I drew my suit jacket over my thickening waist and acted the part. When I was offered the job I was flooded with relief. That night I lay in bed, a sea creature washed up on the shore, and felt the fluttering of my first baby. I held my breath and then exhaled.

8

Becoming Parents

W E LIVED IN Nottingham, where my first daughter, Isata, was born, in a house in a cul-de-sac, with a new cot and pram. It was like playing at being grown-up. Suddenly, we would be parents. But even though pregnancy had been a far greater challenge than I had thought possible, I read all about birth and, with the arrogance of the young, I thought I would get first-class honours in that. When the contractions started, I thought I would manage it all with the steadied practicality of a modern woman. There was no need to be hysterical. Two days later, still in labour, I was crawling over the hospital bed, begging pitifully, 'Someone help me, please', and crying with defeat. The midwives had broken my waters, put me on an accelerating drip to speed up the contractions and all that had happened was an unending avalanche of continuous pain from which I could not draw breath. I had no control at all.

The midwives were supercilious and without mercy. They thought my attempt to take intellectual ownership of the event laughable, and my refusal of painkillers simply stupid. The baby was stuck and I wasn't dilating. A doctor arrived looking younger and more tired than me. He kept blacking out while he was leaning over me and his heavy eyelids would close like lead over his eyes mid-procedure. I thought that perhaps I should prop him up, but I was prostrate with pain. He began stabbing the head of the baby that was still stuck inside to check the oxygen level in its blood. (Apparently, there was too much hair on the baby's head and he couldn't get enough blood on the blade.) I was in an agony of anxiety. What if this repeated stabbing hurt the baby? What if my inefficient body had starved it of oxygen and it lay, killing me, its own life ebbing away as it languished there. I remembered my beloved friend and colleague, Siobhan Kilfeather, and how she had phoned me at work from her maternity leave, her Northern Irish voice earnest with shock: 'It's torture, Kadie. Birth is medieval'. Now I knew what she meant.

At the insistence of the midwives, an irritable doctor came to inject my spine with the epidural. I was crying, and she shouted at me to stop. I had to be told that this was poison in my back and any false move would paralyse me for life. I wondered how I had got into this torture chamber for women and for what I was being punished. I had already been told that, at thirty, I was rather old to be a first-time mother. Now I was being yelled at for being young and silly. The baby inside me was facing upwards instead of towards my back, and I thought of my sister, Isata, and her horrific forceps birth. Stuart and I were left alone as a problem managed for a while, and I lay there, blank with shock.

When, hours later, the baby had miraculously turned and decided to come, they took away the epidural and I followed the waves of pain and panic in a storm of confusion until Isata appeared, brown and with a curly mop of thick, black hair. It was a miracle.

Our reality had changed for ever in that one moment and we were so overwhelmed by love that neither Stuart nor I could articulate anything else for months. I remember giving a speech at the wedding of our dear friends, Dave and Sue, in Wiltshire when Isata was less than two weeks old. I had become a thing that made sense only if I was talking about my baby. I could think about and feel nothing else. My speech floated about the stunned hall of guests as though I were not even speaking a language, and I lost all sense of structure and context. All I could think of was this little warm body, which was the single most wonderful thing in the world. Stuart and I kept seeking each other out to talk about her and look at her. It was the demonstrable thing about our love, and it made us so passionate about each other that we could see only our own faces and the baby that was ours.

I didn't understand how women had babies and then thought about intellectual things. I had so little sleep, with Isata seemingly up all night, that I couldn't thread time together anymore. I leaked milk and gibbered like a fool when friends came to visit. As the weeks went on I tried to look normal by putting make-up on my eyes, but I was so tired I ended up looking like a ghoul. I went to a meeting at Birmingham University before term started, thinking I could get there and back before Isata needed a feed. I sat in the meeting with the other lecturers and professors, with milk, hot and urgent, pumping into my bra and breast pads, and I couldn't remember what I had been saying. When I was pregnant and so sick that I wanted to be hospitalised and left alone in a faraway institution, I read about women who ran marathons while pregnant. Now I wanted those super-mums to just hold their discretion and leave the rest of us hopeless cases well and truly alone. I was a mess…but so in love with my baby and husband that it was all the world to me.

Term began and because I had to put little Isata into nursery, I had to stop breastfeeding her. Separating her from me was painful for us both. She screamed long and hard when the bottle came towards her and my body ached with the pointlessly leaking milk. At the Nottingham nursery, The Mount, I had to hand her over and walk away. It was a beautiful nursery with carers who were bright and efficient, and full of affection. But I was distraught.

Work settled down into Isata screaming until 3 a.m. and me getting up at 5 a.m. to drive to Birmingham, trying to beat the rush-hour traffic but meeting the lorries instead on what was then the single-lane A453 to join the motorway. Stuart would take Isata to nursery on his way to work at the headquarters near East Midlands Airport. I lost a stone in weight, but I didn't know how thin I was until people gently commented. I loved the teaching and I would arrive early, miss lunch to catch up with the marking, and leave for the sometimes two-hour drive to get to the nursery by 6 p.m.

I got ill. Standing on a street corner in West Bridgford, where I had taken the car in for a service, I was suddenly unable to walk or move at all. A cloud had come into my head and I was so unwell I wanted to faint. There before me, unbidden, appeared Stuart. From over the bridge in Nottingham he had somehow known that I was in need and had come without question to scoop me up and take me home. I lay in bed for two weeks, completely unable to get up, so cut down with flu that my mother came from South Wales to look after me and Isata.

Stuart's job took him to London, so we moved to Oxford with the simple logic that it was halfway between Birmingham and London, but this simply made commuting to work a nightmare for both of us. I spent two terms driving in morning rush-hour traffic from Oxford to lecture at Birmingham University. I was sick to my core with the second pregnancy, and every morning I would suddenly wake, heading for the crash barrier, or the back of the car in front, a sixth sense saving me just in time. I *had* to drive because of the nursery school drop-off and collection, as obviously the train was not an option. But when I was face down on the steering wheel, shaking with nausea, I knew I had to stop.

A few years before this, while I was working at Sussex University, I had applied for a lectureship at Fourah Bay, University of Sierra Leone, in Freetown. I was accepted and began making the complicated plans to leave. But then the civil war broke out, heralded by the refugees from Liberia whom I had seen in ragged groups in the centre of Bo while I was there at twenty-four. The choice was taken away.

Stuart had been offered a good position at Gulf Air in Bahrain when we were just married, but I said no as my career meant so much to me and I didn't want to give up my lectureship in the UK. He was offered the job again, and by now I had faced enough near-death experiences to know that it was time to move. It's strange why we make the decisions we do. We could have moved to Birmingham and Stuart could have commuted by train to London. But I thought that wasn't equal or fair, and I was so driven into the ground by hormones and exhaustion that I just wanted to go. That sense of always being temporary, never quite at home, had never left me, so I was happy to go to Bahrain – not listening to people around me who made closed-minded comments about Muslims. Most of my family were Muslim and deserved respect.

Moving Again

WHEN ISATA WAS born, I was amazed by her concentration and the way a light shone in her face when she heard music. It stopped her crying, it held her enthralled. She would pull herself up in her cot and sing, perfectly in tune. Adults constantly underestimate the emotional intelligence of children and their involvement – mind and body – with their surroundings. Children notice change and loss with such depth and devastation from such a young age that perhaps it goes some way to explaining the natural connection that little ones have with music.

Braimah had been born as we began to think about the disruption of moving abroad. With the birth of Braimah, our bright, articulate, happy little girl became a dark force of disobedience. She stared at Braimah and me with a fixed and scorching glare and began having desolate moments between sleeping and waking where she would shout uncontrollably, unable to focus. We began to pack away familiar objects around Isata and she became more disturbed and more unsettled. She began to see an apparition called Tom who would always appear in the same place in the house. She would point at this place with such a terrifying scream that we began to think we had a resident malevolent ghost and became unnerved ourselves. Soon, at the age of seventeen months, she began to look aged and would cower in her cot, all confidence in the world beyond having completely gone.

This was when Isata, so advanced and precise in her speech, began to lose her connection with language. Unable to make sense anymore of her world, the structure of her speech began to bend and warp in astonishing ways. The first things to buckle were her vowels. She began saying pasto rather than pasta; wato rather than water. The letter 'r' became a strange and unwieldy puzzle to solve and she put a kind of Herculean energy into sounding it, contorting her mouth as she did so. Every vowel began sliding out of her control and we would watch her, frowning at herself, as though she knew something was very wrong but she couldn't work out the conundrum.

I was exhausted with proofreading my new academic book, staying up all night with a crying baby and making arrangements to move abroad. Stuart was abroad most of the time and Oxford was a city far away from family and friends. Stuart would leave for Bahrain before me and I would stay at my mother's house in Wales for three weeks before joining him with Isata and the baby. At this point, Isata appeared to suffer further emotional torment. Terrified of cracks in the pavement – Tom having followed her to Wales and with her moments of absent sleepwalking, her panic increased. I kept thinking: but she's less than eighteen months, how can she even understand the change of place and the loss of her father? Am *I* not still here?

I began to wonder if I should get advice from a psychologist who specialised in toddlers, or perhaps a doctor. I didn't, primarily because the pressures of managing two little ones, eighteen months old and a baby, not sleeping, moving home and feeling emotionally exhausted, were too much. One evening, in the middle of a bath, Isata suddenly began screaming. She was rigid with terror and could neither see nor hear us. With the help of my mother and sister, I managed to get her out of the bath where she thrashed around on the floor like a newly caught fish. We were horrified and lost for words. Was this a complete psychological breakdown? Had I lost my little girl? She finally came back to consciousness and I cuddled her gently. She was wet and shaking and couldn't tell me what she had been trying to express. All I could do was to mutter soothing words and stay still.

The terror lurking in pavement cracks and the apparition she encountered in doorways, night horrors shadowing the waking hours and a fear of the outside – maybe these were manifestations of the same thing. Isata lost confidence when the structure of her world didn't remain intact. If her father, if familiar things, could disappear through the holes, then peril was able to engulf her entire being. As an eight-year-old, I experienced that same inability to stand up to the collapse of another home, or bring myself to walk away from what had become safe. My body simply enacted its own crumbling defeat. Was it an unconscious defiance against being taken away again? If I remained unmoving I could find stasis. And Isata, having begun with a toddler's refusal to get dressed, to do as she was told, had become unable to move or to be awake without panic.

Tom travelled with us to Bahrain and took up terrifying residence in a particular doorway, but he began to fade and in his place came the passion for order that dominated Isata's childhood personality. Reunited with her father in Bahrain, she began to centre herself again and Tom gradually receded. We knew that her uncanny intelligence was making her hyper-aware of an emotional world around her she could neither control nor stabilise. The nursery staff in Oxford had told me that her sharpness of mind was extraordinary and the head of the nursery in Bahrain took me aside and assured me urgently that Isata was a genius. But she was also our little girl who needed the people around her to remain solid and constant.

We decided that this kind of intelligence needed something more than a school curriculum and it was at the age of four that Isata began music lessons. Her first teacher, Renate, decided that Isata should learn recorder and music theory, and Isata's lessons with her were wonderful forays into the world of orchestral music, symphonies and concerti. She had a beautiful stereo system in her home and she would listen with Isata while they sat together in this new landscape of music. Isata was fascinated by the congregation of sounds all together that formed an orchestra. The music had endless depth and instruments were in chorus together or pulling apart in layers of harmony. This was a revelation to her.

At home, I would sit with Isata as she completed her music theory. We were already entranced by the speed of her ability in reading and we saw how she loved the ordered patterns of the notes and the precision of the key signatures. She was already singing in perfect tune in her cot and the recorder was a logical ease. Music was easy and fun for her, and she was immediately meticulous and swift, understanding the patterns of the notes and how they built a language. Her recorder playing was clean and clear, and in music she found the same happy play that she entered while learning to read.

Stuart and I loved music, and we focused on teaching Isata to read early and played music constantly at home. When music was playing and children were dancing around her, even as a toddler, Isata would stand stock still, incline her head and listen intently.

But our preoccupation then was her mind. Her spoken language developed very quickly, as did her reading. Isata's preconceived understanding of order, to intricate levels of complication, from a very young age, was fascinating. She was able to see the patterns of things and to impose her own patterns on the world with an unswerving concentration. When she was eighteen months old she would insist on picking up all her soft toys, teddies and little dolls in exactly the right order. When the teetering pile nearly obscured her face, she would carry her treasures to the next room. If one fell or shifted position, the obsessive frustration was extreme and there would be no rest until the pile was again perfectly reconstructed. Everything had its place, minutely, in her world order.

Her sense of humour partly grew out of this passionate understanding of the pattern of things, and what was wildly funny to her as a toddler was a managed subversion of this order. One day, at about eighteen months old, she lay on the mat as I changed her nappy, with her big toddler-size teddy, Bentalls Bear, lying beside her on the bed. I turned around to pick up a clean nappy, and turned back to confront Bentalls Bear on the mat and Isata lying in his place on the bed waiting excitedly for my laughter.

This instinctual sense of creativity and order made Isata startlingly quick with maths, reading and word games. As a small child, she picked up an electronic Scrabble game that none of us adults could understand, and it became such an obsessive object for her that she began beating the machine in every game. Her level of concentration was so deep and so intense that we eventually had to confiscate it.

In Bahrain, I was able to concentrate on the children and know that I was no longer hurtling towards a crash. The people of the island loved children, and if any child were lost in the souk or in a shopping mall, a Bahraini man would place the toddler or small child on his shoulders so that the parents could see their child. We never worried about the children's safety and there was no need for them to be streetwise. I was intending to work at the university there, but Sheku and then Konya were born and the time was pushed ahead. When my hips began melting with painful hormones while pregnant with Konya, or my mind wouldn't work in Arabic classes, it didn't matter so much that I couldn't think.

But I began to lose definition at the edges. I was fading behind the blur of motherhood as though I had never existed. People talked to me as though my limits were obvious and permanent. 'What does your husband do?' And even, 'What do you do?' became questions that would keep me awake at night. I couldn't talk about cookery or art or house decoration because they were not my gift, and more significantly I couldn't see how to find the time. I was play-acting at fitting in, and Stuart and I would laugh in bed at night at what outsiders we were. In the midst of our crowd of friends, it seemed that no one could see us.

I began to get homesick. This was a revelation for me. I was homesick for British culture, for a sense of humour and context I knew and understood. When we came back to Nottingham for Stuart to work as a consultant for British Midland at East Midlands Airport, we listened to Jo and Twiggy on Trent FM and felt at home again.

Now it was January 2002. We had moved into our home in Nottingham four months before, on 11th September. We had come back to Nottingham after three and a half years away in Bahrain, moving in with four children aged five and under. While I dealt with furniture and children, my phone kept ringing with news of one aeroplane and then two crashing into the twin towers of the World Trade Center in New York. It had been a sunny September day, the air very still, and none of us knew what this would all mean.

It was the new year, weather harsh and grey, and I was crawling along the hallway on my hands and knees. I was too ill to stand, and felt weak with fever. Isata and Braimah, aged five and four, were looking at me with interest, while Sheku and Konya, aged two and one, were running and tumbling between the rooms. I knew that I had to sort out their breakfast, but I was sick with flu and two months pregnant. Stuart had had to go to work at East Midlands Airport, consulting for British Midlands International Airways, and my mother was at home in South Wales in bed with the same virus.

Sheku thought that this was a good time to try to ride horseback on me, and Konya needed her nappy changing. I decided that the kitchen was the closest destination and managed to tip Sheku back onto the floor and achieve a crouching position on my feet. 'Are we going to have breakfast now?' Braimah asked, looking steadily at me, head to one side. 'Of course', said Isata, bossily pushing him out of the way and hurtling into the kitchen. Konya padded along, nappy hanging, with her usual look of quiet unconcern. I heaved myself to the cooker and miraculously made the ground rice by concentrating very carefully and very slowly on each minute detail, mixing milk with powdered rice until it boiled and simmered. Now I had to deliver the food to the children.

Chaotic jostling had erupted by my feet, and Sheku had decided that an unwise wrestling match with his older brother would be fun right now. Braimah joined in heartily, with complete certainty of victory, and a stray foot kicked some plates onto the floor. I felt hot tears burn the back of my eyes but managed to get both boys seated, with Isata at the little plastic table and Konya strapped into her high chair. The ground rice, thick and warm with milk, was eagerly eaten up by all of them, happily covering most of the high chair and some of the floor. I grabbed a big cloth, soaked it in warm water and wiped them all down, releasing Konya from the high chair and realising that her nappy had leaked all over it.

The children, released from mealtime, began playing and squealing in the next room, finding toys and each other, and I faced the next task. My head ringing with fever, I managed to coax Konya to crawl up the stairs with me. She obediently allowed herself to be cleaned and changed, and we made our way downstairs again. Exhausted, I lay on the floor. This was always a mistake as it was a signal to all of them to fall and land on top of me, shouting with delight.

The days, the weeks, the months were drowned in the needs of the children. Shivering as I was, each warm body was pressed against me, knocking into me, crawling over me. I knew intimately their hot breath and the soft smell of their skin. I couldn't see past the feel of curled hair on my cheeks and the constancy of their needs.

Now, in Nottingham, I was on my fifth pregnancy, weak with sickness and shuddering with flu. But I looked at each of my unique children, definite and intense with their own person-alities, and wondered at them.

Before ever becoming pregnant, I thought that pregnancy would be all about me and my decisions. I had thought that a baby would tuck snugly into the life already there, already planned. I had thought that I would have four babies neatly fitting into ideas already settled and routines pre-set. When each one was born, those glib assumptions vanished, and I lay there astonished by the force of the person before me.

Nature and Nurture

BACK IN BRITAIN and settled in Nottingham, we introduced Isata to the piano at age six, buying a basic small Yamaha upright with all the savings we had. We were not surprised when she demonstrated perfect pitch, saying immediately, with her back turned, what note was being played on the piano. Within weeks Isata went from a gleeful recognition of exactly what A sharp or E flat meant to a glorious playfulness with keys and styles. She would learn the simple piano piece that was given to her by her piano teacher, make it perfect with both hands together and learn it by heart in a few minutes. The rest of the week was spent augmenting the left hand and the harmonies, developing the tune in different ways, changing the key between major and minor, experimenting with dynamics, emotions, chords and running quavers. She would hear music on the radio or CD and make her own elaborate and passionate performances of them, incorporating melodies, backing vocals, bass notes and echoing top notes, all from memory and interpretation. Then she would perform her own compositions, grown from these ideas, changing the styles to reggae, pop ballad, and classical, adding variations.

At primary school her maths abilities were far beyond those

expected in her school year and her reading level was so advanced that the head teacher called us in for a meeting to discuss how to teach her. We decided that her need for patterns and order also demanded need for security and emotional safety, so we didn't want to accelerate her into an older class and age group. From age six I took her to piano lessons every week, sitting with her four younger siblings in the crowded car outside. When introduced to Mozart, the music immediately made sense to her and we saw her deeply perceptive love of patterns lead her, spellbound, into a world of meaning.

At age nine, she heard that 'the best place to study music is the Royal Academy of Music in London', and incredibly they had a Saturday school for children under eighteen who were too young to study there full time. There was a tough audition and the standard was very high, but she was desperate to go. I contemplated the money and privilege behind those children in the heart of London, the expensive lessons they must have had, the expensive instruments they must own, and the inside knowledge their parents must have. Neither of us had heard before of the Primary and Junior Academy, and I worried about pushing Isata into an environment that we didn't understand, couldn't afford and into which she perhaps couldn't gain entry.

Stuart brushed all this aside and began enthusiastic planning with Isata. She would need to practise harder and we would need to find her the right audition pieces. Having introduced the idea, Isata never flinched from achieving her goal. We listened to recordings and watched videos, looking out for suitable pieces to play and musical ideas. Isata practised, listened and thought about how the music felt and what she wanted to communicate. Stuart and I were learning too. It was more than going to a piano lesson and learning the notes, which she could play perfectly in terms of precision and accuracy. She had raced through most of the piano grades with her faultless memory and quick understanding of structure and pattern. Even though, as a baby, she had no natural hand grip and fine motor skills, she quickly developed lightning fingers on the piano. By age nine, she knew how to communicate joy, brightness and delight. There was a singing, clean quality to her playing that made me think of the sun coming into the room. But now she was to play Mozart's 'Fantasia'. We decided that she should play it at the Nottingham Music Festival, the local music competition that, unknown to us at the time, was in its final year. The adjudicator, Murray McLachlan, listened to her play and asked her about opera. We couldn't afford to take the children to see operas, which were prohibitively expensive. There were no discounted seats at the Theatre Royal in Nottingham as there were at the Royal Concert Hall for the classical music seasons, so we couldn't introduce her to this. This piece, he said, needed an understanding of opera, of ballooning emotion, of grandeur and passion. She needed to hear and to express *tragedy*.

It was Stuart who sat with Isata and helped her to shape the phrases in the music. At that time, working at East Midlands Airport, he was home in the evenings to sit next to her at the piano and work through the details. Stuart's own council-funded piano lessons in London as a child, coaching him beyond Grade 8 distinction, and his parents' own love of classical music, were his foundation.

The morning came for the Royal Academy audition and the train journey to London. I waited in Nottingham with the younger children, aged eight, seven, five, three and eight months, and worried constantly. The result of the audition would not be known for two weeks. Isata came home with a photo of herself standing at the entrance to the Academy on Marylebone Road, eagerly straight and burning with hope. She had played her two piano pieces and her violin piece. She had demonstrated her aural and sight-reading skills and done her interview. Now, we had to wait. Had we set her up in excess hope in order to endure failure? Had it been fair of us to encourage this ambition and desire when it was beyond her reach? It hadn't been easy. Several nights found Isata worrying into her pillow when I came to tuck her in. 'Perhaps I won't be good enough', she would fret. Her Auntie Rhonda said to her quietly, 'Think like Muhammad Ali. "I am the greatest!"'

When the letter arrived two weeks later, a sunny morning in June just after Isata's tenth birthday, I was leaving the house with the six children for the morning walk to school. I had Aminata in the pushchair, Jeneba and Konya holding on to each handle and the boys holding each of their free hands. Isata walked close to me, leading every conversation. As we began our usual morning procession up the street, we bumped into the postman and I was handed a white envelope marked with the Royal Academy of Music. Our procession stopped with a jolt. My hands were shaking as I opened the letter. The children looked up at me and I swallowed. Would all that hard work, all that dreaming, be for nothing? I read, 'We are delighted to offer Isata a place', and relief and delight lit up the morning.

A few months later, when Isata was ten, a family friend, Barbara Carpenter, gave Isata several music books, including the score of a Beethoven symphony, and this was an entirely new encounter for her. The music was written on several levels, in depth, with each group of orchestral instruments accounted for. My mother bought the children the composing software Sibelius, for them to work out for themselves. Within days, Isata had written her 'Piano Concerto in C Minor', complete with three movements and a haunting theme. We were amazed. How could all of this have been in her head? There were new melodies, new ideas, new harmonies and counter harmonies that Isata had sifted through in her mind and carefully written on the screen, line upon line. She played the piano part to us, already committed to memory because it was hers, and we listened to the tinny machine voice of the computer playing the score to us like a cartoon version of the real thing. Isata dreamed of her composition, a reality to her, springing alive on a stage through the multiple voices of real instruments, with herself as soloist, playing her own piano part under her fingers for everyone to hear.

Stuart, never shy and always resiliently optimistic, had no time or patience for caution. He had sent the score to a few orchestras to see what they thought. I loved and was always incredulous at Stuart's refusal to accept limits. There was never any jaded irony about who his children were and what they could achieve. Any suggestion (and there were so many) that Black children could not and should not try to be the best and most celebrated at anything was met with straightforward anger and dismissed. I often wanted to draw in and protect them all from the scepticism of a world that didn't expect them to succeed, but Stuart, bold and brilliant himself, refused to consider it.

I marvelled at, and clung to, that bravery. Stuart would come home from work and tell me the painful barriers that were put in his way at work. There were prejudices that held him back but never convinced him to retreat. Once, early in our marriage, an American boss had told Stuart that he had to wear a white vest under his shirts because his black skin was showing through. Another time, a few weeks into a new job in the Middle East, his immediate boss, a decent and gentle Bahraini, had told him that the executive boss – a White Englishman – had proactively slashed the salary that Stuart should have received because 'no Black man should expect that level of pay'.

Stuart used these sporadic attacks as fuel to his own determination to work harder, to succeed and to hold his children up to the world in the light of his own belief in them. We looked for role models in classical music, but in the UK at that time they were hard to find. Stuart remembered the 1970s, cruel for both of us, and how the media claimed that Black footballers would never succeed in the sport because of their fundamental lack of discipline. Now, dominating the sport and highly visible, those footballers have staked their claim. We knew the cost of doing this, but Stuart would not compromise. He watched Isata, who was unaware of her own singularity, and he would have done anything to conserve her unsullied joy in the music.

The conductor of St Bartholomew's Orchestra in London answered and said he would gladly arrange for his orchestra to play Isata's concerto. I looked at Stuart with wonder and understood what bold belief in something meant.

The afternoon of Isata's concerto debut with St Bartholomew Orchestra came with a sense of breathless unreality. *Nottingham Post* had taken up the story of Isata writing her own piano concerto and it had made the front page of the newspaper. The concert would be taking place at the Waldorf Hotel in London. Isata had the easy excitement of a child doing something wonderful but not unusual, as though she were being taken for a trip to the pond to sail the boat she had made from scraps and twigs.

On the stage in the hotel ballroom, she walked in front of the adult orchestra as a small eleven-year-old in her three-quarter-length white dress, watched by a big audience, among them a crowd of friends, cousins, aunties and uncles, parents, grandparents and siblings. She was bright and eager, childlike in the simplicity and directness of her performance, at the centre of her own drama. When she played, every note of piano and orchestra memorised, every note articulate and loved, I knew she was where she had to be.

This love of composition, linked so closely with performance, was a bright thread through the children's childhood. One week in the summer holidays, staying with their grandparents in

London, the older three composed several string quartets and piano trios for fun. They were eleven, nine and eight, and this week was a gift for them to spend how they liked. Given total freedom from school and routine, they huddled over Sibelius, that immeasurable gift from my mother, and composed together with such vivid energy and delight that when they came home and performed for us what they had created, we wondered at the excitement of it all. Later, this grew into the compositions and arrangements created together as a group of seven, learning all the time how music is an act of communication and sharing, their distinct personalities competing furiously to produce a chorus of instrumental voices.

In the midst of having a house full of very young children, there is a constant battle for structure. The only way I could manage the wonderful chaos of several strong personalities was to balance a sense of humour (they were all so funny and so interesting) with a determined attention to routine. The morning pre-school order was planned to survive the tyranny of the rogue nappy change, the random tantrum or an insistent desire from one or more of the children to wear inappropriate clothes. While I dealt with spilt milk or an incomplete PE kit, I would be laughing over Isata getting a word subtly wrong, or Braimah furrowing his brows over a vexed question about what he would do if he couldn't find his football in the future. I would pluck Sheku down from his climb up the front of the bookcase and halt the journey of baby Aminata being pushed helter-skelter by Konya and Jeneba between rooms in their dolls' pram. I would often reach the front gate, procession complete, to find that Sheku had sneaked several toy cars up his school jumper, or Konya had her shoes on the wrong feet, the baby was hungry again and Isata had forgotten her book, and I would stop for a moment, defeated.

The evenings were carefully mapped at an early stage. After

the voracious mealtime, there was reading and writing, and everyone had a music session on the piano or on their stringed instrument. The boys would often practise their remarkable gymnastics in the hallway while waiting their turn, while I sat breastfeeding and listening to one of the girls at their instrument.

Night after night, in the relentless after-school routine, I sat with each of the children in turn, listening and helping them with their music practice. Stuart would also be sitting with children in turn if he was home in time after work (and not working abroad). When Stuart approached a piece of music, he loved the drama of the big picture, while I was forensic about the notes, the timing and the dynamics, which had to be clean and accurate. I made sure each child didn't smudge a running passage with blundered notes, or crash through a phrase that was meant to be quiet. But I was also tired. It was a condition so constant it was simply a fact of life. I thought for a while quite seriously that perhaps I had developed narcolepsy because every time I sat down in a waiting room, in the opticians with one of the children or even at the steering wheel, I would drop off. But there was no time to consult a doctor. Even the *thought* of sitting in a chair in the surgery sent me to sleep. While I was sitting and listening to a child practise, I often found myself waking up with a jolt, mid-breastfeed, to find one of the girls calling me, exasperated, to pay attention. If I was sitting with one of the boys, I would suddenly stir to hear Braimah or Sheku gleefully playing a crazy composition for fun, taking full advantage of my exhaustion to break free. I asked many a time, 'Have you played all of your scales?' Or 'Let's finish going through this piece now'. And they would answer, 'Yes, of course', or 'I've been practising this piece over and over'. It was later that I found out how much they fabricated, laughing among themselves at their regular victories.

My knowledge of music was enough to start all the children on their instruments. I knew the keys, the notes, the strings, and I had Grade 5 theory, Grade 7 piano and Grade 5 clarinet and violin. What I didn't have was any substantial education in classical music. I didn't know who the famous musicians were, or the difference between a good and a bad recording. But I remembered beginning to practise for my Grade 8 piano, and longing for someone to teach me how to play all of Mozart, all of Mendelssohn, to understand the technique needed for each era of music and knowing that I was out in the wilderness, looking in.

I lost Stuart's enthusiastic evening presence when Aminata, the sixth child, was born and Stuart got a job based in London. The punishing daily commute, leaving before 5 a.m. and returning home by 8 or 9 p.m., meant that he had to sometimes stay overnight. Even when he came home he was too late to listen to the children practise, or diffuse the tempestuous rule-breaking of the boys and share the emotional demands from every side. Every day, I stood next to the washing machine in the draughty boiler room, with the usual mound of dirty clothes, Aminata on one arm, and cried.

There were times when the tiredness, the unremitting demands of six little children, would make me wonder if I could get through the day. Then one of them would say something shockingly kind, head on one side, looking at me, or Braimah would play a piano piece with a completeness that seemed to come from nowhere, and I would carry on.

When I had recovered from the flu, sizeably pregnant with Jeneba, my fifth child, after that freezing winter, I managed, at last, to tuck all four children into bed. Sheku was knocking Action Men and dinosaurs together under the duvet, Braimah had finally stopped laughing with him over an energetic joke, Isata had put down her book, and Konya, sweet-faced and thumb-sucking, had closed her eyes. I began tackling the next huge load of washing. The washing machine was downstairs, so I had to carry the heavy yellow laundry basket down the stairs, above my unwieldy bump. My knees were buckling with tiredness and pregnancy sickness, and my distorted control over my body was having its usual effect. I always lost sense of where my body began and ended, and clumsiness began to dominate. But the days were packed with jobs and duties, and I had to get through them. Disorientated and wobbling with the bulky basket, I slipped and fell thuddingly down the stairs. At the bottom, basket and clothes everywhere, the pain in my ankle and leg was extreme. I cried, holding my ankle, lamenting that Stuart wasn't there. But I had to get the washing done, so I crawled along the floor, put the clothes back in the basket and somehow carried on. In the next few weeks my leg burst out in violent varicose veins from thigh to foot, which had to be operated on several months later because it hurt too much to stand. I knew then, packed with bandages, and woozy with the anaesthetic, that there are, perhaps, moments where the self has to come full centre. But as a mother that can be an impossible lesson to learn.

I have often been asked, as though it's a mystery that needs to be probed, so unusual is it, why we have seven children. For me, it seems the simplest and most natural desire. I didn't have an urge to stop having children after Mariatu, but we stopped merely because Stuart was too worried to have more. I would have had the younger three closer together, but it was Stuart who pushed back against this. He was the one who, separated from their warm voices and vivid bodies, got up at 4 a.m. through the winter to face the grey reality of earning the money to feed them. Before we got married, Stuart announced that he would like three children, because he had always liked the idea of having a brother himself and three seemed like a good number. I immediately bristled and insisted on four. I had been one of four, and it seemed the perfect number, a family enclosed and rounded, like four walls against the wind. Stuart agreed, and we joke that we ended up adding our two numbers together and getting seven.

My longing for the fifth child came partly from the realisation that I was suddenly unlocked from the private, faraway cage of my own body, doors shut around me and my babies, and I was expected to walk out into the world again. It also came from the inexpressible joy that having children gave me. They are a magical reality, utterly palpable and real, and brimming with possible futures. I wanted to listen to everything they said, understand all their grief and make them a home that never crumbled. Perhaps I felt that the bigger the family, the warmer the home. The more siblings I could give them, the fuller their sense of identity would be. And perhaps, just *perhaps*, my anxiety about who I was could dissipate into them.

They have a father who is as present as any father can be. If he couldn't always be there physically, he was doubly there emotionally. The children have always known that. Often, waiting to play in a concert that means a lot to them, the nerves building, Stuart will rush in, impossibly, from a plane or train, ready to hear them. I wanted that bond to repeat itself as many times as possible, each moment standing as a monument against the immovable fact that my own father couldn't rush in last minute to be with *me*.

Another reason, I know, is the miscarriages. I had five miscarriages in order to have seven children. I mourned each foetus for as long as I remained not pregnant. When I was pregnant with Isata, I took Mum on a holiday to Jamaica as a 'thank you' for organising the wedding so beautifully. I was bowed down with sickness and I must have been a tedious companion. Trying to give her an exciting time, I went with her to climb a waterfall. I was just less than three months pregnant with a small bump in my swimming costume, and I realised while we were doing this that it was not a good idea.

Afterwards, I began bleeding and didn't stop, so a local doctor was called to the hotel to see me, Dr Minnott. He announced that I would have to attend his clinic for an ultrasound. This was far away from the fenced-off private beaches. We sat in a waiting room with the local people we would never have met otherwise, and I had an extraordinarily clear ultrasound scan. Little Isata, perfectly formed, thin and full of life, was waving and kicking and clapping, her hands sticking together each time in a slow-motion gesture. After that, I really was a tedious companion, making sure I walked slowly and rested, getting weaker for the sake of this baby I had seen.

During my second pregnancy, the same thing happened, but I thought it would be resolved as it had been before. I was driving up and down the motorway to work from Nottingham to Birmingham every weekday, leaving at 5 a.m. after Isata had screamed until 3 a.m. I got thinner. This time, the bleeding got worse and I had to stop, halfway to Birmingham on the hard shoulder, prostrate with the flooding.

I was too distressed to talk to Stuart's Mum when she tried to console me over the phone, then regretted not talking to her because I needed her so much. A couple of months later, I realised that I was pregnant with Braimah (when Isata was eight months old) and, looking up at the Eiffel Tower on a quick break with Stuart and suddenly feeling sick, I was full of fear. When the bleeding started, Mum accompanied me to work because I had a pile of books to carry, but although I was sick, all was well. There were miscarriages between Braimah and Sheku, Konya and Jeneba, and two between Jeneba and Aminata. The worst was the fourth miscarriage. After Jeneba had just been born, I didn't stop bleeding. The doctors were brought in to put me on a drip as I started shaking and turning cold. It was a very peaceful feeling for me, and I grew steadily distant, calmly watching Stuart anxiously holding baby Jeneba as I felt my body shake. Two weeks later, the bleeding started again and I ended up back in hospital passing blood clots the size of babies and needing a womb scrape and a blood transfusion. I refused the blood transfusion. I had heard of the scandals with infected blood and I knew that my situation was borderline. I think they were so aghast that I had five children aged six and under that they wanted to give me any help they could.

Stuart wanted no more trauma. We now had more children than we had agreed to and he was content. He was managing to keep going with consultancy work for British Midlands International Airways, but he felt the lack of security and we had the largest mortgage of everyone we knew. I had been living in the tyranny and the miracle of my own body for so long that I couldn't see past it. The children I had were all so close to me and I was with them all the time in a life that revolved around breastfeeding, nappy changing, group baths, meals and bedtimes. It was overwhelming and absolute, and they were the entire fabric of my life. I had long forgotten the difference between my body and theirs, and their needs were always paramount. When my brother, James, spoke to me with concern and asked me if I were going to start doing something for myself, perhaps go back to work or write another book, I looked at him with incomprehension. That other self that I had once been was swallowed up now in this wonderful sacrifice to the children and I was at once consumed with happiness and too tired to think. And when I was well, the intensive, gnawing longing for another baby had begun again.

There is nothing rational about wanting children. I hear criticism of those women who will do anything, at any age, to have children by any means, and I feel nothing but sympathy.

That longing, born of nothing but love, is neither selfish nor moral. It simply is. I had five children and yet, there I was, aching with desire for another, and the desire was no less fierce and all-consuming than it had been for all the others.

Even as Stuart argued against it, I became more stricken with longing. I saw in my head all the time the baby I couldn't have. I couldn't understand how Stuart could let me suffer in this pit of mourning when I was panicked with the loss of this baby I wasn't allowed.

I got pregnant and was triumphant. I was going to have the sixth baby and I was joyful. The sickness was the worst I had ever suffered, and it felt like a punishment for pushing Stuart into a situation he hadn't wanted. That Christmas of 2003, I lay on the settee in my Mum's lounge and wanted to go into a coma. I was so ill I could barely lift my arm. It felt worse than flu and I was drowning in the sickness. At three months pregnant, I staggered to the ultrasound scan alone. (Stuart was at work and I wanted to enjoy this moment of seeing my baby on screen by myself, with no anxiety beside me.) The radiographer looked without expression at the screen, doing the usual machine measuring and analysing. I waited, wanting to see my new baby and planning the future. 'It's bad news, I'm afraid', she said and turned the screen towards me. The baby was there, perfectly formed. But instead of the waving and slow-motion clapping that Isata had done, this little one sat still and its little arms sagged down in front of it, as though it had fallen asleep with exhaustion. There was no heartbeat.

I lay in bed, night after night after that, reaching out to my dead baby, trying to cuddle its little body to me as though it were there in the bed with me. Although it had died, my body would not let it go, so I had to go into hospital to have it removed. I ate nothing from the night before to be ready for the first shift of operations the next morning. But I lay there until late afternoon because they had other priorities. The ward was unfriendly and the nurses were without pity. Eventually, I was taken into the operating theatre, desperately hungry and desolate with misery. Afterwards, with the woman in the bed next to me inconsolable because her urine catheter was now leaking over the floor, I pleaded for food. One nurse briskly told me that there was no food and left me unable to move in the bed. Stuart came in for the evening visit, tired from work, and I asked him for something to eat. He was furious that I had been left hungry, and food miraculously appeared from some fridge somewhere. I still remember the taste of that tuna sandwich, intense in flavour simply because I was so hungry, but mercilessly stinging the inside of my mouth, which was full of ulcers.

I bled continually for nearly a year, getting pregnant briefly and bleeding again. The hospital doctors told me that I had a 'dysfunctional womb', but there seemed to be nothing they could do. I bled for the two weeks of our summer holiday in Wales and tried to focus only on the happy bundle of children that I was lucky enough to have. And I *was* so lucky. So why did I still reach in the dark for that baby who had died silently inside me?

We were due to go to Antigua for Christmas 2004. Just before we left, still bleeding continually so that I could never leave the house without sanitary pads, I lay in the dark in bed. Stuart was away for work and the children sound asleep. I prayed to Mary, mother herself, and asked her if she would heal me and give me the gift of another baby. I asked simply and fervently and humbly. And a miracle happened: she appeared and said, 'You only have to hope' – and I was filled with peace. I didn't tell this to anyone, embarrassed, of course, to admit to a religious experience and very sheepish in front of my own family, who had been slightly bemused by my conversion from my Welsh Baptist upbringing to Catholicism. But this was *real* for me. I immediately stopped bleeding and two weeks later, in Antigua, I conceived, giving birth to Aminata the following September.

For me, all my children were fated and gifted. I never understood when people would say to me how relieved I must be when the school holidays were over. I thought of what my Auntie Jen said, that she didn't have children to get rid of them. Seven children has always felt right, and each and every one of them is a miracle I can't explain.

11

Of Troth and Allegiance

S TUART AND I, young and naïve, imagined we were in control. Each child arrived, a bright jewel we knew intimately and pledged to preserve. But knowing intimately is not the same as knowing completely, and we were often knocked off our feet in wonder at something one of our children said or did. Even aspects of who they are can emerge from a hidden place beyond our notice. We had clear ideas about what a parent was and how to plan the future. We only had to write the plot and direct the proceedings. Wasn't it as simple as that?

So fierce was each flame of self-possession that we thought we saw the entire child at first glance. The rest was a matter of upbringing. If we were firm and loving, they would respond with perfect obedience and remain directly in our presence.

I remember the first time Isata said no to us. She was about a year old and we had told her to pick up her dropped toy. She stood, staring straight at us, and refused. The ground shifted. We saw her experimenting with new and innovative ways to test the limits. After we were shaken to the core by Isata's first 'no' as a very small toddler, we began asking questions. Hadn't we been firm enough? Why was she not conforming to the framework we had set? Other surprises had preceded this. She didn't sleep at night for five months, screaming until the early hours when I had to get up to drive to work at dawn. She had no instinctive hand grip as a baby and she refused to give up breastfeeding when I had to return to lecture at Birmingham University. We found these 'wilful' choices to go against us extraordinary.

From then on, what we imagined as a perfect structure of rules and expectations sprouted a forest of wild undergrowth and clamouring branches we had to battle through. As the family grew, the children nurtured between them a powerful group identity which was built on sharing, equality, kindness and love. It also fostered collaboration, gang secrets, loyalty and a bond to each other that lay outside our reach. They learned to value generosity, wit and integrity, and they also built a network of subversion, triumphs and in-jokes that Stuart and I could never hope to penetrate. Sometimes we're allowed to peek into their world and learn a funny story they kept from us, a rule broken or a sibling protected, and it makes us laugh. We know this is where their restless creativity has been allowed free rein, and where they learned to express their gifts in unfettered spaces.

It all seemed so obvious. Parents laid down the rules, showed the way and formed the growing personality. How could it not run smoothly? We had to learn that parenting is a constant conversation between one's expectations and the powerfully present person before you. We knew what behaviour we expected and there was no negotiation here. Respect and politeness had to be shown, particularly to adults and relatives. Never would any swearing and uncouth language be tolerated, and we demanded fairness, sharing and above all kindness to siblings. We could not, however, dictate personality. Each of the children was so definitely himself or herself that we knew we couldn't own them for long. Our job was to provide a consistent framework within which they could grow, feel certain and safe, and against which they could test their strength. They would playfully and surreptitiously subvert every rule they could and learn valuable life lessons.

It wasn't always easy to work out their motivations for acting contrary. They would devise elaborate acts of subterfuge to hide a lie or break a rule, or simply do the opposite of what we said in plain sight. We have a video of Sheku, for example, below the age of one, standing with Braimah in front of a cabinet of DVDs. He tries to grab one and I say no. He looks me directly in the eye with a mixture of innocence and defiance and, putting his hands behind his back, tries to grab another. Braimah, standing next to him, stares at him and gives him a push. Without taking his eyes off me as though daring me to see, Sheku reaches again for the DVD.

As parents we operated as most institutions do – with strict laws and by-laws – while knowing full well that within that tight structure there was quiet room for hidden disobedience and secret societies.

We concentrated on what they delighted in doing and on what they were good at. This led in many possible directions: to sport, academic achievement, writing stories, but *overwhelmingly* it flowed into music. Our choices for them were constrained by time, family commitments and money, but we couldn't ignore the natural gifts they had and their shining preoccupation with music. Yet each child has their own story.

Braimah, our second child and first boy, was born so strong that, at his birth, he began crying when only his head had emerged. He was physically confident, talented at football and gymnastics, and with a natural sense of balance and stamina.

We couldn't afford tennis lessons, but when he had a chance to play, he showed excellent hand–eye coordination and he could always dance. We have a video, taken on Christmas Day when he was three years old. Stevie Wonder's 'Superstition' was playing and he began to dance. This was a *performance*, playing joyfully to his audience, an extraordinary display of music moving fluidly and creatively through his body, and it spread a celebration throughout the room. He is a natural comic actor, always at the centre of a social gathering, able to imitate any voice or characteristic and make everyone laugh.

As a child, Braimah was also the one who would come, thumb in mouth, for affection, and the one who was always thinking, always contemplating the world. Born second to his older sister's sharp and quick command of language, Braimah developed a gentle stutter with the exact timbre and tone of my brother Steven's voice as a child. This stutter claimed him at times of conversation or speaking to older people, and persisted through his teens. Yet, like Steven, he never stuttered while delivering a speech and he is still always pushed to the front of the stage to address an audience, his voice loud and clear and his jokes perfectly timed.

His first instrument at age five was piano, and he had a concentrated, careful approach. Sometimes, if he got stuck on a passage for a long time, he would go to bed in frustration, wake up the next morning and be able to play it perfectly. When he decided, at age seven, that he would like to play the violin, I was delighted.

When Braimah picked up his first, cheap, half-size violin, we all waited for the inevitable screeching of the child player. But the sound that emerged was immediately sweet, immediately pure and direct. He played with a singing tone that grew sweeter and stronger every day, and his tone and intonation seemed to come from somewhere deep inside. I marvelled at the fearless physicality of this active boy, playing football, learning karate, ice-skating with friends with perfect balance and then quietly picking up this cheap violin and playing something that spoke with such depth and stillness.

Soon, he was playing with Isata accompanying him on piano. They had always been close, playing imaginary games together, constructing elaborate projects involving props they made themselves, or Jenga and Lego pieces. Now, listening intently to each other and understanding each other's personalities, they played duets.

It is impossible to trace Braimah's development as a violinist without Isata and Sheku. Their relationship with music was indistinguishable from their relationship with each other. When they practised their separate scales and studies for their teachers, it was in the knowledge that the others were doing the same. The pieces they learned to play were shared by all of them. Isata accompanied both boys, and both boys played the piano parts for each other. They adapted pieces played by the others for their own instruments, or created harmonies and counterparts to play together.

At first, playing together was simply and naturally an extension of their exuberant games; tumbling, imaginative games down the stairs and in the garden; secret plots in their bedrooms. They were always banded in furtive rebellions against Stuart's and my rules, involving the younger ones in elaborate schemes to undermine our control. We knew this was the case and thought it very funny. We loved the fierce loyalty they had to each other, always covering up each other's transgressions and demonstrably upset if one of them faced punishment for answering back or breaking someone else's toy.

We thought we were in full knowledge of all their schemes and tricks, allowing the sibling secret society to function by pretending to be in the dark. Then there were moments where we would suddenly realise that they all inhabited a world they owned supreme. One of these moments of revelation came when they were very young, the older ones still at primary school. We had a strict rule that they were allowed on the computer only if they had maths homework to do or research for a school project. We didn't want them to be roaming the internet or wasting time on computer games. The television was never switched on during the day or after school. We allowed special treats of perhaps a DVD with all of us sitting together to watch on a weekend evening or to watch *Doctor Who*. It wasn't practical to have television or computer games because there was just no time to fit it in and the children never expected or asked for them. They were fascinated when their school friends would talk about the number of television programmes they watched after school or the amount of hours they spent on Xbox. How did they have the time?

Stuart and I would have teenage babysitters – usually the sons or daughters of close neighbours and friends (George, Grace, Graihagh, Rachel) – who would sit in the house so we could have an evening out. If out alone, we would spend the evening talking non-stop about the children. Later, the older ones were the babysitters, with a mixture of expert care and delighted misrule, or the patient and creative Sophie or Kassie. When they were little, the children were always asleep, used to an unvarying routine of early bedtimes and unbroken rest. The computer was password protected and the house quiet when we left. They were always cheerful when we kissed them goodnight and left the house, smiling angelically up at us as we tucked them into bed.

Then I came across a diary entry that Konya, seven at the time, had made a year earlier in a notebook she had finished with. I never read their diaries, always very respectful of their need for privacy in such a big family, and remembering how important that had been for me when I was a child in a close family of four children. But Konya was little and the diary was no longer in use, page open. I scanned the innocent, childish writing and gasped. She was triumphantly detailing a trick that they had all carefully planned and carried out months before. She described how Isata, Braimah and Sheku had rigged up a system where Isata's phone had been balanced, hidden on the settee and angled to film the computer keyboard. I had been called to type in the password ('Excelsior') for homework. After that, they had a video of the keys I had typed and the magic password. For almost a year, they had happily said their sleepy goodbyes as we went out, then immediately jumped out of bed and grabbed the PC. Stuart and I laughed for a long time at our parental innocence and the realisation that there are always competing family narratives, and ours is merely *one* perspective.

Another regular act of rebellion that we didn't discover until a long while later was the phenomenon of 'Matlock Mondays'. I drove Aminata every Monday in rush hour to Matlock, an hour and a half there and an hour back, in order for her to have her hour lesson with the wonderful Jo Percival. She was a violin teacher I had encountered at the Derby Music Festival and lessons with her were well worth the journey. Having lost Siân Evans who had moved away, Jo coped with Aminata when she was still little and reacted to her with humour when she chatted brightly and without shyness. Jo was loving and kind when Aminata would erupt suddenly into tears of uncontrollable misery at not being able to play something, her mercurial personality – drama followed by tragedy – a constant source of bemusement. While we were out of the house for the evening, I imagined the settled order continuing: homework, practice, Mariatu tucked into bed and soothed by Konya in her loneliness without Aminata to cuddle to sleep. I later discovered that Mariatu was indeed bathed, put in her pyjamas and comforted to bed, but then the homework and practice were abandoned for delighted feasting in front of a DVD. The television – never switched on during the week – was watched avidly by five happy, loud schoolchildren who would look out for the car headlights as I came up the drive, race to clear away the evidence, and look sleepily or sagely at me when I entered with their little sister. This wild and regular evening of riot while I was in Matlock with Aminata ended abruptly when she auditioned successfully for Junior Academy. She began lessons with Nicole Wilson every Saturday and I was no longer absent on those 'Matlock Monday' evenings.

It was this creative, subversive and secret language of brothers and sisters that I could see and hear when they played music together. They knew instinctively how to play with the rules to create new sounds, how to harmonise and complement each other's ideas and how to challenge each other into more daring feats of imagination. I still often see flashes of humour between them, a grin, a raised eyebrow, a knowing joke when they play as an ensemble. Sometimes, they would cover another's mistake by adapting their part, or stifling a laugh with a rogue musical phrase. Through their own secret games they developed a language of music that was part of that world.

Often, they dared each other to put something rebellious into a performance and wait to see if Stuart or I noticed. We have been at performances where we would suddenly notice a new trill, or a sly insertion of an earlier tune in the wrong place, accompanied by a smile across the stage if more than one was playing, or a raised eyebrow into the audience. Once, Sheku dared Jeneba to insert a 'Tierce de Picardie' (a major chord at the end of a minor cadence) into the last chord of her Chopin 'Ballade No. 2' at a concert at Southwell Minster. She was thirteen at the time and Sheku sixteen, and when the unexpected major chord rang out in the big church, instead of the minor, I felt a frisson of pleasant surprise but didn't guess in the moment quite why Sheku was quietly laughing.

Stuart and I tried hard to give them opportunities we could not really afford. The school they attended, Walter Halls Primary, was a vibrant city school with a diverse mix of children. They had to learn to deal with strong personalities, assert themselves against bullying and realise what an unacceptable swear word was. I gently fielded the endless demands for them to go to other houses for play after school and politely rationed this, but I knew it was important for them to have a community of friends. The school was run by an inspirational head teacher, Pete Strauss, who was passionate about music and organised Music Nights where children were encouraged to perform on instruments they learned in school or to sing. He used the school budget to fund talented music directors such as Vicky Manderson and Catrin Jones who would coach the choir and put on musical theatre shows.

The state budget could not cover learning an instrument before age nine or ten, and couldn't stretch to one-to-one lessons. We knew we would have to pay for private lessons if we wanted the children to learn early and advance. Braimah tried clarinet lessons in school at age nine and ten, but he was preparing for his Grade 7 violin exam and had passed Grade 5 theory, and the group lessons had to be pitched to the least skilled member of a beginner class. It was sad to see all of Braimah's peers robbed of the chance to progress and having to pay for lessons which would have been free when I was at school. Pete Strauss was a wonderful head teacher, making the most of the budget and filling in the gaps with his own energy and belief in the children, no matter who they were. Pete would play recorded classical music, for example Yo-Yo Ma's Bach cello suites, as the children walked into assembly, creating a calm concentration offered equally to all. (Since the time the older five children left for secondary school, there has been barely any budget for music and other creative arts, although the choir continues under the direction of Andrea Cox.) I wonder how different the children's response to music would have been had music not been integrated into the school day.

I remember one Music Night with the school hall packed with children and relatives, all excited to hear the choir and see their children singing and performing solos and ensembles. Stuart and I were with our close friends, parents of the children in the football team and parents interested in music. The children's friends, many from families who knew little about classical music, loved to see them play. It was Sheku's turn to take the stage with his cello, accompanied by Isata on the old upright school piano. He was a small eight-year-old with his half-size cello, and he clambered onto the stage with his usual calm, slightly distracted manner. A look at Isata and they began. Around us, his football friends, teachers and parents watched, transfixed. He looked at everyone in the room as he played, insisting that they come into his world and listen. It was impossible not to concentrate on every expression he made, and each note was played with such meaning. Yet the whole narrative of the piece was never lost, and Sheku, with Isata, drove us all to such an exciting conclusion that the room erupted at the end. No one could understand the alchemy that changed the small scruffy schoolboy into this beautiful intensity on stage. Within the context of his school and among his classmates, the cheap half-size cello had been transformed and everyone drawn into the spell.

Being allowed to bring their music into assemblies and Music Nights to perform in front of their friends, and to be celebrated by their teachers and head teacher, was a vital source of affirmation and encouragement. At their secondary school, Trinity, the older six have also always had the chance to play with their friends, facilitated again by inspirational head teachers, Mike McKeever and John Dexter, and more recently Mike Shenton and music teachers like Vicky Manderson.

Neil Bennison, events manager at the Nottingham Royal Concert Hall, was also intent on making classical music available to everyone. Free group tickets arrived at the schools for evening concerts to see famous musicians play, and we would go with groups of their school friends. The Go Classic cards were launched, which offered £5 tickets for concerts for young people and made it possible for us to take all the children regularly to hear live classical music.

Stuart and I began tightening our budget in order to pay for the music. We had moved into a house built in 1905, with big, cold rooms and two landings with lots of carpeted (soon threadbare) stairs to bump and slide down. We arrived with four small children and needed the space. Maintaining the house became an impossible task. The old wooden windows kept needing repair, old chimneys needed cement and repointing, a creaking water boiler suddenly burst and flooded the hallway. We carried on, patching together what we had to and studiously ignoring what we couldn't afford. There was rarely a discussion about priorities. The children were thirsty to learn and their obvious talent was a demand that we couldn't morally efface. Stuart's mother watched them when they were very young and said, 'Their talent is a great responsibility for you, a burden you have to shoulder', and we understood that we had a duty to fulfil. At that time, when we had four little ones and then five, all shining with energy and potential, Stuart looked at me and said with a deep breath, 'This is not even a decision for us to make. Here they are and we can't let them down'. I responded, 'Yes, your Mum's right. It *is* our burden and our job. Every day'.

Sheku began the piano at age five. I used to drive them all at rush hour after school to their early piano lessons in Arnold,

Nottingham. This was close by but involved sitting in long traffic tailbacks at that time of day. I had five children at this point and we would all sit outside in the car while the older three went in, one by one, for their lessons. We thought that it was important for them to have the structure of the weekly lesson so that they and we would have an external teacher to work for and a professional dimension to the learning. Also, I didn't have the confidence to think that I could teach them completely. While one was in his or her lesson, I would be reading with each of them. Jeneba, a small toddler in her car seat, would inevitably need the toilet and I had learned that little children do not fit neatly into preordained plans, as she either wet the seat or l had to hold her suspended over the gutter. This serial-reading practice wasn't always easy. Strapped into their car seats they didn't always want to cooperate but had to anyway. I remember Braimah, cross and scowling, looking at the Dr Seuss book and complaining, 'Oh Red Fish Blue Fish, and all that stuff'.

The children all learned the piano quickly and I soon realised that these limited lessons, once a week, were not enough. They each practised the scale or piece they were set within a day, consigned all to memory, and wanted more. Isata, playing simple half-page pieces of childlike music in her lesson, memorised the whole of Beethoven's 'Für Elise' at home and we knew they needed fuller challenges. It was time to move to a teacher who expected as much as we did, assessing each child not by age but by hunger and ability. I also wanted them to take up the violin.

I hadn't forgotten or overcome my unfulfilled desire to play the violin, so Stuart bought me, as a surprise, a violin for Christmas. I was delighted, in awe of the beautiful wood touch of the instrument, the sound of the plucked strings and the magical bow. But I had no idea how to play it and make it sound like the sad, sweet songs I had heard. I began violin lessons once a week during the day, while Jeneba spent a couple of hours in the local nursery, and I put all the determination I had time for into learning all I could. As I already knew how to read music, I concentrated on becoming proficient with string naming and the principles of tuning without the guidance of a keyboard or finger holes. I experienced the leap of faith it took to listen and remember where the fingers of the left hand stopped to make the correct note. It was a surprisingly physical experience and I didn't have the developed muscles needed to hold the violin for any length of time, or to move the wrist or arm in the right way to play vibrato. Everything hurt and nothing came instinctively. I had to think and work through my body as well as my mind. I did my Grade 5 exam at the end of a year of learning the violin, passed with merit after ballooning into the exam room, seven months pregnant with Aminata, and had to stop playing after she was born. But I had learned enough to help Isata and Braimah when they started the violin, and to teach Sheku for several months because we couldn't afford more lessons. It also made me remember, as an adult, what it meant to learn an instrument from scratch and to appreciate just how demanding and complete the learning is both emotionally and physically.

Sheku, sharp and quick, was also impatient. Braimah was playing well and Sheku, at nearly six years old, was behind his older brother. I tried patiently to guide him, but he didn't want to listen and was naughty in maddening, undermining ways. I would be explaining a fingering problem or showing him how to hold the bow and he would rudely begin playing, unable to slow down. The sound he made didn't inspire him, and although he could learn very quickly, he rebelled. I would be left at the end of every lesson crying with frustration. Now, when Sheku talks about his time learning the violin, the duration always shrinks. The several months became three, two, then one month. The last time I heard him discuss this period of violin lessons with a journalist, it had become two weeks in his memory.

Sheku was easily as gifted as his siblings, and to me the violin was a captivating instrument. I was determined to carry on teaching him. Isata and Braimah joined in the Stringwise weekend course in Nottingham for young string players. This involved two weekends of orchestral learning, ending with a concert to parents. We sat in the semicircular Nottingham Albert Hall in the audience, just above the cello section. Sheku sat, rigid and attentive, staring all the time at the massed cellos, and uncharacteristically unmoving. We would spend every Sunday at Mass in The Good Shepherd and, later, St Teresa's Catholic Church, with Sheku unable to sit still in the pew, often crawling, whispering and writhing out of sight by the kneeler. (I would simply be grateful that no one could see him.) Now, though, the dreamy whispers and restless shifting had stopped. At the end of the concert he turned to me, his face alight, pointed to the cellos and said, 'I want to play *that!*'

A cello hadn't been in our plan. Stuart had played cello to Grade 6 as a schoolboy, with piano as his passion. He saw the cello as a social tool, allowing him access to the local youth orchestra. We both looked at Sheku's face and knew we had to listen. He was rarely expressive in this direct way and we understood he wouldn't change his mind. We didn't know any cello teachers so we contacted Windblowers, the Nottingham music shop, and they recommended Sarah Huson (now Huson-Whyte), a young performing musician who had graduated from the Royal College of Music and lived in Southwell. We phoned her, arranged for her to give Sheku lessons at home, and found out from her where to rent a quarter-size cello.

When we brought the cello home to Sheku, it looked big next to his little body. He touched it quietly and with reverence. When he had his first lesson, he concentrated intensely from beginning to end and we could not stop him practising it, often on his own when I had to sit with the others. Stuart and

I watched, amused, through the open door to the room where he kept the cello. He would be totally absorbed, moving quickly from string plucking to the bow, playing with a kind of dogged fervour which was addictive to watch. If he saw someone paying him attention he would immediately change how he was playing, throw his head and body back and perform to whomever it was, watching them intently for a response. He always sought an audience, setting up a demanding communication between himself and the watcher, an irresistible connection which felt like a bewitchment.

When the boys played duets, Sheku was a typical younger brother constantly throwing a challenge at the older. For Braimah and Sheku, the wit and humour was as important as the music, and intrinsic to it, and I could hear and see the flow of their conversations while they played, as though they were sparring and jousting with their instruments. When Isata joined in this musical banter, she created a sparkling virtuosity that threw its own challenge and acted as an intense focal point for the music. They have always played together with a natural understanding, and their unfaltering listening to each other has always been a form of love.

Both boys, like Isata, began going quickly through the Associated Board of the Royal Schools of Music (ABRSM) grade exams. It was a valuable framework for learning and progress, giving them goals and points of achievement to spur them on. They made it a fun competition between each other, teasing one another about how high a distinction they could each achieve, and it gave Stuart and I clear markers as to how well they were doing and what techniques they needed to master.

Isata arrived at the Primary Academy at age ten, brimming with excitement from the early train and having Saturdays full of orchestra, choir, general musicianship, chamber music (music played in variously sized groups, from duets to larger ensembles of instruments), composition and her piano and violin lessons. On her first day, Stuart and I sat nervously in the Royal Academy canteen. We watched other parents, who all seemed to know what they were doing and who all belonged here. We sat, the only Black parents with the only Black child, and we didn't know if Isata was good enough. Even here, beyond the audition, beyond her acceptance, we worried.

Isata appeared at the canteen doorway after her first piano lesson with her teacher, Patsy Toh. Patsy was serene, kind and amused. She was also extremely pretty, older than us and very impressive. We soon realised that she had a sharp sense of humour and was keenly perceptive, which made her slightly scary. When she began talking about Isata's obvious talent and how we should consider a full-time music school for her, we were filled with such warm excitement that it felt like a dream, like that first day with the acceptance letter in my hand.

Patsy was an extraordinary teacher. She took Isata's bright talent and her quick mind and taught her to look deep into what she was playing and to express what she found there. The in-depth technique needed to touch a note in the most effective way, to round the wrist at the end of phrases and to develop from the small, clever child into a sophisticated musician was all achieved through Patsy's dedicated, perceptive teaching. We were in awe of her.

At the end of that first term, Isata had passed her Grade 7 with the highest marks in the UK across all instruments for the year. At the end of her third term, she had passed Grade 8, also with the highest marks in the UK, and was presented with two ABRSM Gold Awards for the same year, receiving the news in one letter. The following term, now eleven, she won Nottingham Young Musician as the youngest ever finalist, and the Nottinghamshire (Clement Pianos) Young Pianist competition, winning an upright piano for home and two digital pianos for Trinity School. It was only a month later that we sat in the ballroom of London's Waldorf Hotel and listened to Isata's piano concerto being performed by her with St Bartholomew Orchestra, and the glowing dream of a possible future emerged before us.

When Braimah, at age ten, gained his Grade 7 distinction on violin, and Sheku was about to take Grade 7 cello, they were determined to audition for the Primary Royal Academy as Isata had done two years before. We asked the boys if they were sure it was what they wanted. 'You'll have to practise a lot and work harder if you get in. Just look at Isata'. We were asked lots of questions by other parents at the school gates. One parent said, 'It's not fair of you to push two Black city boys to audition for a place like that when they just want to play football'. Another said, 'You're setting them up to fail'. One parent asked us what it was like to be such pushy parents. Crestfallen, I asked Stuart if we were taking them out of their own context and trying to wedge them into an environment that wasn't theirs. He just laughed. 'Who says it isn't theirs?'

The following Sunday morning, Stuart and I were woken at 5 a.m., startled to hear the sounds of a half-size cello and a half-size violin being played in two different rooms – a bedroom and the bathroom. When we opened each door we saw eight-year-old Sheku and ten-year-old Braimah practising with grim determination in the early gloom of dawn. This pattern remained, the boys supporting each other in their self-imposed regime for weeks, turning down camping trips with friends and games of football in the park because they wanted so badly to get through those Academy doors.

One parent we knew chided us directly, 'You shouldn't give these boys unreal expectations. Look at them. They don't belong there. It's cruel to give them unreal hopes'. He saw the boys throwing their energy into ambitious sliding tackles on the pitch and laughing with friends, and couldn't match these boys with the ones who got up at 5 a.m. of their own volition to perfect a semiquaver run.

When the morning came for their auditions, I began to think: What if these parents are right and all this encouragement is unfair and misplaced? Just because Isata had done so well, did it signal some kind of genetic destiny? Were we innocently leading the boys on to catastrophic failure? We sat on the train with the two of them, my mother having driven from South Wales to look after the other children, and tried to be upbeat for our sons. This *must* turn out to be the great adventure and golden chance they saw it to be.

Dominic John, the accompanist for the auditions, rehearsed with the boys and took each one into the audition room in front of Krystyna Budzynska and Jonathan Willcocks, while we sat outside and worried. They had practised their piano pieces as well, and we had listened carefully to their violin and cello pieces, performed several times for us. On the train afterwards, still not knowing the result, we discovered that we had boarded the wrong train and were charged an additional £150. And we didn't know if it had all been worth it. I still remember the hostility in the guard's face and feeling small and stupid, miserable at parting with money we couldn't afford.

The envelope arrived two weeks later, neat, white and bold with the red words 'Royal Academy of Music'. Had we done the right thing, encouraging our sons to walk through the marble entrance hall, past the busts of Beethoven and Bach, to audition for a place each? The letter, which I read with breath held, began with, 'We enjoyed meeting the boys and hearing them play', and then it welcomed both to Primary Academy. I sat down and let that breath out. We had made the leap of faith, taken the risk and landed on warm ground. We had believed in our children.

Two terms later, at age nine, Sheku was ready to take his Grade 8 cello. He was playing a rented three-quarter-size cello.

When he played it, the sound was much bigger and fuller than the instrument, and there seemed to be no separation between Sheku and cello. Isata was busy preparing Mozart 'Concerto No. 20' to perform with an orchestra near Nottingham, so we employed an accompanist from the university to play the piano parts. He came to rehearse with this little boy in our house, looked at Sheku and asked how old he was. We told him that Sheku was nine, and the accompanist sat, disbelieving, at the piano. After the rehearsal, the accompanist stood at the door, a look of awe on his face. 'But people *need* to *hear* him', he said. Sheku gained the highest marks for Grade 8 cello in the UK that year, and a letter arrived from the ABRSM exam board awarding him the Marguerite Swan Memorial Prize. The examiner wrote in the comments at the bottom of the exam sheet that it had been a privilege to hear him.

We knew the children's blinding musical gifts demanded hard work and talented teachers. We were very lucky with our children's teachers. Sarah Huson used to say she looked forward all week to teaching Sheku and listening to what he'd done with the pieces she'd given him. A teacher who responded to what she had before her, she let his own voracious pace lead the way and entered Sheku for an exam every term, loving his serial distinctions. Ben Davies (at Primary and Junior Academy) says Sheku didn't talk to him for years, and he soon realised that 'Sheku didn't do small talk. He'd come in, maybe grunt hello, take out his cello and play. It was through the cello that he could be articulate and say what he wanted to say'. Both teachers allowed him to grow into his own voice, while being insistent on the technique he would need to express this voice. These teachers made a long-term commitment to developing the musical ability they found. It takes such time and attention, such understanding of how different children learn, such listening in that conversation between teacher and student.

The trust and the bond that builds up over time is always there. I can see, if I watch and listen to Sarah's or Ben's students, and those of Hannah Roberts, Sheku's current teacher, a wonderful unity of sound and technique that marks out those who have learned from the same tutor.

Exams and auditions are not the only moments of recognition for musical children, and we have learned to cope with the tension of the live performance. Parents who say they are totally relaxed and even happy when their children perform are a mystery to me. It's like a woman saying she feels well in pregnancy. For me, these occasions are fraught with a miasma of suffering. I try to act with cheerful confidence but very quickly feel the rictus of nerves taking me over. While my children perform I become stiff and find at the end that I'm sweating and shivering at the same time. The weight of the preparations that came before – the practice where something went wrong, the shoes that didn't fit, the lost rosin, the sore throat, the mislaid piano part, the late train – all remain like a weight on my head. Then there is the harsh reality of the moment, expanding like a waking dream in slow motion when your child walks out on stage. The pressure in my chest of not being able to help, unable to either take over or run away, means that I can't eat for hours before an important performance, and I have to *force* myself to speak.

The children, while learning from their teachers, also learned from each other. One child would always help another with a difficult technique or musical idea. This required an easy honesty born of their sibling relationship, and they listened carefully to each other. Braimah's passion is intonation, and he will persist with Sheku or a sister until they have a passage perfectly in tune. Isata's ears are sharpened to accuracy, and she always came down hard if one of the others played a lazy run of notes without individual clarity. Sheku has always wanted to hear the overarching phrase and how it echoes or changes another. Konya's interest is life and wit – how does the music spark into something alive? Jeneba plunges into the depth of the piece and wants intensity and meaning. For Aminata it's drama and for Mariatu it's expressiveness and joy. Of course, all these preoccupations are shared and exchanged, but personality and music are closely allied.

Krystyna Budzynska recommended the older three as a piano trio for a children's programme called *Yo Gabba Gabba*. Krystyna has been our guiding friend for years, ever since Isata arrived at Primary Academy at age ten. She was fair, direct and often scary in her honesty and lack of sentiment when it came to auditions and assessments. If one of our children fell short in anything, she told us the truth. And her advice has always been correct. For this programme they were to play the piano, violin and cello (at age eleven, ten and nine), to showcase a family playing music together. As they did this all the time, we saw it as an opportunity for an interesting day out in a television studio. They would get some new clothes to wear and perform the third movement of Haydn's 'Piano Trio No. 9', the Gypsy Rondo, a fun, dance-like piece which was easy for them to play.

We still have a recording of that performance. They each introduce themselves with the high voices of childhood, still young primary schoolchildren. They look at each other, and Isata begins playing with the definite weight of the chords which throws down the cue for the boys. They follow her and join in with their own musical personalities, unchanged from then to now: Isata's sparkling precision on the piano keys, leading her brothers with precise command; Braimah's serious expression and singing sound, leaning into the bow; and Sheku's darting eyes and mobile face, sparking with every response. It's a strange thing, comparing their trio playing as small children with how they play together now as young adults and seeing the completeness of their communication even then.

This was the children revealing how 'we play together as a family', and playing music was an organic part of family life, rooted in the routine and the wildness of every day. Stuart and I tried to manage the restless energies of our little children in a regime dedicated to tending the remarkable natural abilities they showed. The children relied on the rules and regularity we constructed, using them as a boundary within which their imaginations were free.

I have always managed by trying to get out of bed about three quarters of an hour before the children wake up, setting my alarm to 5.40 a.m. on weekdays. (With a noisy baby or toddler in the house, the waking time was often much earlier.) Then it was a battle to get through every hour, making sure each child was washed, dressed, fed, understood, loved and disciplined.

We didn't have a crowd or a cluster of little ones, but rather several very different personalities who needed attention. There was always one particular child who called out for special notice at different times. Stuart or I would hear something they said or a repeated misbehaviour that signalled trouble. We had to focus carefully to find the source of the discontent, distress or confusion and then work out what to do. Each of the girls has suffered a grim period of being bullied. I found myself alone, crying with anger after I came up against the emotional lockdown caused by bullying. I saw how crushed and small it made them, embarrassed and ashamed. These onslaughts from the outside world are better dealt with in childhood and adolescence, even though my instinct was to bring them home and tuck them in around me. I can't protect them from relationships that squash their self-esteem or from gossip which embeds its own internal truths. But always the family is a place of safety where the bond of allegiance is never broken.

There was always one child who we needed to worry about more than the others, who was temporarily naughtier than the others, or more distressed. We accepted whichever child it was who posed a challenge to the settled order and targeted the problem as effectively as we could. That one child might regularly do something naughty to upturn the calm flow of events, or sit silently sad and apart. Each behaviour needed extra moments of attention.

Every stage of the family routine was punctuated with statements that became mantras, used to herd the children into action, such as 'wee-wee, wash hands', 'come on, ten minutes to go', or 'shoes, coats, Vaseline!'

When the school procession around the pushchair was complete and the primary schoolchildren left at school, I would begin the regime of clothes washing, cleaning, tidying, cooking and errands, all piling up and sliding hopelessly into longer and longer 'to do' lists of endlessly undone tasks, constantly made impossible and necessary by the noisy presence of babies and toddlers. By nightfall, when Stuart came home, it was increasingly difficult to account for the day or my weeping exhaustion. It often seemed as though my job was to maintain a kind of slowly degrading status quo. The kitchen was tidy at the beginning of the day when Stuart left for work, and it looked the same when he returned. The children were in their beds when Stuart left in the morning, and asleep again when he came home. What was hidden from view was the turbulence in between these hours. I had no emotional or physical energy left at the end of the day and felt as though I had fought a war of attrition.

Being absorbed in the overwhelming task of motherhood didn't make me forget what it was to have an identity. At night, about to sink into the oblivion of sleep, I tried to remember what it was like to be at the centre of myself. When I had a profession it was proof of my place in the world. I saw myself reflected in the mirror, whole and separate. I walked into the room with a face. Now, I had evenings with Stuart at rare dinner parties or gatherings where someone would ask what I did. The hot misery rose and I was left a hollow thing wrapped in my unfashionable clothes. An elasticated post-pregnancy waistband seemed always to tighten on me as I stuttered an answer about being a full-time mother. Motherhood is like a cloak of invisibility. I was stripped of singularity. Lost behind a biological screen of pregnancy, breastfeeding and babies, I often felt a dull sense of shame. But Stuart had to commute and travel round the world for work, either with airlines, hotel companies or advertising, and I wanted to be present for the children. I found myself justifying this, rehearsing the reasons behind my choice and then feeling so tired that I didn't know if I had *chosen* at all. The financial pressure on Stuart as the sole earner felt insupportable and the pressure on me to remain at home was tough. At times it felt like naked courage, but still I fought to stay with them.

Leaning on each other, we would sit in a concert and watch one or more of the children take their place on the stage and play something they had practised long and hard…and we would smile, look at each other, and say, 'Well done'.

12

Family, Identity and Kindness

S TUART SPENT LONG hours as a child playing cricket with his cousins in South London streets, or football in the parks, or free badminton with his sister, Rhonda, in school holidays. I wanted the children to walk up hills and run through forests, climb trees and play ball games. The culture and environment had changed since Stuart and I were children. The traffic was more dense and dangerous, and parents no longer allowed children to roam the streets, parks and woods alone. The days I had in Caldicot, building dens in wild land and cycling with friends or siblings to Wentwood, were long gone. So Stuart and I would take our children for days out in Nottinghamshire and Derbyshire, or country parks nearby where they could kick balls and chase each other.

We did try to be practical parents, attempting to take them cycling in Clumber Park with bicycles tied up on racks on the back of the car. We kept getting stopped on the roads because one or more of the bikes would start hanging precariously off the back, and if there were a puncture or the chain came off one of the bikes, we were like fish out of water. We would look admiringly at our neighbours, Vicky and Steve Manderson with their children, bikes perfectly bracketed on the back of their car, all practical jobs done. The cycling was kept to holidays with my mother, where the children would ride their bikes to Caldicot Castle and spend their days in the fields and woods. I loved the brightness and energy in their faces after a day outside, their voices too loud and their physical limits tested. Their games were expanded to fill wide, open spaces, and they had been free.

The intellectual intensity of music learning meant longer hours of testing different physical limits. The concentration and muscle stamina demanded to play a piano, violin or cello to a high level is *another* challenge. We tried to keep a balance between the two activities. It's difficult to be a brilliant musician without being physically fit. It's difficult for a musician to be creative if her body is sluggish and her mind kept indoors. If there's no outlet for strain, the hours of practice twist the body into knots of anxiety.

But time is limited. We found that the hours in the day devoted to school and then to homework left precious little time for music practice. The children had to learn to play when they were wrung out with tiredness at the end of the day. Saturdays at Primary and Junior Academy were early and long, and Sundays began with Mass in the morning and practice for the rest of the day. I worried that the endless days of children rolling down hills in the grass and making up wild games in the woods were slowly disappearing. The struggle to maintain any equilibrium between the long weeks at state school, the travel demands of music lessons, the practice time and the children's psychological and physical well-being is an intense one.

For a number of years, while conversations at the school gates turned to the relief of the approaching weekend, we gathered ourselves together for the hardest morning of the week, Saturday. Before Isata left for London to take up her full-time scholarship at the Royal Academy, five of the children were making the Saturday journey to Junior Academy. Now, the younger three travel with me to the Primary and Junior departments. We have spent years bracing ourselves on Friday nights for the relentless and dogmatic timing of the Saturday-morning routine.

The clearest way to illustrate this family routine is perhaps to focus on the era when the older five were travelling to London, at the time when Stuart would travel with them (a role we have exchanged over the years). Mornings have always been a brutal fixture in my day and I find them very painful, so knowing that I *have* to wake at 4.30 a.m. fills me with stress for at least a day beforehand; I always need at least half an hour to be able to communicate on a rudimentary level with the children – and much longer with anyone else. Stuart in the morning is torture for me. He always manages to begin addressing me with questions, which are like a woodpecker tapping, echoing, in my skull. I would stumble in a precise order from child to child, giving each a ten-minute chance to get to the bathroom and have time before the next one joined them. The boys were last and the most challenging. It always took several determined attempts to get them out of bed and thumping heavily down the stairs.

None of them can function at all without breakfast. This is a crowded affair with growing teenagers colliding grumpily with younger ones in the small kitchen, one stirring porridge on the cooker, one making toast, one frying an egg and another spilling muesli on another's plate. The table, seating only six crammed together but often used for nine, would be all elbows, jostling and grumbling. In the midst of this I would pile the bread for sandwiches and divide them all into five wrapped packs with a bottle of water each.

The tyranny of the clock would always overtake us. My mantras would begin as it got close to 5.30 a.m.: 'You're supposed to pack your bag the night before!' 'Where is your cello?' 'Why is your instrument not in its case?' In the days where I stayed at home and breastfed the youngest one, or took the two youngest to piano lessons, Stuart would be levered out of bed ten minutes before leaving, hastily wash and begin chiding everyone for not being ready. I would lift the two little ones, complete with creased pyjamas covered by jumpers, into their car seats and begin reversing the car into the street. Invariably, Braimah would have forgotten something and Sheku would be limping sleepily after the car with one shoe on.

At the train station, the crowd of five children would be woken up and hurried out of the car in the dark, rucksacks and instruments on backs, sandwiches packed, and the whole parade following Stuart up the station steps. As he fumbled to print out the tickets I would sit for a moment, watching. The 6 a.m. train would leave the platform, engine roaring, and I would contemplate the miracle of the achievement. Then I would turn to Aminata and Mariatu. At that time they were both learning piano and violin. We made it our special time. Little ones respond beautifully to plans and routines, and to have a whole day carved out especially for them was a treat.

It would begin with an interesting breakfast, perhaps scrambled eggs with fried onions, or ground rice, or cheese on toast, complete with black pepper and chilli flakes melted in. Then I would get them washed and dressed and give them a special reading time in the big bed they shared, or playing time involving their teddies and dolls. This was my chance to get all the school uniforms washed and the endless school and work shirts. The washing was always at least two loads every day, and often three with bed sheets, towels, underwear, PE kits and pyjamas.

Once a washing load was on, with dry clothes from the day before taken off the hanging clothes dryer and folded into heavy washing baskets to be taken upstairs for unloading and putting away, I would tackle the kitchen. The children were disciplined to clean up their own dirty plates into the dishwasher, but after the morning rush, there was advanced debris. After the dirty crockery, pots and pans were dealt with, I had to clean and wipe every surface and sweep the floor. Then the music duties would begin. Aminata would have an intensive forty-five-minute piano lesson followed by Mariatu's half-hour, during which Aminata revelled in her books. They would then swap over for violin lessons.

In the summer, they went out into the garden to play while I cooked the main pot of food for lunch and the family evening meal, after which I would deal with the next washing load. We would go outside to the park in spring, or in the colder weather take a walk around the streets close by, the girls skipping ahead to collect conkers or riding their scooters. If there was hair to be done (always a major undertaking), I would unplait the small, tight braids in front of a children's DVD, then pause the film to wash one girl's hair with the shower hose as they sat in the bath, working through the conditioner and oils as I tried to detangle the forest. The rest of the film was a great distraction from the Afro comb, raking painfully through the curls with hair grease. I would drag perfect, straight lines and squares into the scalp as I worked the braids back in.

Having five daughters, I always wondered at how much more time mothers of girls with straight hair had. All those hours of unplaiting, washing and detangling, oiling and combing, parting and plaiting that girls with Afro hair and their mothers endure…in our case added up to hours of lost practice time! I imagined the extra technique they would have mastered and the pieces they would have perfected in the time their heads were clamped between my knees, having the knots taken out and the patterns put in.

I am still hairdresser for my daughters, partly because a

professional hairdresser would be far too expensive, and partly because I've realised that what I thought of as a debilitating, time-devouring chore, leading to ripped and sore cuticles and fingers for me, has yielded other treasures. It has been the time where we sat down and shared films and documentaries together, where we talked endlessly, often when the rest of the family were in bed. I hear individual anxieties, excitements, preoccupations. Each daughter has private and exclusive time with me while I care for their hair, with patterned precision and detail, and in this way I am caring for them.

Once the hair was done and the little ones had eaten their last meal from the big pots of chicken stew and rice on the cooker, full of onions, tomato and Scotch bonnet peppers, or dark-red palm oil, plantains as a treat, it was bath time. They would sit in the bath together, Mariatu at three or four years old, Aminata at six or seven, splashing bubbles at each other and filling the bath with rubber ducks, plastic frogs and empty, frothing bubble-bath bottles used to make 'soup' and 'ice cream'. Dressed in pyjamas and wrapped in dressing gowns, they would put on their socks and shoes and climb into their seats in the rusty nine-seater car for the 8 p.m. drive to Nottingham train station.

We waited in the car, listening to Classic FM or a music cassette tape (the car was too old for CDs) until the older five bundled off the train with Stuart and clambered in. The old car instantly filled with the noise of nine people. They jostled into their seats, instruments piled into the boot, bags at their feet and everyone trying at full volume to recount their day at Junior Royal Academy. Fascinating but overwhelming, like the sudden roar of a great wave in a hurricane, crashing into the space inside the car. I would try to decipher girls' voices under the loud male tones, all competing for attention, each trying to tell the same story in their own way, or continue someone else's, or tell a shouting tale known only to them. Stuart's voice would dominate but not deter everyone else's, and the youngest girls would shout about their day along with all the rest.

I would manage to hear parts of detailed descriptions of lessons, performances and competitions that had taken place that day. Lots of very funny incidents where someone's teacher (usually Ben or Druvi de Saram) had quipped about something quirky in their playing, or Patsy had smiled at something which had been played in a curious way, or Sarah Pickering or Nicole Wilson had told a funny story. There was always something to laugh at, or gossip to relay, or a piece of music that someone wanted to sing.

By the time I'd driven home through the Saturday-night stag and hen parties, the end-of-football-match crowds or the teenagers off to a gig at the ice arena, I was exhausted. They all raced in through the narrow back-door entrance, crammed with piled shoes, dumping bags and instruments while I yelled over the noise to tidy them up, then they would descend, plates in hand, on the pots of food. Seeking refuge upstairs, I would peel off the little ones' dressing gowns and tuck them quietly into their king-size bed in the lamplight. 'What was your favourite thing today?' I would ask each of them (and I still do). A long and involved story would ensue from Mariatu, always first because she is the youngest, constantly interrupted by Aminata. Then they would suddenly share a joke which I would have to quieten, or a tickling match would break out, which I had to quell in the interests of settling them down. We added a prayer or a gentle song – either 'Amazing Grace' or a Mende lullaby.

One of the older ones would inevitably crash into this sleepy serenity and leap on the bed wanting to chat, cuddle, tease and be part of the snuggle. Sheku would often be lying in wait for me when I entered the room, gleefully hidden under the duvet by the girls and pouncing just as I began the quiet routine.

I would then go downstairs, try to organise everyone into

cleaning up the kitchen and then finishing it myself, Stuart now stretched out on the lounge settee. The noise would be growing upstairs. More stories, jokes, jostling for bathroom space, girls climbing into bed to read, boys sharing a piece of music together on a speaker. I would move from room to room, tucking in each child in their shared rooms, revisiting the day with the same words: 'What was your favourite thing today?' I then finished (and still finish) with the mantra, adapted to each of their particular ages and interrupted by kisses to each cheek, 'You are the best, most loving, most gorgeous ten-year-old in the whole, wide world'.

When all the children were in bed, all seven either sleeping or talking and laughing secretly from pillow to pillow, I would go downstairs to Stuart. I very rarely intervened in the surreptitious chatting and playing that went on after lights out, pretending I heard nothing. This was the children's private time, their world created like a secret garden beyond us. The children belonged to each other as much as they belonged to us, and I was careful not to interfere as long as the silent pact remained that it was under the radar and contained. Sometimes I would hover quietly outside the door, hearing the giggles and whispered secrets and remembering how it was with me and my sister and brothers when *we* were young. If parents make rules and represent authority, they ensure the continuation of that authority by allowing these secret free societies.

And now the time belonged to Stuart and *me*. We would curl up on the settee together, often with a blanket, and talk through the day. Stuart always had interesting gossip to tell me, or a funny observation. This was the time to discuss each child, especially a problem or a celebration. Perhaps one of the children lacked confidence or was finding performance challenging. It was here that we talked through our observations and agreed our strategies. We reassured each other or else talked through our increasing alarm. We usually ended by making each other laugh at just how interesting the children were.

To lengthen the time together, we watched a DVD, tired and relaxed, my legs on Stuart's lap, thankful that the 4.30 a.m. alarm wouldn't sound for almost a week.

Nothing has changed with bedtime routines, or the way everyone interacts when they are together. I still wake every Saturday between 4 and 4.30 a.m., but the four elder children are now full-time scholarship students at the Royal Academy and the three youngest are the ones who make the Saturday trip to London with me. Until very recently I took Konya, Jeneba and Aminata every Saturday while Stuart stayed home with Mariatu.

As the years have gone by, we've worked out different patterns for each parent to have particular time with the children or with a child. For me, it's always been established with the early days of learning an instrument and the concentrated attention needed for every note. It's been established with the early days of breast-feeding, intimate care, washing, dressing and bedtime routines. We've both shared these things, but Stuart's gift has always been adventure. He enables sport, exploration, trying and daring new things. He is spontaneity, risk and careless confidence. I am routine, safety and consistency. But whenever genuine physical danger has threatened, it has always been Stuart saving each of their lives, in the nick of time, with his clear vision and uncanny sixth sense.

Stuart has an inexplicable connection with the children, and this strange bond first revealed itself when Isata was four months old. We had decided to move her cot to the next room so she could get used to a proper sleep routine. In the middle of one night, Stuart suddenly sat up in bed and said, 'Isata's ill'. I watched, bemused as he left the room. He came back with a baby in the throes of her first fever. Later, when she was a toddler and we were packing up the car to leave her grandparents' house in Catford, Stuart suddenly ran from inside the house, into the road, where Isata had wandered unknown to us, and grabbed her within seconds of being hit by a car. He saved Braimah from drowning twice with sudden lightning bolts of intuition, Jeneba from choking and Sheku while hanging from the T-shirt around his neck from the top of the garden gate. Any child in trouble and it is Stuart who responds to the emergency. He has a kind of decisive thinking and a courageous lucidity of mind that can be simply breathtaking.

The world he inhabits, guided by reflexes, intuition and optimism, is both magical and alarming for me. He achieves flashes of brilliance and bravery on which I breathe caution. Yet he is always right. I am a dreamer, but carefully hedged in with pessimism, believing utterly in my children but cautious about the world. Stuart will leap gloriously headlong and unselfconsciously into impossible scenarios, all caution to the wind, and – unbelievably – succeed. But this can often create precarious situations. He crashes around the house, often unaware of the edges of his body, hitting his head and bumping into objects. Constantly moving, he often reverses into people standing behind him during conversations, or changes direction in a wild jerk. Most things broken in the house or car are broken by Stuart. Yet he has always been a beautiful dancer and expands horizons that I didn't know were there.

His so-called sector days with Mariatu, which were perfected when she was too young for Primary Royal Academy, are built around Stuart's mathematical mind. He will not embark on running, walking or even a day without a mathematical analysis. His particular understanding of time is a gift that I find irritatingly paradoxical. He keeps a detailed calendar but is continually surprised by an imminent event for which he has made no practical plans. He is unpredictable in his attitude towards money and finances, and yet rigidly lucid in his analysis of it. He veers wildly from vaulting optimism and generosity to mathematical doom, unable to map a smooth path that takes in the coming ups and downs, or even predictable costs, and yet he skids to an equilibrium out of the blue. I always proclaim, 'But maths is not life'.

The contradiction is that I exist in a poetic fog of unmanageable time, and he believes in grids. Yet he is blessed with the grand vision and the big dream. I live in the careful rhythm of everyday needs and conservation, knowing exactly and neatly the earthly limits of my own vulnerable body. Stuart risks everything, without limits, but in the end he lands on his feet.

A 'sector day' is divided into events that are measured exactly in units of time. All is discussed and mapped out beforehand. Mariatu, eyes shining, enters into the wonderful unfurling of the day ahead. Half an hour is allotted to the park run. Half an hour to walk back. Interesting-breakfast sector: half an hour. Walk into town: thirty-five minutes. Exploring: forty minutes. A cinema film...and so the day unravels. Practice: one sector. Listening to music: another sector. Doing maths. Nature documentary. Somehow the relentless planning adds a sense of adventure akin to spontaneity. 'Dad days' are inspiring. Consequently, Mariatu is passionately and vocally always on her father's side.

Our approach to the children's music learning has also been a mixture of careful planning with experiment. We insist on routine and hard work, yet make adventurous decisions. Buying Isata a piano at age six was a conscious plan to give her the opportunity to learn. Encouraging her desire to audition for Junior Royal Academy was a risky leap into the unknown. Starting Sheku on the violin was a carefully calculated plan to keep costs manageable as Braimah and Isata were learning violin and could pass on expertise, instruments and music. Allowing Sheku to follow his own dream of learning the cello instead launched us into an uncertain and more expensive future. Insisting on careful equality between the children dropped us into the chaos of escalating debt and unmanageable promises. But, against all odds, we kept those promises.

Looking back at the years of children being born and growing up, it's easy to invent, retrospectively, a narrative for our family. As parents, the ultimate goals in mind cannot be as precise and defined as to map out any clear direction of travel. We didn't decide at the beginning that our seven children would become musicians and pursue a professional music career. We still don't know for certain what paths they will all take and what changing decisions they will each make about their lives.

When Isata was born, we simply saw her as being born into an extended family of loving grandparents and great grand-parents, cousins, aunties and uncles, with long histories from three countries – Wales, Antigua and Sierra Leone – to all of which she belonged. At first, she was us, our ideas and dreams, our experiences and identities. The first time I walked out of the house alone, no new baby attached to me, simply to post a letter, I felt at sea, as though I had lost my own self. When I had time to look in the mirror as a new mother, I would be shocked to see my own face, not hers, close up. I would search my own skin for her newborn baby rash.

While they were individuals, the children also had their places within the family. They would forge different alliances and make strategic close partnerships when they played together. They tested their strength against each other, pushing and jostling for space. The boys would wrestle each other and compete at football. The girls would boss each other about or quarrel over toys. The boys would annoy the girls or be annoyed by a younger one who trotted into their room and took something. Aminata was adept at this. Born into a family of five older brothers and sisters, she would toddle around the house, alive with curiosity.

There was nothing subtle about Aminata. In order to elbow her way into this developed sibling world, she learned to project her voice above the crowd. She would regularly hit notes like an opera singer, holding forth in her high chair or deafening every conversation with her entry into a room. She always had something to say, loudly and excitedly, interrupting every settled train of thought. Her expeditions into bedrooms always led to an inexplicable disappearance of a doll or toy car, and when questioned she could not retrace her steps. The older five thought of her as a roving vehicle of mayhem, dominating every space in an attempt to be included.

Irritation with this toddler tyrant changed as she grew. What was an unacceptable intrusion at inconceivable decibels became increasingly entertaining. Aminata was always acting. Her room entries demanded attention, and she showed us different characters with exaggerated mannerisms and uncannily accurate accents. She was very funny. Her position in the sibling community was as the centre of a drama. She began duo acts with Braimah where they would plan scenes to act for us, livening up a tired school evening with a hilarious mini show. Her voice projection lent itself to singing, and she decided that singing was more important to her than violin. She sang everywhere and all the time, clear, full and in tune. (Now she divides her time between singing, violin and piano.)

Outside the house, Aminata is a shy fourteen-year-old, desperately self-conscious but able to tell stories that make us laugh about moments of embarrassment she's encountered. She is deeply self-critical, worried that her abilities lag behind her older siblings and yet, with Grade 8 distinction on violin at age eleven and Grade 8 piano at twelve, they do not. She is simply younger. When she walks on stage, the often closed and muted violin practice at home suddenly takes flight and she shines, smiling and projecting excitement, with a sound as clear and full as her voice. I often wonder how differently we would all see her achievements – simply normal to us now – if she were the eldest child.

An example of this dual personality is her recent performance of Bruch's 'Violin Concerto No. 1' with Djanogly Community Orchestra in Nottingham. For weeks, Aminata decided that the whole thing was an impossibility, something she could not ever achieve. Even one week before, she had not memorised the concerto and was crying pitifully every time it was mentioned. I kept up a steady expression of optimistic enthusiasm, knowing that this was her regular approach to impending performance, but I began to worry. Bruch's concerto was a huge undertaking for a child just turned fourteen, and perhaps I had wilfully deserted my post as a mother. In the rehearsal a few days before, she pulled a music stand close to her body and stared nervously at it through the whole of the last movement. Perhaps this was a disaster I had to halt in its tracks.

The day arrived for the performance and, to add to the alarm, Aminata's violin looked in need of repair – strings, bridge and pegs in unsustainable tension with each other. Would they finally implode during the concerto, along with Aminata's miserable psychological state? In the green room beforehand, a warm annex of the large church, where Aminata cowered away from the sold-out concert about to begin, I cuddled her and looked at her unhappy face. Had I pushed her too far?

As I waited in the audience following her introduction, Aminata walked in front of the orchestra, put the violin to her chin and played with all the self-possession, determination and excitement of someone *born* to perform. She played with no music stand, effortlessly from memory and totally in commu-nication with orchestra and audience. As the crowd cheered her back on the stage, I sat stunned as usual and felt like those mothers who throw their newborns in the swimming pool to see them swim, naturally, heads above water.

While all the children are in many ways constructed within this sibling framework, they are all immeasurably supported by it. Jeneba and then Aminata were bullied for a time at primary school, a heartbreaking scenario for any parent, where your child comes home diminished and afraid, raw with shame. The older children, especially the boys, were wild with fury and marched into the school, looking for the offenders. I managed to calm the situation down and the school teachers dealt with the issues, but it was taken as an offence against the family and a deeply personal attack against them all. Once Braimah, as a student, incensed by a friend who had not treated Isata with respect, grabbed him by the neck of his clothes and slammed him angrily against the wall. He was restrained by others, but this friend was never forgiven. They all rise quickly to any insult against a sibling. Where they can tease each other mercilessly, they will not accept a slight from outside. Their pride in each other is palpable. They expect hard work and commitment from each sibling, stricter than I am if they feel another is being lazy. And they beam with excited satisfaction at another's success.

This sense of family identity has also built an impenetrable wall of collusion against us as parents. Fierce loyalty is embedded between them and they still doggedly keep each other's secrets. I often see the girls in some huddle of gossip together that shuts down on my approach. One boy will, without fail, leap to the indignant defence of the other if we dare to complain about either of them. They understand the lived pressures of the incessant practice needed and the psychological toughness to balance student deadlines, concert preparation and sheer exhaustion. They understand the competitiveness of life as a musician and a conservatoire student, and the battles needed to get to that point. Konya and Isata sometimes meet simply to cry together when the pressure mounts, and Braimah and Sheku share everything. I often see them wearing each other's clothes, and a charger or comb or shirt belonging to one is usually in another's bag.

They like making each other laugh. They also like making *us* laugh. When we can sit and have a meal together, or be on holiday as a family, or meet on Saturdays in the Royal Academy canteen, they are hugely entertaining. The early shock when Isata asserted her personality as a toddler has developed into a constant source of joy. When they tell a funny story with a witty or eccentric view of life or give vivid impressions of each other or of us parents, it makes us laugh all the time. We love the children dearly, but we also *like* them hugely, seeking out their company jealously as they grow into adults.

We all have nicknames, coined by the children and born from the essence of a character trait they all find funny, on the family Facebook messenger. These sharp, sidelong images so immediately convey who the person is that the shorthand becomes more expressive than the actual name.

I am 'Fraying Jumper' because I always wear old clothes around the house, used to being in the midst of domestic work, or lying on the floor with a child, or cooking.

Stuart is 'Mr Big Shot' because of his grandstanding about work and his impressive world travel. He's known in the family as the 'pontificator', the wicker chair in the bathroom having been 'Daddy's chair' because he used to pontificate there while they had their group toddler baths.

Isata is 'Clara Schumann' because she has released an album of Schumann's piano music and has been so deeply embedded in Schumann's music and life for months that it has become her own affectionate title.

Braimah is 'Pardon?', the perfect reference to the fact that he never seems to know what's going on, is always the last to realise a concert date and takes an age to answer messages. It's also a lovely memory of the little boy, brows furrowed, endlessly questioning and overthinking.

Sheku is, 'What a Final', a very affectionate reference to Clemency Burton-Hill at the BBC Young Musician and all the media attention he has had. It's funny precisely because he doesn't wear any of it like a mantle, is totally unchanged and shrugs it all off, so we can tease him and wait for the wry smile.

Konya is 'Spangly', a word Isata coined to express the sudden elongating growth spurt that Konya went through between fifteen and sixteen, changing from the skinny little schoolgirl with the bulky rucksack that seemed bigger than her, to a six-foot teenager. 'Spangly' invokes the memory of her crashing into doorways and her arms and legs seeming to be all over the kitchen as she tried to get used to her extended limbs.

Jeneba is 'Hanging Lip' because of her tendency to speak dolefully and with extreme seriousness. She loves the quiet and intense conversations, wanting to plumb emotional depths, a quality she brings to her piano playing.

Aminata is 'Maggot', a word she uses pertinently and with arch naughtiness against her siblings for marked insults.

As yet, Mariatu is too young for social media, but when she enters she will probably take over. Her family name is 'Maz Baz' or 'Mazza Beast', because she is everyone's pet.

We have promoted values of fairness and kindness, essential in a large family. They, independently of us, have applied these on a general basis. They also share a quality of humility which is independent and sincere. Constantly reminded that each of their talents and skills is achieved within the context of siblings who are equally or more brilliant in particular areas, and that everyone constantly improves, they have consistently been generous to those outside the family. As they have become more skilled with their instruments, it has raised their appreciation of others who work hard and have the courage to perform, or who achieve other things. They always find something to admire in another's performance. If Stuart or I are even slightly critical of others, they become very cross with us. We are often pulled up short by their disapproval of our attitude and we are instantly silenced and pleased. It is as though they are now teaching us the values of kindness and humility that we thought we were teaching *them*.

13

Talent and Sacrifice

W E WERE NAÏVE and inexperienced parents of classical musicians. We were also naïve and inexperienced parents for Isata, our first child, feeling our way, making ill-informed choices, having to guess whose advice was right for us. We were a paradox: a large, Black family who wanted to train in classical music. As parents, we expected our children to be close to us. I walked the older children to primary school every day with their baby and toddler siblings in tow. They came home from school every day to join the younger ones and we ate together in a babble of voices and energy. This was our home, and everyone had their place.

But Isata was gifted. We took her to music courses and competitions, and the people around us, the ones who understood the world we were stumbling into, asked which music school she attended. When we answered that she was at a state comprehensive school, which we loved, we were met with incomprehension. Urgent advice came our way that Isata could not succeed without music school, that we were throwing away her gifts by leaving her to languish in an education not tailored to her potential. When we looked into these specialist music schools, we could see that the academic curriculum was cut to a core minimum, to allow music and practice to fill more time. Choir, orchestra, chamber music and instrumental lessons filled the spaces left by shrinking art, PE, drama and extra science. The twelve or more General Certificate of Secondary Education (GCSE) subjects required at Trinity would be replaced with five, and pupils would be set free to expand and accelerate in music.

This seemed wonderful. But there was no such school in or near Nottingham. We would have to send Isata away to board. All my emotions rebelled. How could we send our own child away from us, away from the context of family in which she had been nurtured and in which she belonged? It would be like unwrapping a bandage on my chest and exposing a wound. I would not let her go. Isata's eyes shone at the prospect. She had read all of J.K. Rowling's *Harry Potter* novels over and over, as all of us had, and for her, magical talent was like musical talent. It was a gift that singled you out, made you special, but for which you had to work and learn and train hard. To win a place at music school was as romantic as being mysteriously chosen for Hogwarts. She wanted to be transported to this imagined castle of music where she would make friends with others, magically talented like her, and play music all day.

We explored the possibility of moving close to one of these specialist music schools. Patsy, her teacher, recommended the Purcell School of Music, north of London in Hertfordshire, because she also taught there and Isata could keep the same teacher. If we lived close by, Isata could go to the school in the day and still come home to us all. I envisioned welcoming her back into my arms every day, her face lit up by the advanced music she had studied all day with no restraint. We researched house prices in Hertfordshire and laughed. We would have to move to a tiny terraced house with seven children, the walls so close to our neighbours that no one could practise their instruments again. Chetham's School of Music in Manchester was also too far away, and there Isata would have to leave Patsy.

I happily put the idea of music school away and we went to see Mr Mike McKeever, the extraordinary, dynamic head teacher of Trinity Catholic School. He immediately understood. Trinity was an outstanding state school, at once creating its own family of mutual respect and equality and celebrating those with particular talents and achievements. Any pupil who excelled in a particular sport, or out-of-school activity, did so with the admiration and support of everyone, and the entire school would share the pride. He suggested giving Isata a full day off school every week to put in extra practice and focus fully on her music. The school would tailor her timetable to make this possible, and she would be given practice time in school on other days. As a comprehensive school, they had to rely on a piano that had been kindly donated in years gone by, and there were no dedicated practice rooms, but the teachers rallied round to make everything possible.

We were very happy. At the end of each school concert and the annual prize-giving, Mr McKeever would spread out his arms to the hall, everyone ecstatic at the collective talent, cooperation and joy that had ignited during the evening, and he would declare, unabashed, 'Trinity pupils, I love you all!' This was no ordinary comprehensive school. Since the days of head teachers Mike McKeever and John Dexter, the school has undergone a restructuring of power that imposes ideas from a new, distant authority, and funding for music has been harshly slashed. Consequently, the academic prowess of the school, along with the sense of pride and of collective endeavour, is under threat. The confidence and self-worth that the older children gained in the school should be available to everyone for the generations to come.

But we still encountered those people in the classical music world who were perplexed by our decision. Why would we deny Isata the superior music education she needed? What if we were shutting the castle doors for ever on Isata's progress, limiting her to a truncated knowledge frustrated by lack of time? Could we deny her this opportunity? We looked at the details. Everyone told us that funding was not an issue, that specialist music schools had government funding, means-tested to each applicant. When we explored this it became clear that Stuart's job, at which he worked so hard, would make it impossible for us to afford the fees. Had he owned his own business and was paid via dividends, or had a sizeable inheritance or trust fund, these fees would have been ignored. But his *taxed* salary was entirely relevant. We approached Purcell and asked if family circumstances or the number of children could be taken into consideration, but the rules were rigid. If we allowed Isata to audition and she won a place, all our money left after mortgage, household costs and food would be lost to the fees. We would not be able to respond to household emergencies or maintain our car, and the younger children would have less. The fees over two years could be put towards the grand piano we so desperately needed, and that could serve all of them.

But Isata begged us. It would be a dream come true to be given this chance. Stuart and I had always done everything we could to shoulder our responsibilities to our children. We had made the decision to not dwell on our future struggles, but rather to give all of ourselves right then and there, trusting the determination of our future selves to climb the bigger hills. We knew in that moment that we would look back on this denial – saying no to Isata – as a failure.

We prepared Isata for audition. I thought that perhaps she wouldn't get in as the process was tough and competitive. On the day of the audition, we entered the cool entrance to the school, buzzed in through the imposing barrier of the gate. Everyone was reserved and clipped and posh. They were friendly but not personal. Isata was just one possibly gifted child like many others there for audition, and the school was full of international talent. We were shown around Purcell. The rows of practice rooms, each with an excellent piano, were stunning. There was a concert hall, a recording studio and chamber music rooms. I thought of Isata there, with access to all these facilities on a daily basis. But the dormitories were box rooms, with four bunk beds in each and shared bathrooms on narrow corridors. All the money was spent on the music, and I wondered if there was love. I waited anxiously while Isata went in for the audition and exhaled when we left, feeling the stretch of every long mile between the school and home.

Isata was offered a place for the following September, when she would turn fourteen. I remember sitting on the back doorstep, just looking at the small back garden and smelling spring in the grass, overwhelmed with misery. It was wonderful that she had been offered a place. It was terrible that she had been offered a place. I saw the sacrifice as my duty as a parent, and I tried not to resent the musical gift that had made it necessary. I looked at our mediocre pianos and the messy music room with the dog-eared grade and scales books leaning off the shelves. I looked at the small cellos and violins, the viola that Isata played, and felt stripped bare by it all. Why had it led to me losing my child?

We met up with friends who had a talented cellist as a son. He had auditioned for Chetham's School of Music in Manchester and won a place. They were caught in the same trap as us: not poor enough on paper and not rich enough to hide their wealth. They couldn't afford it and sent their son for an audition at Eton College instead. Eton took into account all their family circumstances and their son went there at hardly any cost.

During the week leading up to Isata leaving, I didn't sleep

well. It was early September and still warm. Daisies covered the lawn and the air in the house was still gentle. I carefully washed, oiled and plaited Isata's hair, putting extra love into each braid to make it last over the three weeks until she would be home. Stuart or I would see her every Saturday at Junior Academy once term began, but that seemed even worse – like waving at her over a fence and not letting her back in. Nanna had been confused. 'Why would you send away your own child?' I secretly agreed. It was an abomination, but what choice did I have if I were to be the mother Isata deserved?

As the days moved closer to Isata leaving, I began to panic. I panicked about the escalating debts. I panicked about the house we could not maintain. I panicked about the family, its perfect structure disintegrating. The night before I was to drive her away, I dreamed that water was seeping into the walls of our house and running down beside the stairs and onto the landing. The fabric of the bricks was soggy and crumbling, and I couldn't keep them solid and safe. I woke with my whole body trembling and feeling transparent. It was a beautiful day. The sun was shining over the green garden and little Mariatu was just over a year old, her tiny plaits in colourful bobbles. We all crowded together on this glorious family Sunday, taking photos and smiling. But it was a mournful day and I would not be consoled. Mariatu was saying goodbye to her sister and I drove Isata away on a wave of family excitement. She was following a dream and I had to wave my white handkerchief from the dock.

Every instinct I had told me that this was a story of sadness. I felt forlorn as I listened to Isata's animated chatter in the car, as the M1 took us inexorably south. The school sat in quiet lawns on the cruelly beautiful day, and the parents' meeting was a long wake where we slowly said goodbye. It was time for me to leave. As Isata was taken away by her new energetic group of girls, I walked out to the car. It looked completely out of place. It was a big nine-seater. Bright red and unashamed, it took its place next to the BMWs and Mercedes, all driven by parents with wealthy voices. The international students had flown in.

I wondered if Isata would be completely out of place, or was this where she was *meant* to be? I was somehow ill equipped to be her full-time mother because the talent she had was too urgent, too needy, too greedy. This was my sacrifice and my gift to her.

I drove back from Hertfordshire along the sunny M1 with eyes blinded by tears. The aching never stopped. When Isata came home for the exeat weekend, I was half maddened with missing her. Every time she came home I cooked a special meal and she left the following morning to head to Saturday Junior Academy for the day. We would have a painful Sunday morning when I was invariably weak with grief and unable to enjoy the completeness of the family because she was leaving that day.

Through the first winter, I drove Isata all the way back to Purcell with the road clogged with traffic and the spray freezing on the windscreen. It was always dark before we arrived and I had to take her to the door, watch her use her digital pass to enter and say goodnight as she walked alone along the evening corridor. Then I would sit in the car in the dark and sob, ridiculously, unable to drive until the mourning was over.

I sympathise with Isata over the emotional weight of those drives. I wanted to get everything I had missed packed into those three hours, to hear all she had done every hour away from me and to give her all the love and attention that I had been unable to give. She wanted to shut herself down and recharge her mind before going back into that intensive melee of teenage life. I was banned from the world in which she existed away from us – the intrigues, the competitiveness, the unkindness of teenagers away from home, wrestling with the turbulent demands of their own skills and ambitions. Some, far away from their own countries and emotionally immature, would struggle, jostling and elbowing others for space in this world of many geniuses.

I would repeatedly ask Isata, 'Do you want to stay? Are you happy? Would you like to come home again and leave Purcell?' She would always laugh and say that she was happy and wanted to continue. I knew then that it was *me*. The witch had come and stolen Isata and I could not bring her home again. I couldn't tuck her in at night and ask her what was her favourite thing that day. I couldn't make sure she had eaten a healthy evening meal at teatime and watch her take her place in the sibling order of things.

I also couldn't follow what she was doing academically in school. They had a parents' evening after school midweek in one of those terms, but it was impossible for me to get there, and they didn't seem to expect it. Hardly any parents could come because it was an international boarding school. I tried to communicate over the phone and by email, but parents were not an integral part of the fabric of this world. I did receive Isata's results for the exams at the end of year 10, when she was fifteen, and I was horrified. The marks were shockingly low. I eventually got a response from a couple of teachers who basically told me that she wasn't very bright and it wasn't her fault.

At this point it seemed to me that the school didn't know Isata at all, and she was being allowed to slip in and out of their surveillance, caught in a feral web of teenage rebellion. She would turn up at Junior Academy looking worn out and hardly able to play. In retrospect, I realised that it was the feverish dormitory of girls and gossip that had kept her awake – not the lonely hours in a practice room that I had conjured up in my mind. I had watched the film *Black Swan* and lay in anguish at night, picturing Isata walking along shadowed corridors to enter the solitary confinement of the piano in its small space, alone.

It's fascinating how, as a parent, you can convince yourself that someone else knows better how to nurture your child before they are adult. I didn't understand the world of professional classical music or how to properly cultivate an environment where an undeniable musical intelligence could flourish. I thought that this large, happy mass of siblings, screaming with delight as they sped downstairs on the settee cushions, was a sign of an unsuitable home. I thought this gang of shouting children collecting jars of shining conkers on wild autumn nights was so unorthodox a setting for a bona fide classical pianist that I had to save Isata from it.

I remember one exeat weekend where we all sat together for Sunday dinner. I was inarticulate with the pressing, choking presence of Isata's departure. Aminata, six years old at the time, came to the table wearing a toy princess crown on the top of her scruffy braids, a crown meant for a two-year-old girl and comically small. Isata laughed and said, 'Why are you wearing that ridiculous crown, Aminata?' Everyone laughed except for me. I exploded, completely unreasonably, scolding Isata for her rudeness and telling her that her behaviour was totally unacceptable. The room was silent for the meal, now a properly funereal event. I was venting the pain I felt because Isata was leaving by unleashing a fury of words towards her. They directed themselves at her because she was the centre of that unbearable sorrow, and my mind could not process her laughing expression with the howling wilderness of my love.

At age fifteen, Isata applied for BBC Young Musician and was knocked out at the first audition. We were shocked. She had got through to the second round at thirteen. Could she have gone backwards? She did win the Iris Dyer Piano Prize at Junior Academy, but as I watched her enter the room with a ladder in her tights and heard her slightly flustered playing, it was as though she were a shadow of the pianist she had been. She was tired.

Meanwhile our debts mounted. Stuart worked impossibly hard and managed, after staying up late every night researching and developing his expertise, to get a better-paid job so we could manage our costs and the needs of the other children. The school fees immediately increased to more than the salary rise after tax. We were defeated. People told us of parents who had given up their jobs in order, paradoxically, to afford the fees by becoming eligible for the government scholarship. We heard of parents who divorced so that the scholarship could be claimed by the mother who didn't work. Neither move was palatable. We had been brought up to work proudly for our own children if we could, and we would never even *pretend* to give each other up.

At fifteen Isata was asked to take part in the ITV show *Born to Shine*. The producers came to Junior Academy to audition potential musicians and Isata was chosen. Her role was to mentor a celebrity who would learn a piano piece in a competition against other celebrities with a mentor in dance, singing and performing arts. Her celebrity was Nick Moran, who Isata knew as Scabior in the last two *Harry Potter* films. He was a talented actor and director, and interested in music. She had a wonderful time meeting Nick and engaging with the producers. Adeel Amini, whom we all adored, was our main contact, and Isata was filmed with Nick at the piano and performing in the studio. For her spotlight moment, Isata, fifteen and wearing a bright yellow dress which showed off her rich dark skin, sat at a grand piano on prime-time ITV1, playing Chopin's 'Fantaisie Impromptu'. It was a glorious performance, brilliant and electric. She chatted with the host, Natasha Kaplinsky, and we realised, astonished, that Isata was a media natural. She was totally at ease on stage and in front of the camera, quick and funny, articulate and warm. We didn't know that her beautiful performance on the piano, commanding and perfect, would be followed by this easy, sparkling presence on stage. Her wit and relaxation in such settings has developed further over the years, and she is as much at home talking and presenting as she is playing the piano.

Isata was filmed with Nick Moran at Purcell, and she seemed so at ease in her new world and so confident with her piano skills that we felt sad. As we struggled with the fees we couldn't pay, we knew that her time there had to end and we had no choice but to bring her home.

I also looked at the other children. Braimah, while Isata was not at home, had become the eldest. It made him strut around the house, heady on his new-found position, but his mood was darker and less gentle. I could see that he missed Isata's direction, and he missed *her*. It also impacted on Sheku, who watched Braimah weighed down by the new burden of being oldest child. Konya was now the eldest girl and, at eleven, still with her sweet full mouth and goofy teeth, had to step into the role of responsible girl against the growing bravado of her big brothers. They had also lost their pianist. With no sibling accompanist to play their solo pieces with them at competitions, festivals and music exams, the boys would sometimes accompany each other, or we had to hire professional pianists at a spiralling cost. They were excellent, but we missed the ad-hoc rehearsals, often in pyjamas, where so much did not need to be said and communication was telepathic. It did encourage greater creativity between the boys to play duos with cello and violin. In the absence of a piano accompaniment, they would develop harmony, counterpoint and creative musical conversations with growing inventiveness. But Isata was a significant musical force, and they needed her.

Our mistake was not to value the context we could give to Isata. We hadn't understood the safety and intensity of the musical life she had at home, in our own house of music, with its shared inspiration and framework of mutual respect. The sharing and experimentation that existed between siblings who trusted each other and were not in competition was invaluable. They had always explored classical music together and listened to each other for encouragement and ideas. And they looked after each other. The secret or wild games they played together, the mealtimes shared and the routine wrapped around them like a safety blanket were all fertile ground for them to bring to music something with life and energy and love.

The landscape of music school did make Isata tough, and she had learned a lot, but I felt that she needed boundaries, personal attention, understanding and family. Slowly, her cultural landscape was changing. She did not eat tea at 4.30 anymore; instead, she wanted 'dinner' at 7 p.m. She insisted on straightening her hair, which made it thinner and more brittle, and I thought of all those hours I had taken over all those years, moisturising, nurturing and plaiting it. Her vowels started elongating into a more southern, 'received pronunciation' mode, and she grew impatient with the idea of church on Sundays.

We spoke to Isata as the second year drew on and explained gently that we could not afford to keep her at Purcell. She was crestfallen, caught up in the reality that she was in and wanting her friendships to continue. Stuart and I both still felt that we were taking her away from a context of success, but the cost of it was just too much. I was sorry for her and sad in the face of her gracious acceptance. But I was also elated. We were going to bring her home.

We approached Trinity, asking if Isata could come back for sixth form, and they were full of warmth and welcome. The office staff at Trinity seemed to know who everyone was. Mr McKeever, the head teacher, knew every pupil by name or reputation because he was interested. Each pupil had the chance to shine while being part of a celebrated whole. They all belonged to each other. I confessed that Isata's GCSEs would be sparse and the marks depressed from the level of her abilities. She already had an A* in GCSE Music which she had taken early in year 8, and Music, English and History would be her A-Level subjects. John Dexter, then head of the sixth form, was full of confidence in her. The GCSE results would be irrelevant because she was coming back home and they knew her. I was beaming with relief. Isata would come back to a school with which we were all connected. She was returning to a family who saw her as an individual and was proud of her.

Coming home was a relaxation back to normality. Konya was delighted to have her big sister back full time. Braimah had to adjust to this challenge to his new, brooding masculinity. He was fourteen and growing tall, and he now had to take second place as top musician in the house. Before Isata had left for Purcell, the boys would join together to beg Isata to sleep in their shared bedroom with them so they could plot, gossip and talk until late. Now these relationships had to be renegotiated as Isata settled back into the family full time. They found their way back through music. Isata, Braimah and Sheku began playing as a piano trio again, but this time in greater earnest. They all had more experience at Junior Academy, at summer chamber courses and at Purcell, and they developed this further with extra coaching from Patsy Toh and Ben Davies, and locally from Sarah Huson and Siân Evans. Isata played more duo repertoire with the boys as well, and they played as a string quartet with Konya. For me, hearing them play again together, with all the lively conversation and excited debate about how each bar should be played, made me feel as though I had been pieced back together. They expressed themselves through musical taste and influence. Isata brought with her the chamber music coaching she had at Purcell, expecting a high level of response from her siblings. Braimah, Sheku and Konya acted to question, enhance and add to these ideas, always in a concentrated tussle for dominance. There were arguments over effective dynamics – should this phrase grow or echo another? The character of a piece, which instrument was to the fore and what style or bow stroke or tempo was fitting – all was up for lively debate and demonstration. The music was alive and full of energy.

We were also calm and certain that none of our other children would go to a music school. We were a family and their music would be nurtured at home. It was necessary for them to foray beyond the house for lessons, and engagement with the world outside was critical, but here was their base and home, and we would not send them away until they were eighteen.

14

The Importance of Failure

ISATA'S PIANO PLAYING began to blossom again out of the fragmented personality of puberty, and her performances coalesced into a more definite character. She regained her sense of direction and her results at school dramatically improved. She went back to a circle of friends whom I understood and who supported and liked each other. They had known each other since year seven and I felt that Isata could operate back in a world that didn't thrust adult challenges at her. She entered BBC Young Musician at seventeen and won through each round until she was chosen to play in the Keyboard Category Final, televised at the Royal Welsh College of Music and Drama in Cardiff. She practised with a burning focus for hours after school. Each time I listened to her, her fingers were quicker and more brilliant on the keys and showed breathtaking dexterity. Isata had the facility to play anything, such was the level of her technique.

I think I was out of my depth. The journalists began entering the house to celebrate her success at getting to this televised moment of the competition, and the BBC cameras arrived with searching questions about how she would feel if she won through to the Final. I was overly excited, dazed by her success and unsure how to help her. I was still slightly intoxicated on having her back with us and felt blissfully relieved that she had been put back into the heart of the house. We felt complete. Here she was, back in the organised jumble and chaos of family life, with little Mariatu, now four, running in and out of the piano room and spreading her crayons at Isata's feet as they pedalled, still managing to get to the BBC Final. It felt like fate.

I stayed up all night to cut and fix the hem of the long dress we had bought for her performance, its rich blue folds flowing all over the floor as I tried to curb the length. I stayed with Isata for the two days that she had to be resident in Cardiff for the Keyboard Final, having help for school runs, collections and teatime from Matilda, the lovely teenage babysitter who lived in the next street and who took over in Nottingham when Stuart had to be at work. Stuart brought the children to stay with Mum in Caldicot for the evening of the Final. It was an almost surreal experience living in a bubble of cameras, interviews, BBC make-up sessions and meetings with the other candidates, who were strangely friendly. They were each in direct competition with the others, but also in the same stormy boat of teeteringly high hopes and the promise of something wonderfully and yet maliciously close. To have come so near to the final stage of the competition – the top five pianists – was an unreal achievement. Each candidate dreamed of the possibility of climbing to that winning pedestal. To slip at this stage meant a very long fall.

We all had vertigo, especially the long-suffering parents. With our children, we had worked for a long time and come a long way, but who knew what the evening would bring? We had been witness to the long hours of practice. We had invested the time, the finances, the hope and the emotional strain needed to get each of our children here. And Isata, at seventeen, was still a child. Each parent recognised themselves in every parent's face and felt a mixture of empathy and desperation. As the evening came closer, Stuart, my Mum and sister, my niece Kadie, and the rest of the family arrived and we sat in the central café area of the Royal Welsh College of Music and Drama, waiting for Isata to finish with the make-up team and to have her final interview. BBC Young Musician is a hugely significant competition. There was so much dedication and hard work required from each talented young person playing an instrument at such a high level. The competition makes public the consistent focus that young people can demonstrate, and the sheer wonder that can be generated by teenagers revealing the result of such punishing practice. All this is not glamorous. There are no quick and easy rewards, and everyone has to learn to listen to advice, to pick themselves up after a fall and to learn from failure.

Isata appeared on the balcony in her long blue dress, with sparkling studs on the straps and bodice, and a shining clip in her black hair. She looked beautiful. The rehearsal had been perfect and I had sat listening intently in the empty concert hall, not realising that the camera had been sweeping over me too, catching my serious, glum-with-suspense expression. While Isata warmed up in her practice room we all queued up to enter the Dora Stoukzer Hall. I had kissed Isata's cheek, her face burning with anticipation. She reminded me of when she had won the Clement Pianos Nottinghamshire Young Pianist Prize, and the presentation was at the Trinity summer concert, and she couldn't wait to get to the piano and play. I could see her there at the side, eleven and small, trying to stop herself from marching to the piano mid-introduction to play Chopin's 'Fantaisie Impromptu'. As soon as she could, she had walked too fast to the piano and played with such unbridled brilliance that the entire sports hall-turned-concert hall had risen to their feet en masse. She had learned 'Fantaisie Impromptu', a mature and intricate piece, from scratch in one week, secretly, in the piano room with her Dad, wanting to keep the project in seclusion from me. On the night, she walked blissfully in front of the crowd, playing the virtuoso and beautiful piece entirely from memory, beaming afterwards at the surprise gift she had given so lovingly to me. Tonight, she was ready again, longing to give all she could to the waiting audience and brimming with excitement.

She was the third performer, right in the middle, just before the interval, and she caught everyone's attention. The cameras crowded round us all in the central area, wanting to know how we felt, wanting to know how her stunning performance had affected us. We were puffed up with pride and hope, looking at our amazing daughter's face and feeling that this was the moment where all the daily struggles would blaze in an apex of meaning and destiny. But Isata didn't win. The prolonged deliberation of the judges, making us all suffer with uncertainty, ended with a different name, Martin James Bartlett, being called. It is a terrible thing to have to stand by and watch the disintegration of a hope. Isata was devastated but brave, staying to talk politely with the judges afterwards, accepting the commiserations of everyone. One audience member came to tell her cheerily that she was brilliant but it seemed right that the person who had been in the Final twice and who was also brilliant should have won, and she was sure that Isata agreed. We nodded politely, but it seemed that this happy homily was not to end soon, so I extricated Isata as smoothly as I could. It seemed extraordinary that *anyone* would not understand the depth of shock and disappointment that drowns a young person when they lose a competition so significant in their field, so mythic within classical music.

In the hotel room later, Isata lay on her bed, diminished with despair. A whole future had been blasted away with one announcement. All her hard work, all her dreaming, seemed to have come to nothing. We went back to Nottingham and Isata got out her A-Level books and concentrated on studying for the exams. She was practical and efficient, refusing to dwell on a closed matter. I admired this because I, of course, was drenched in misery. We watched anxiously to see how she was coping and stood united in such overwhelming sympathy that we all suffered. When the Keyboard Final was televised two months later, fresh and new to the rest of the country, we had to go through the moment all over again and accept the commiserations of friends and acquaintances whom we hadn't told. Then Isata was informed that she had won the Walter Todd's Bursary with Jess Gillam, the young saxophonist who had not won the woodwind section. They were to be honoured for being the two most promising musicians who had not got to the Grand Final.

We took the train to Edinburgh for the Final and walked through the beautiful city to Usher Hall. It was a bizarre experience to be backstage with the three finalists, all pacing or rigid with focus, talking but looking only towards the performance to come. Isata and Jess were floating weirdly at the sidelines, so we wandered into a spare room to keep out of the way and ended up disturbing the previous winner, Laura van der Heidjen, who was warming up for her return performance. Jess and Isata, with their one parent each, were people of no significance, the ones who had *not* made it through the glittering door of consequence. They were not the ones who would walk on stage to perform with the backing of a full professional orchestra in a showdown of prowess and artistry. Before the final announcement, they did have the chance to walk onstage and to be honoured for their achievement. Just before they were due to walk on, Jess, distressed, noticed a ladder in her tights. Luckily, having experience as Isata's Mum, I had a spare pair in my bag and both girls could walk in front of the cameras with dignity.

I thought only of our humiliation on that evening. Isata and I laughed hard and long afterwards at the vagaries of the trip. How funny it had been when we got lost backstage and found ourselves with Jess, stuck in the victory vanguard of cameras and presenters who were following the winner, Martin James Bartlett. How we had tried to find another route to the after-drinks room where we could congratulate the performers – only to end up somehow outside on the street, trying to make a circuit of the building to get back in the right door! We laughed about the dinner before the competition where we had sat on the edge of the table with nothing to say and with absolutely no relevance. The wilderness of failure is a very lonely place, but Isata and I, relaxed out of the camera's glare, giggled for hours in our pyjamas.

It seems strange now to see both Jess and Isata with their debut albums, both with Decca Classics, both successful recording artists. For Isata, that moment of failure, huge in its consequence, made her into a more compassionate and thoughtful person. She took her eyes away from glamour and worked to get excellent A Levels, clever and canny in her organisation. Having won the Elton John Scholarship to the Royal Academy, she worked with passion and dedication to be a better pianist, facing the first term of self-doubt and bruising hours of practice with humility. She was invited to speak at the Success Talks at an art gallery in London because the organisers saw her, the first Black pianist to get to the Category final for BBC Young Musician, as a glowing success story. They invited her to be recorded giving a lecture on the secret of success. What emerged was an incredibly moving talk, a revelation to me, on the merits of *failure*. Isata began by saying that she had been invited to speak knowingly about success, but she wanted to talk about a far more significant thing. Failure was that which built a person and led to real ambition and hard work. Without failure there was no success, and she didn't see herself as a successful person but as someone who knew how to look failure in the face and learn from it. She spoke with grace and a quiet thoughtfulness that was magnetic. While talking about failure she was more impressive than I had ever seen her. Her life before BBC Young Musician had seemed like an inevitable ladder of achievement. She had known that if she worked hard she would get the highest distinction in the country for her music exams, be the best pianist wherever she was, be the cleverest, the one with the scholarship, the prize, the one chosen. But now here she was, having worked herself mercilessly, and she had not won the prize.

Isata grew up and became more giving and more generous. Having had to survive at Purcell, she had been forced to become tougher and less communicative. Now she became a wise counsel for her sisters and always ready to sympathise and comfort. When home she gave lessons to the younger ones and advice to the boys. She was kind and understanding, ready to take a sister to one side and hear their adolescent crises or help with a piece they were learning. I worried that this softer Isata was more vulnerable, but her work ethic was steely. She began running in Regent's Park behind the Academy and she became leaner and fitter, saying that it helped her to practise for longer hours and stay strong. Her playing improved swiftly, with more power and expression at the piano.

At the beginning of Isata's second year, Sheku decided to audition for the next BBC Young Musician competition and Isata would be his pianist. He had to choose the right repertoire and they had to practise together to get the ensemble as intuitive as possible. With Isata as his partner, Sheku won through the first and second rounds, and Isata was ecstatic. This was going to be Sheku's time, and she would be right by his side. Her love for her brother made her work on the music with extra intensity. When Patsy Toh, Ben Davies and Krystyna Budzynska gave them masterclasses on their Strings Final programme, she hung on every word. At the Strings Final, I knew Isata would look after

Sheku. She was as desperate for him to win as he was himself, and she was fiercely proud and protective of her little brother.

When Isata joined him for the Rachmaninov 'Elegie', she knew everything he wanted to say, and she sang it with him, a duet of intense communication. We knew the years that were behind that one performance, the perfect understanding between the two and the love that gave it energy.

Since then, Isata has been Sheku's duo partner and travelled the world with him. Their communication has always been full of humour and based on the frankness and lack of reverence of any brother and sister, and yet full of mutual respect. Isata always tells us funny stories, rolling her eyes, of Sheku in every plane, train or car, letting his head drop immediately onto his cello case and sleeping soundly for the whole journey. She calls him the most boring travelling companion.

Isata has gone on to win major solo prizes at the Royal Academy. She also entered the Harold Craxton Chamber Prize with Braimah and Sheku, a prize that celebrates the blending of different instruments with piano to create a harmony, a conversation and a musical understanding that together makes something unique. Just before they all walked into the competition room for their turn to play, they were interviewed by the American network CBS, which was making a documentary on the family for *CBS Sunday*. They chatted and made jokes, talking about themselves as a family to the television crew. The interviewers were surprised when the three suddenly stood up and announced they had to go and play right now as the time had come for their chamber piece. They walked in, looked at each other and played with such bewitching tenderness, so in tune with what each wanted to say, that they won.

At Isata's graduation, after her four years studying as an undergraduate at the Academy, I turned up after the train had been delayed, shining with sweat. It was a hot day in July and the graduation was to take place in the grand St Marylebone Parish Church opposite the Academy. I had jogged uncomfortably up Euston Road and Marylebone Road (as the traffic made the taxis too slow) with my new dress tight on me, and I had to change out of my trainers into high heels at the Academy doors. I suddenly saw Isata. She was resplendent in her graduation gown and mortarboard pinned to her hair. I stood, rooted to the spot, overwhelmed that she had done it. She had achieved her first-class degree and here she was, graduating from the Royal Academy of Music. I had never seen her look so beautiful. For me, it was the culmination of all the years at Primary and Junior Academy, all the painful early mornings catching the train to St Pancras on Saturdays, all the bleak mornings meeting her here after her train journey from Purcell via Watford. It was the culmination of all those phone calls home when Isata was struggling with trying to impress Hamish Milne or Carole Presland in those weekly piano lessons, and the tiredness that made her despair. It was the conclusion to that wonderful day when she played her Final Recital on the stage of the Duke's Hall, with the panel of examiners sitting inscrutably at the back of the audience, while Isata played for an hour without sheet music and without a break. I was brimming over with emotion and so frightened that I would embarrass Isata that I barely spoke.

Having run from work, Stuart joined me, panting as he entered the church and while I helped him with his tie and fanned him with the programme. As John Suchet from Classic FM presented the ceremony, we waited with bated breath for Isata's turn to collect her rolled piece of paper that claimed her receipt of the degree. Afterwards, we saw Sheku across the road, cello on his back, searching for Isata among the crowd of students in gowns thronging the steps. He was longing to congratulate her, having rushed from a lesson to see her. He was beaming with pride.

15

Doors Flung Open

THE DOORS TO the outside world had always been firmly shut after school. The warm smells of food, followed by a flurry of homework and long hours of intense music practice, kept us all locked in together. I moved from one room to another, each with a child ferociously concentrating on a page, a bar, a note of music, often frustrated, often elated, often exhausted. My role was to enter, listen, give advice, exhort or comfort. With the younger children I had to spend more time. Here, the basic mechanics of holding a bow, tuning accurately, posture and fingering were critical. We would painstakingly work on a passage to achieve the right sound, repeating a rhythm or a shift over and over again. Shifts have to be practised with patient determination. Being able to slide the finger swiftly and lightly up or down a cello, viola or violin string to hit the required note perfectly and beautifully takes long, slow-motion practice. Being able to sit or stand with a cello, piano or violin for any length of time takes long months of building stamina and muscle. Also, the training of concentration and extended focus has to come with unbending routine.

A house of seven children grappling with the demands of classical technique cannot be an open house. After school, a big pot of hot stew had to be ready on the cooker and the children would eat voraciously and then attack what had to be done.

This was not a house of lonely soloists. The children often burst into each other's spaces, giving advice, remonstrating or simply singing and celebrating another's efforts. There were regular spontaneous moments where a duo or a trio would spring up. What began as a solo on the violin would be joined by an improvised accompaniment or a cello harmony. A classical string quartet would flow into a reggae or jazz beat and everyone's voice was loud. Sometimes instruments were swapped and the children would play their second instruments to try out a different part of the music. Sheku would often take a violin and play a violin tune, holding it like a cello on his lap. Braimah would move from his violin and accompany Sheku on piano, or sing astonishingly accurately in mock opera style. Often an instrument would be strummed or rapped to provide percussion.

Whenever they launched into serious trio or quartet practice in order to prepare for a concert, there would be prolonged shouting. Perhaps Isata had an idea that was being ignored, or Sheku was grandstanding, flying into a solo routine in the midst of an ensemble piece. Braimah would want to perfect one bar of music and finesse the collective tuning exactly, and Konya would want to perform a dramatic flourish to the end. And then the collision of intellectual, instinctive and emotional reactions would suddenly coalesce into a melting moment of such intense harmony that I, passing through, would sink onto the stairs and sigh.

But then, in 2015, we were approached by *Britain's Got Talent* to appear on the show. Our immediate reaction was disbelief. A TV phenomenon, but did they really want a group of classical musicians on? Would they be able to support the children? After several discussions and a meeting with the producers, we agreed they should take part. One of the ways to introduce classical music to the general public was to play it for them, perhaps breaking down some barriers to a perceived art form of 'privilege'. Viewers would see Black people playing classical music for the sheer joy of it.

At the televised auditions they decided to play their own arrangement of Brahms 'Hungarian Dance No. 5', adapted by them for three violins, two cellos and a piano. (Mariatu was only five and at a basic stage with the violin, so she was to watch with her parents from the audience.) They took the music and each other seriously, Braimah as always being the perfectionist in the group and playing the lead violin. It was just another concert but more relaxed as they could turn up in their casual clothes, and we treated it as a day out in London. When we arrived, we were all amused by the intensity of the excitement backstage, crowds of performers warming up in the huge backrooms of the theatre. There were dance groups, mime acts, singers, dogs and people with faces thick with stage make-up. We were fascinated by all the theatricality and the way the interviewers and cameramen were stirring everyone into unreal expectation. It was like a day of carnival.

Twelve-year-old Jeneba was the dreamy one of the group. Piano was her main instrument, but she loved to play cello and breezed through Grade 8, with distinction, almost absent-mindedly. But we knew how distracted she could be and warned the others to watch out for her. We sat in the packed audience with television cameras trained on our faces as well as on the stage. When it was the children's turn, they all walked out with Jeneba trailing behind looking happily half asleep. They all sat and looked at each other while the judges waited. Suddenly Jeneba woke up and scuttled off the stage with her cello. There was a loud buzzing of voices around the audience and muttered speculation amongst the judges about what on earth was going on. (She had left her cello spike holder somewhere backstage and we groaned with relief when she reappeared.) The others just sat there, waiting as though she had just run upstairs at home, and on her return they began playing with all the attack and gusto they always had. It was a burst of energy from their connective playing, a small insight into what they wanted to express together. I heard in it the years of playing wild imaginary games together in the hallway or on the stairs. I heard the whooping of chases in our walks together through the Welsh countryside and loud arguments over Monopoly.

The audience roared and sprang to their feet, and the four judges rose too, Simon Cowell grinning and winking with a thumbs up. When it was aired, it was heavily edited, with just the beginning and the end colliding with itself like a bright firework of a piece. We learned then the power of television as an editing tool, but they had won a place in the semi-final. The children felt very much like ambassadors for classical music and they concentrated on a piece they loved playing together – 'Czardas' by Monti. They worked on making the piece as tight as possible. It was a courageously virtuosic piece which they played with ease and joy. When the producers heard it in the run-through it was rejected as being 'too classical'. The children then spent weeks writing and arranging the harmonies for a medley of classical pieces, which would be shared and adapted between the players, flowing from one piece to the other with a witty centrepiece for a popular violin part from the Clean Bandit song 'Rather Be'. It was an intensely creative project which they saw as their own domain, and it was rehearsed and organised with such generosity to each other, each having a moment to take centre stage.

But this was a big television show, which has its own agenda and which creates its own audience expectation. After they had resisted the pressure to walk on stage with white string instruments and play only pop music, the producers lost faith in what the children wanted to do and we knew before the semi-final that they wouldn't be promoted to win. I was proud of their obdurate sense of musical identity, refusing to be moulded in an alien image.

16

At the Precipice

B Y THE TIME we sat in the audience at Sheku's BBC
Young Musician Final and watched him play the
Shostakovich concerto with the BBC Symphony, we
all understood the nature of sacrifice and the elusiveness of
immediate success. We all understood the way in which the
child's personality and experience created the adult. Sheku was
still the naughty boy who climbed the gate at age five in search
of his football and got stuck at the top. He was still the boy who
broke as many rules as he could and walked down the path to
primary school with his cars and Action Men hidden bulkily
under his school jumper. But in that moment, on stage, he was
someone and something else, alive with music and communicating truths he couldn't speak.

But this moment, our son poised on this cliff edge of possibility, had come about not just through practice and dogged
hard work but also through dreaming. The practice regime
could not have been sustained without visions of a possible
future. Children need role models, an idea of what they can
become, worlds they can inhabit. We gathered examples of
inspiring classical musicians for them to watch and listen to.
They spent long periods of time on Sundays and holidays

marvelling at the performances of Itzhak Perlman, Maxim Vengerov, Marta Argerich, Jacqueline du Pré. They all had favourites with styles and tones they loved: Yuja Wang with her stage charisma, Daniel Barenboim with his supreme confidence, Heifetz and Oistrakh with the immediacy and simplicity of their sound. We listened in detail to Ashkenazy's Chopin and, watching *Fiddler on the Roof*, we endlessly repeated Isaac Stern's dramatic opening solo. Sheku learned how to play with vibrato while watching Jacqueline du Pré and Braimah listened closely to just how Michael Rabin broke his heart.

But these were icons from another world, another culture. Heroes who absorbed their particular magic from traditions far removed from us. Beside them we placed Muhammad Ali, Nelson Mandela, tales of escaping slaves, Bob Marley. African music, reggae, rap, Welsh male choirs, Country and Western, Welsh folk singing, all entered the house with equal status. It didn't occur to the children that there was a door they couldn't open or a hero they couldn't emulate.

They looked in awe at the Decca Classics labels on the old records or new CDs and wondered at the long gallery of classical stars who recorded with Decca. There were names passed into legend: Brendel, Rostropovich and more recent, young stars like Benjamin Grosvenor and Nicola Benedetti. They examined the concert halls they played in and the instruments they played. It seemed they all had artist managers, and signing to an influential manager was like signing to a big football club. These agents paved the way, opened the doors, protected and negotiated. The concert halls, the record label, the agent – all were mysterious elements of a life to strive for. But so much was out of reach. Some paths were impossible to follow. They were not born into families with legacies of money, tradition, travel. But they watched BBC Young Musician every two years and dreamed of one day arriving.

It was Isata who opened the door for Sheku to reach the Final, demonstrating how far she herself had come and giving him all the time and skills and love she had. It was she who proved what was possible. And now it was time for the announcement – the winner of BBC Young Musician 2016. My face fell, wanting to prepare myself for the blow and needing to survive it. Dobrinka Tabakova was making a beautiful speech about the meaning of music, what it was and the dangers of settling for mediocrity, and the loss of that meaning in society. There was a trembling understanding of the tender mystery that lived in great music.

A sense of the significance of this moment, this day, was growing in the room. And then I heard his name, Sheku Kanneh-Mason. The world stopped. I wanted to stop. I wanted to crawl to the margin and watch, invisibly, while the room erupted. I wanted to sit in silence and look at my son, my husband, my family, and hold it all like a pearl in my hand. Everyone stood and applauded. Sheku's sisters cried, sobbing and clapping. Sheku was looking at Ben Davies, at his school friends, at his brother and sisters, and at his Dad, and he was so happy.

The world swooped in to look at Sheku. Suddenly, the family was in all the major British newspapers. There were photos and articles of not just Sheku, but also the context from which he came. In many media photographs, Sheku sat with the cello surrounded by his siblings, all playing a classical instrument. Journalists and television cameras came through our front door and stared at the rooms, cluttered with sheet music and filled with four pianos, many music stands, violins, books of music theory and the rushed, busy detritus of seven classically trained musicians, all still teenagers and children.

Into our shared private world, full of our own distinct idiosyncrasies, came a shock of cameras, microphones and journalists. The children's private space, hidden behind the doors of home, was suddenly opened up for all to see. For Stuart and I, it felt as though we were watching a past life being explained and narrated. Every piece of film was a memory of how things used to be and what we were losing. Every photograph of us together was a wonderful realisation of a past lived without special scrutiny, as though we had been years asleep and now were forced awake. The children's musical life had been aimed at performance, but now the unperformed, the unselfconscious parts of their lives were thrust up on stage. It felt like a kind of enchanted violence.

17

Revelations

EACH CHILD HAS multiple stories to tell, and our responsibility as parents is to give them the tools to tell the ones they choose. The ability of each child to astonish with who they can be and with the choices they make shows that parents are simply blind guardians, stumbling on with specks of knowledge and bundles of hope. To be gifted is not to show all your treasures at once. Every child is astonishing if allowed to be. We expected excellence born of dedication, and that expectation was invaluable. But we were never in control.

One of the many mistakes parents make is to sum up their children entirely on how they are constructed within the family. Family does have a huge effect on personality, but it can make us short-sighted. Isata was older and therefore always expected to *act* as the eldest. She was never indulged as a 'little one', and she was expected to be responsible, sensible and cleverer than everyone. Already by the young age of seventeen months, she was a 'big one', and by the time she was six, she had four little brothers and sisters to be older than. We never saw her as the six-year-old that Mariatu was, the indulged baby who was everyone's pet. On the other hand, Mariatu is expected to be like the others. She goes to bed later than they did at her age, is taken to concerts late at night and has to follow a practice regime already set in place. While Isata was listening to nursery rhymes on car journeys with her siblings, Mariatu was listening to the Sibelius violin concerto. While Isata climbed trees and ran through the woods of Sherwood Forest every weekend, Mariatu practises her cello, does park runs and watches her siblings in recitals.

When the family is all together, each child assumes his or her place in the order of things: Isata is in charge and precise about everything; Braimah is elder brother and spokesperson, either big brotherly or witty and satirical; Sheku is the cheeky little brother annoying his sisters; Konya, the middle child, plays a double role as Isata's confidante as well as second pianist and violinist; Jeneba is both bossy sister to Aminata and immature sister to the older ones; Aminata is funny and dramatic but unsure of herself; and Mariatu is at once eager to please and knows exactly who she is.

As they grew up, these points of status shifted only in terms of allies, teams and couples. At first, it was Isata and Braimah as the 'big ones' and Sheku and Konya firmly together as the 'little ones'. Konya was the perfect baby, pretty, thumb-sucking, quiet and always at my knee. Sheku, very affectionate, was also an engine in constant motion, brain ticking over to explore and to find gaps in our field of vigilance. While Konya silently and steadily observed, Sheku would be clambering onto the garage roof. Then Sheku joined more firmly the Isata and Braimah trio. Then it was often two boys and two girls. Then it split into younger girls and an older trio. Then Konya was in the older quartet or in the Konya/Jeneba duo known as 'the girls'. Aminata and Mariatu were the giggling little ones, playing with their dolls and teddies, and now often it's the Jeneba/Aminata duo with Mariatu as the rather serious, thoughtful youngest trying to act bigger.

All these benign factions and treaties, set within the overall order of siblings, created personality traits that have lasted. Isata still has a solemn sense of responsibility and a work ethic born of high expectation, and she is cast as the one who all the girls go to for secret advice. Braimah is a natural leader and teacher, crafting all the rehearsals with a searing eye for detail. Sheku spent his childhood determinedly trying to be as good as his big, sporty, handsome brother. His competitive spirit was honed by being the smaller one trying to kick the ball as hard or run as fast. His creativeness was sharpened by finding ways to win at games, or dares that belied his size or age disadvantage. Often, Stuart would play football, cricket or ball throwing and catching games with the boys in the back garden or the park. As Braimah was taller and older, with natural sporting talent and perfect balance, he would always outplay Sheku, and Stuart and Braimah delighted in teasing Sheku by throwing or kicking the ball just above his head or just to the side of him. Sheku would stand enraged, frustrated by his inability to win a point, looking for any loophole or space through which he could win. But it made him a fierce competitor and fiery player on the football pitch.

When it came to board games (an important part of family life), particularly during our summer holidays in Wales, Sheku was a fireball of determination, ferociously trying to win at any cost. Isata, very quickly unbeatable, reached a point where we couldn't play some board games with her at all, not even with the incisively clever extended family of cousins, aunties and uncles. Isata had a lightning connection between brain and hands, able to think at extraordinary speed, connect word patterns immediately and snatch at them with breathtaking alacrity. Games like Take Four and Anagrams became pointless sessions of watching Isata take over the board in what seemed like seconds. She also presided over Scrabble and even Monopoly, fiercely competitive in a hotly motivated family. Sheku, a flaming point of anger, resorted to all sorts of ingenious methods to cheat his way to a win. It was always him with cards under the table or rabidly hanging on to a point in his favour that he didn't deserve. Braimah would often be seen calmly and wryly switching off, while Isata bitterly hung on for justice. Stuart would be ruthless in his own way, just as determined to win, and I would look for a reason to get a cup of tea and some much-needed solitude. Sheku's need to prove himself and his ability to work at everything with no deviation came in many ways from being the third in the family. He could stick at any game, whether table tennis, football, chess, for as many hours as he had an opponent, and he would play the cello for as many hours as he had an audience.

This pattern of fierce competition and intense cooperation was set and continued, each child perfecting skills of creativity, commitment and improvisation. I was happy to let them roam free in their private world, understanding this as their safe space and knowing that the patterns set then would endure. They never broke ranks, covering up for each other at every turn. Once, Braimah was sent home from primary school, dazed and with a big lump on his forehead from a cricket bat. He refused to say who had whacked him, realising this had been an accident and not wanting the culprit to be in trouble. After quietly asking him, we discovered it was Sheku, trying too hard to be the best player again. Braimah's refusal to betray his brother was done simply and without sentiment, as though the obvious and natural course of action for which he expected no particular praise.

Chess was a favourite of the older three for years when they were children. Stuart would love to play games of chess with each of them and they soon began to play amongst themselves. This developed into multiple games of chess with multiple boards, all going on at the same time. They created games with seven boards set out on the floor of the boys' room, which the three of them played and which lasted for days. This invented game was called 'Attackers', with rules strict and intricate, taken very seriously and a complete mystery to Stuart and me. We marvelled at the boards and pieces and the children's avid concentration, day after day, on this game of patterns and competition, strategy and wit. They also developed games of intense cooperation spilling onto the landing and involving the younger children as helpers or collaborators. The 'shop' was an important game, demanding the production of carefully drawn and cut-out 'money', selling goods at different prices to other 'buyers' in the house. The goods for sale also displayed artfully constructed props and a lot of noise. I tiptoed with resignation through the piles of things that accumulated in and outside their bedrooms: chessboards and the 'shop'; the creation of 'Superland', with more props as well as fascinating superpowers and names; the Lava Game, which was essentially every cushion, pillow and soft toy in the house sliding with the children down the stairs; 'I need some support' – the game of hanging precariously on to radiators and doors in teetering bundles of children; and the autumn/winter Dark Game, played mostly inside the house, entailed lots of crashing about, stumbling and shrieking with the lights off. I found myself plunged into darkness while carrying a basket of laundry up the stairs, or shut into a room, ironing, while mayhem erupted around the rest of the house.

Konya, the quieter addition to this older trio, arrived as the intended baby of the family. We had planned four children, and here was our fourth and last. She was two weeks early, small, pretty and sleepy. We were living in Bahrain at the time, with Stuart working for Gulf Air in the midst of the hot, humid summer. July temperatures were regularly close to 50 degrees Celsius (122 degrees Fahrenheit) and the humidity was overpowering. We didn't need to switch on the water heater over the summer months because turning on the cold taps would result in boiling water coming out into the sink or bath, billowing with steam. We would rush to the air-conditioned car and fall into the seats with our bodies already soaked with sweat, and when the car doors shut, the air conditioning was a matter of life and death. The children couldn't play outside in the summer. The slides and swings, all made of metal, were instruments of torture under the sun, red hot and ready to take off a child's skin, and the swimming pool in the compound was a deep hot bath, threatening to produce a deep faint if plunged into. Into the marble cool of the hallway we dragged a bouncy castle, a plastic slide and a plastic-ball tent, and the children played in the air-conditioned house.

When Konya was born in Awali hospital, after I had been taken by surprise by my early labour, I was forced to sit inside watching the fierce and unremitting sun outside the big window while Konya's big sister and brothers dived into the bouncy castle or squealed down the slide near me. Stuart brought the three little siblings to visit their new baby sister when I was still in hospital. Sheku was fifteen months old, Braimah was two and Isata three. I was exhausted from the birth and the children bounced excitedly around me. I felt myself rising to a panic. I was blinking back tears, desperate in the blast of all this noise and activity. How was I going to manage this?

My mother and niece (Kadie, my sister Isata's daughter) came to visit when Konya was a few days old. Kadie was twelve years old, and I always thought of her as the first child. She was astonishingly clever, walking before she was nine months old and talking at around the same time. Her abilities at maths and reading, as well as her sharp and articulate speech, made her a very special person. She was the beginning of our next generation and loved by all. This 'last baby' I envisaged in Konya made me feel I had climbed to a summit and needed simply to take stock and rest. Konya was quiet and undemanding, happy to sleep where the others had always been awake and crying. I revelled in her sleepiness and the way I could feed her, put her in her cot and concentrate on the loud energy of the toddlers and Kadie's interesting, intelligent talk.

As Konya grew through babyhood, everyone revelled in making noise for her. I remember her sitting through her first and second Christmases in my Mum's house in Wales, surrounded by siblings, cousins and relatives, with the squeals and shouts and movement going on around her, simply sitting without a sound. We thought her silence indicated complacency and a gentle lack of spark. Her soft, full mouth and big eyes made her an attractive and uncomplicated addition to the family. She walked months later than the others and didn't speak much when she was very little. She would be happily pushed in her pushchair, looking as though she were not particularly engaged, and her Grandad, Stuart's father, called her 'Beauty Box' in her sweet charm. I decided this pretty neatness suited the 'baby' of the family and it made life feel a little easier when dealing with Isata's intensive talking and the boys' incessant physicality. As I sat breastfeeding Konya in the living room in Bahrain, I would hear dishes crashing and smashing on the tiled floor of the kitchen, and my visiting mother or Stuart would have to run and snatch up Sheku. Or Braimah would be daring wild somersaults on the bouncy castle while Isata set up energetic and intricate adventure games all around us. Sleepy Konya was just what I needed.

Then, I was forced to acknowledge that this compliant, sweet-faced baby and toddler was not Konya's whole story. As usual, I had to wash, oil and plait each girl's hair, a time-consuming job needing patience from both me and each little girl. Isata, miserable at the process, endured the need to keep still. With Konya it was like trying to pin down a raging animal. When faced with something she didn't want to do, she was shockingly

Above, left: My parents
(Megan Edwards and A.B.
Kanneh) in Birmingham,
1959.

Above, right: My mother,
now Megan Kanneh, hold-
ing me as a two-year-old in
Magburaka, Sierra Leone.

Left: My father holding
Steven, Magburaka.

strong and completely unmanageable. From when she was still
under two, Stuart used to have to hold her down for me so that
I could sort out her hair, and she screamed so hard I thought
the Social Services would come round. Often, she would fight
so fiercely that she would simply flop from the energy expended
and fall asleep in my arms. I had never known a small child so
stubborn that, in order to fight their corner, they used every last
ounce of their strength.

Once she had started primary school, she would get into
arguments with me or even my mother when she came to visit.
To refuse a direction from any of their grandparents was a
step further from refusing *our* directions because of the extra
amount of respect due. I was aghast. It became a pattern that she
refused to walk to school and stood, stock still, staring pierc-
ingly at both of us. We tried the fail-safe method of managing
a small child by threatening and then carrying out a walk away
from her, even turning a corner if we were not on the main
road. She never budged. I, or my mother, would be forced to go
back and see her, and she would be standing in the same place,
staring rigidly back at us.

It was soon clear that Konya was a force to be reckoned with.
She had learned the magnetic charm of the baby and knew how
to use her beautiful smile to get what she wanted. This manipu-
lation was surprisingly clever to us who had thought of her as
a simple, clear landscape. She also had granite determination. I
was potty training her when I was heavily pregnant with Jeneba.
Konya was not going to be the baby of the family after all, and
I couldn't let her reach the age of two without this step towards
independence. My mother very soon took over. Konya decided
by herself that she would use the potty, behind our backs and
on her own terms. Then for months afterwards she refused to
use anything else. We had to take that red potty everywhere and
to everything. It sat in the bottom of the pushchair because we

knew that she was not going to bend to our will. Even at Goose Fair, with Jeneba wrapped on my chest in the baby carrier, we had to take the potty with us.

We realised, to our surprise, that Konya was creative and clever. Shadowed by the loud blaze of her elder siblings, we had failed to see her gifts until they simply appeared at our feet. She suddenly began producing beautiful artwork and had a flair for drawing. She was good with her hands and loved my sister, Isata, showing her how to sew, knit and make things out of fabric or other materials. I thought sewing and craftwork were execrable occupations, and I was amazed at her talent. Then she showed an uncanny ability to fix things. If we found anything not working, whether a computer, radio, toy or mechanical object, she steadily watched our frustration. Then, when we or one of her siblings discarded the object as unfixable, she quietly approached it, head on one side, and took it apart. Before long, we heard the whirr of electrics or cogs in motion and the thing worked.

While we were visiting Antigua when Konya was about five years old, her Grandma and Grandad's front door had a broken lock and handle. They warned us not to touch it in case it either locked us all out or jammed open. We used the back door instead and steered clear. Then there was a shout because Stuart's Dad noticed Konya silently fiddling with the handle and working her fingers over the lock. When challenged, she quietly stepped away, interested rather than alarmed. Her Grandad ran, annoyed, to check the handle and lock…and everything was fixed! It worked perfectly for the rest of our time there. Since then, if something isn't working, we all turn to Konya who unerringly corrects it. Sometimes her long fingers grabbing at one of our mobile phones as though she can't resist experimenting can offend my sense of ownership. Then she always points out something intuitive and helpful to obvert a clumsy

Above: All of us in the garden. Nottingham, summer [to] right: Braimah, Sheku, Jeneba, Aminata, Isata, Kor[…] Front: Mariatu and I.

Below: The House of Music in lockdown, spring 2[…] right: Sheku, Braimah, Isata, Aminata, Konya, Jeneb[…]

In Nanna and Grandpa's kitchen in Caldicot, South Wales, circa 1976. Back row, left to right: my grandfather (James Edwards), grandmother (Ivy Edwards) and mother. Front row, left to right: me, Isata, James and Steven.

Outside Nanna and Grandpa's home in Chipping Ongar, Essex, circa 1973. From left to right: my grandmother, grandfather, James (sat on the car), Isata, me, my mother and Steven.

My brother, Steven, in front. Back, left to right: cousins, Ansumana Konneh, Konya Seisay, Isata Seisay. Kenema, Sierra Leone, August 1984.

Isata, James, Steven and me as teenagers in the 1980s.

Steven, Isata, me and James at my wedding.

Above, left and right: Stuart and me at our wedding, 7 October 1995.

Left: Stuart's parents, Arnold and Enid Mason, on their wedding day, 28 March 1959.

Four become five. From left to right: Isata and baby Jeneba, Konya, Sheku and Braimah, Nottingham, August 2002.

Den in the garden! Summer 2007. From left to right: Jeneba, Konya, Isata, Sheku and Braimah.

Aminata's baptism, early 2006. From left to right: my mother, Megan, Idris (nephew). Back: Steven Wyatt (sister Isata's partner and Idris's father. Isata – sister – is taking the photo); me, holding Aminata; Stuart, Kadie (niece), Deacon John Wakeling. Front: Braimah, Isata, Jeneba, Sheku, Konya.

The future Kanneh-Mason
Trio. Braimah, Isata and Sheku
with their music awards,
March 2006.

Stuart helps Sheku practise,
October 2005.

Jeneba learning piano,
September 2005.

Baby Mariatu with Braimah's
violin, 2009.

Above: Sheku's bus in Nottingham, the picture shows his winning performance for BBC Young Musician 2016.

Below: the Kanneh-Masons play at the Royal Variety Performance, 2019.

Stuart and the children, Nottingham 2009. Left to right: Stuart, Konya, Jeneba, Braimah, Isata holding Mariatu, Sheku and Aminata.

Rehearsing, 2017.
Left to right: Aminata, Konya, Jeneba (at front), Braimah, Isata, Mariatu and Sheku.

Around the dining table at the home of Enid and Arnold Mason (Grandma and Grandad) in Hodges Bay, Antigua, 2019.

operation or irksome glitch, and I have to acknowledge that she has a different way of looking at things.

As Konya grew and I noticed her becoming ever more involved in reading and writing pages and pages of stories, I also noticed her face getting closer to the pages. She would spend afternoons drawing beautiful pictures of dragons, fantasy men and women, or portraits of her siblings, incredibly accurate in showing an expression, mood or essence of character, making each face unmistakable. She saw right into everyone around her and was astute at understanding mood and personality. My brother, James, called her 'poppet' because of her charm, and when she developed teeth that slightly stuck out because she sucked her thumb, she was even more endearing. She added to this a kind of nonchalant lack of awareness of time and space. We quickly realised she had very little geographical sense at all, and almost no concept of time. It was as though she were happily lost in a world of indistinct boundaries through which she swam in her own way. If we were driving to my mother's house in South Wales – a regular three-hour drive – Konya, even by age ten, would pipe up from the back when we had driven for only two minutes and were one street away: 'Are we nearly there yet?' She could not negotiate distance or place, and this never seemed to improve. Once she began at Trinity School at age eleven, she had to catch two buses into the city centre and out again to Aspley in another part of the city. Luckily, she had her older siblings to travel with, but catching the bus home from her last lesson was an endless trial. The buses departed from the Upper School gates and no one could get her to understand where these were in relation to Upper School, although they were simply in front. Even after managing the journey several times, Konya would get lost and confused. I waited at the end of the day for the inevitable phone call from Steve Manderson, assistant head teacher, to say that Konya had missed the bus again. I regularly packed the younger three in the car and drove in school rush hour to pick her up.

We wondered why she had no sense of the geography around her. One day she went running around Mapperley Park, our neighbourhood, with Stuart and the boys. She was left behind a little bit and Stuart began gesturing to her from the top of the road. He couldn't understand why she was slowing down and became agitated with her. Later, she announced that she had seen a strange man waving his arms at her and had no idea who he was. I began to understand the reasons for her face constantly close to her book pages and her head almost in her breakfast bowl. We had all thought that it was an endearing Konya quirk. At about thirteen, I took her to the opticians and found that she was very short-sighted. Suddenly, with glasses, she could read piano and violin music without being comically close to the music stand, and her fingers could move more quickly over the keyboard. But she didn't find a new relationship with the world around her. She had spent her childhood detached from any visual geographical sense, so she had learned to do without it. When she was sixteen and had been going for extra maths lessons next door with Vicki Black (who refused to charge a penny) for two years, she looked over the back-door fence and asked whose garden that was. She couldn't relate the direction she took out of the front of the house with the proximity of our neighbour's house to the back garden, and she was perplexed by our disbelief. I suddenly understood the courage it had taken for Konya to leave the house and deal with the world outside. I knew why she had been so distressed when arranging to meet her friend at the cinema in the centre of town, which was a few streets away from the bus stop where she waited every school morning.

As a young child and on into secondary school, Konya was small and thin, with delicate features and legs and arms so slight and slim that she weighed a feather when picked up. She looked like me, with lighter skin than the others, so I assumed that her smallness and neatness of body was *me* and expected her personality to be the same. My Auntie Mini, when she visited from Sierra Leone, saw Konya and Jeneba as carbon copies of my sister, Isata, and me at the same age: Konya was the bossy older one expecting order and Jeneba was the wilder, more physical and wilful child. Konya was one of the youngest in her school year, being a July baby, and when she started school we had the sweetly funny sight of this tiny girl with stick-thin legs carrying an oversized rucksack. Because she was worried about forgetting things, not having a natural sense of day and time, she would pack all her books for every subject of the week in her bag every day and totter off to the bus. I saw her disorientation in the world as a form of innocence and her ready smile as a kind of apology.

When Mariatu was born, Konya quickly fell in love with her tiny sister. A firm bond cemented between them and I would find Konya curled up with Mariatu reading books with her and talking quietly. Konya became a second mother to her, and Mariatu soon grew to prefer Konya's kind and loving attention. They would share all sorts of secrets and promises, and Mariatu looked forward to the next chapter of whichever book Konya was reading to her. They read all seven books of the *Harry Potter* series together, wound round each other on Konya's bed, and the big sister had endless patience and humour with the little one. I was amazed to see how the one we had thought of as the baby had become such a responsible and soft-hearted big sister.

Konya loved music and played with natural ease. We simply expected a certain standard early on and took no special notice of it. Then she took her Grade 8 piano at age eleven, an age that, in terms of the other children, we saw as average, even though we would have seen it as exceptional had she been our first. We were blinded by the fact that we treated Konya and Jeneba as a duo and entered Jeneba, then nine, for the same exam at the same time. They both gained high distinctions which we decided was exciting in Jeneba's case because of her age and was, in Konya's case, the norm. The following year, at age twelve, Konya gained an even higher distinction mark for her Grade 8 violin, with celebratory comments from the examiner. I noticed she had a magnetic flair with the violin and was beautifully expressive and virtuosic when she played. I wondered if she should make the violin her main instrument because she played with such fluidity and energy, and joy flowed from her with seemingly no effort or thought. I think because her older and younger sister were both pianists, it was what she chose. Or maybe because the challenges of the piano were greater for her, she developed the desire to play that instrument more than the violin. She was adamant that she wanted the piano to be her first study, but she was also equally adamant that she would not be a musician. She was going to forge her own, individual way and be a writer. I looked at her thin, long, spindly fingers on the piano keys and the challenges she had with technique, getting the muscles developed in these long digits, and thought that maybe she was right, but somehow I sensed these words did not come fully from choice but from her place in the family. It was as though she saw herself as a spare part, caught in a compared duo with the precociously gifted Jeneba, and with an accomplished piano trio ahead of her. I worried that she was limiting herself with choices born of jostling comparisons with her siblings.

As Jeneba chose to audition for Primary Royal Academy, Konya refused and instead began having lessons in Belper with the brilliant Beate Toyka on Saturdays. Beate gave her the attention and detail she needed, and she even had an internal slide down her staircase that Aminata and Mariatu could play on while Konya had her lesson. I was deeply impressed that there was someone else whose house belonged as much to the children as to the adults, and Beate's kindness to the children, coupled with her insistence on teaching to a very high standard, was admirable.

Konya began playing with real excitement and charisma. She won several prizes at the Derby and Grantham music festivals and there was a sparkling freshness to her playing that seemed full of optimism. I sat down and talked to her, explaining that no one would force a decision on her but that I wanted her to be in a position to make a proper choice when she was older. She agreed to give the Junior Academy audition a go, but reiterated that she would study English and not music at university. I said, 'How wonderful, Konya! But you can do both for now'. After all, what would happen to her self-esteem if she were the only child not playing music at a high level? Was she really in an informed position to choose the outlands, beyond the others? For me, siblings had to be able to communicate with each other and understand a shared, secret language. What if Konya were banished from this world by her own misguided lack of confidence and, as the years went on and her skills dwindled, could not regain entrance? When she auditioned and was accepted to join the Junior Academy at age twelve, Stuart said she should have a teacher who celebrated her musicality and allowed her to develop at the pace she wanted. Druvi de Saram loved her, and she loved him. He would come into the Royal Academy canteen after their lesson together and talk about how music flowed from inside Konya, with no obstruction. Konya said the lessons were full of humour and Druvi would deride 'damned boring pianists' and praise Konya as exciting. Her desire to play well grew and Druvi never prevented her from playing pieces she wanted to play. She gained Highly Commended in the first Iris Dyer Piano Prize she entered at the Academy and began practising harder.

Then she began growing. I first noticed when she started getting stuck, bumping into the door frames every time she tried to enter a room. She began crashing about in the kitchen, as though she no longer knew the length of her limbs or fingers. It became uncomfortable getting breakfast next to her because she seemed to spread like a spider into every corner and over every surface. That was when Isata coined the word 'Spangly' to describe her elongating limbs. Then came the untidiness. I was shocked: I had thought of her as neat and ordered, and here was this wild, spangling creature whose possessions began spreading uncontrollably around her room and the house. When she walked, her legs danced under her in a way that reminded me of her Dad. In fact, everything about her began to remind me of her Dad. She was untidy, her voice was continually and always at full volume, she dominated every room and was utterly unconscious of the space she took up. The quiet little child who could be tucked away in the pushchair had become this loud, tall person who made a mess wherever she went.

As Konya grew taller (she grew a foot in a few months) she became very funny and very witty. We were all taken aback. Her comments and stories were dry and amusing, and put her at the centre of attention, as though she had stepped out of the shadows and claimed her place. When we went on holiday, she was the family chronicler and wrote very funny narratives of our days with incisive and accurate character summations. She listened and understood all our ways of talking and being and could write about us with alarming accuracy. We laughed out loud at her sidelong view, and those stories provide such a clear view of our time as a family that they are now a precious archive.

But it took her a while to accept this new, tall body, and her body itself also seemed to go into shock at the sudden change. I began to hear sporadic screams from Konya at random moments around the house, and there she would be writhing on the floor, one of her legs stuck out at an awkward angle. I would have to gently smooth my hand over her knee to try to unlock it. This took patience and time as it would be tightly stuck and taut with pain. This became a repeated drama, and I took her to the doctor, then the hospital, and she was given a course of physiotherapy. Apparently, her body had grown tall before her slim little legs and slight knees had time to build up any muscle. I did the exercises with her regularly, stretching, bending, walking up and down steps, massaging. In the end, I thought running was probably the best thing and we began running around the many hills of Mapperley Park.

For a long while, Konya was the hopeless runner in the family. She was always last, trailing behind with her weak legs whenever the children ran together. Stuart despaired and thought she would never keep up. The others, including Jeneba, sped past her as she staggered on, and we decided she was just not built for running. Then she began catching up. We would see her pale, determined face appearing over the hill and not stopping until she ran seriously over the threshold. And then the balance was tipped. The girl who outgrew herself and walked hunched and ashamed of her height into school, and who could barely hold herself up, was now one of the best runners in the family. She was nearly six feet tall, strong, slim and striking. She still crashed around the kitchen and carried a bag fit to burst with spilling objects. But she began to hold herself as though she belonged in this new body.

The teeth that stuck out and gave her the loveable quality of the little girl were surveyed by the orthodontist. She was offered braces and took them affably, but first came the retainers, big plastic teeth shields that sat on her palate and behind her bottom teeth. They made her dribble and she was unable to speak properly. As we came out of the appointment and into the street, she began crying, her words slurred and almost incomprehensible: 'I'm so mish-rable' (miserable). She held a tissue over her mouth and I was full of compassion. 'You don't have to go into school', I said. 'Stay home and get used to them first'. But she had gone through the teeth extractions and she was determined to get on with it, so she went straight into school. Teachers angrily accused her of eating in class and then were sorry when they heard her explanation. I was impressed by her ability to face this new suffering without evasion. Her mouth hurt when the braces came in and she couldn't eat anything but soup for three days. She didn't dwell in self-pity but got on with it. The optician kept insisting on thicker glasses, and Konya cried at the limitations of her body. She tried contact lenses and, even after several appointments, she couldn't get them on her eyes without crying with the sensitivity. I tired of sitting there for every contact lens session while Konya sat gripped with distress as the optician 'bullied' her. My mother began to join me to give some moral support. We changed opticians in a saga with no evident end. I wondered how to gently extricate Konya from this cycle of failure and wondered how she could bear to continue on this path of inevitable misery. (My mother agreed that Konya could never achieve this painful victory.) Then in one session she simply conquered it. Dogged in her insistence, she placed the lenses on her eyes and all at once she could use contact lenses, and she walked out of the opticians with all-round vision.

When the years of braces and the months of contact lens try-outs had ended, Konya suddenly emerged as a surprise. She appeared in the house as though from nowhere, this tall, slim model-like girl with a huge, magnetic smile. Her sense of fashion was stunning and she wore everything with a kind of abstract coolness that looked almost indifferent. And she could wear anything. If she walked into a room, she seemed to fill every corner with personality, and I realised that she wasn't me at all. Meanwhile, she had changed her mind. She was going to be a pianist – with only eighteen months before the auditions to conservatoires such as the Royal Academy, the Royal College, Guildhall and others. No one had thought this was possible. She hadn't been training with that in mind. To play musically and with joy can take you to a certain level and no further. Konya hit a wall in terms of technique, and her entire approach to the piano needed to be stripped down and rebuilt. How she pressed the keys, rolled the muscles in her arms, the power and strength of her fingers, her understanding of advanced phrasing and varying weight of touch, the flow of thought and feeling from shoulder to fingertip – all had to be remodelled. Everyone around us was doubtful. Her new teacher, Sarah Pickering, emphasised that the window for change was too small. The journey to conservatoire needed to be longer and planned earlier. Did we need a plan B? Perhaps she should apply to conservatoires that didn't demand the standard of the Royal Academy or of the Royal College? But I knew that if a child wanted to aspire to something, the worst thing a parent could do would be to say, 'No you can't', or 'Aim lower', and I wouldn't say it. I argued with everyone that Konya had a will of iron and a stubbornness that would win through, and failure was better than giving up. I also had complete faith in Sarah. She had taught chamber music to Sheku, and we all thought she was brilliant, efficient, precise and intensely musical.

The journey began. Konya had to learn some basic and difficult technique, which meant hours of exercises and studies, and playing pieces that seemed far below her abilities. At first, I could hear how she was being reined in, forced slowly and painfully to retrace her steps. A lot of the work was meticulous and time-consuming, as though she had to recondition her body and thought processes to approach the music from another place. Sarah asked in-depth questions about key, modulation, context and structure, all of which had bearing on how every phrase was expressed, every key pressed, every gesture enacted. It was about understanding as well as building up muscle and stamina.

Time was pressing on and Konya had to apply for the expensive auditions. The cost was approaching £100 for every audition, and it was the lead-up to Christmas, when money was always tight. I helped her to write her personal statement. When we sat down together, she had so much to say that was surprisingly impressive. She had already achieved a lot as a musician. I had been looking at her under the towering shadows of Isata, Braimah and Sheku. They were travelling the world as a piano trio, and Konya had been self-consciously writing herself out of this narrative for so long that we had begun to believe in her absence. But here she was on paper, a significant musician with real desire. She applied to three conservatoires: Royal Northern, Royal College and Royal Academy. The Royal Northern was in vibrant Manchester, and I thought that maybe it would be good for Konya to attend an excellent conservatoire in a big city other than the one with her siblings.

I began to notice a big change in her playing. The sometimes overly bright tone of her sound, delightful when she was a child, had become more considered, deeper and more rounded. The music swam and flowed from her fingers as it hadn't before. When she played Debussy or Ravel, the Impressionist splashes and soft smudges of the pictures she expressed made sense, as though another line of music had opened up underneath the surface and had been allowed to grow. When she played Haydn, there was a brightness and joy that gave space to nuances and tenderness that before lay hidden, and everything about her playing seemed to have swelled into vision.

Konya entered Nottingham Young Musician. It felt like her time and she was ready. At the Final, she wore a long black dress, studded with sparkling sequins around the bodice and neck, that reached the floor. She had recently started leaving her hair unplaited so that it sprang around her head in a thick, crowning Afro that made her seem even taller. She was like a tall, lit match with her black hair ablaze round the edges from the stage lights. When she played, her sound filled the Djanogly Recital Hall at Nottingham University with a new self-belief. I watched her arms almost rippling up and down with the music, inviting us to join her hypnotic dance. She was playing with her body and allowing the notes to join and flow together. James Bailleau, the adjudicator, said, 'Konya, the next step is for you to pin us all against the wall with your virtuosity', and I understood what he meant. She learned from Sarah how to open up the channel between the music in her head and its expression through her hands and body. Now she needed to take off the reins and let it free. That courageous, carefree piano playing and the witty virtuosic performances that characterised her violin playing could be allowed to storm the stage again, now that she had worked so hard to build her technique. Her playing was beautiful, and she won the title, and as she stood, holding the trophy, I knew she had a chance.

Then the day of the Royal Northern audition arrived. I felt a horrified sense of responsibility for the organisation of train tickets, timetables and the practical decisions about shoes, clothing and music books. Konya would play without music but needed to have the sheet music with her. They would interview her about the pieces and instruct her to begin at different points, indicated by technical terms that she had to know: exposition, recapitulation, modulation to the relative major. I thought of

Konya as the innocent one whose confused geographical sense of the world extended to the music. Would she understand the markers and signposts? If they dropped her without warning into the passages of Bach or Ravel, could she navigate her way without a map in her head? I was full of panic and concentrated mercilessly on every detail of what she took with her and the timings of every moment, from the waking alarm to the arrival at the Royal Northern. I woke an hour before her, got myself ready and went through each already-organised item. Konya was reverberating with nerves and electric excitement. This was it. The first audition.

We got to the train station in good time and I saw the train. This part was straightforward. I had caught the train with them every Saturday morning to London for years. We climbed aboard and settled ourselves in good seats. Konya got out her headphones to listen to recordings of the pieces that she would be playing and spread out her books. I had done the first part of my job and Konya caught the train in time. After a while, sitting in the comfortable warmth of the carriage, the usual announcement from the guard came over the loudspeaker about where the train was going, the number of carriages, the buffet car, the threats about having the correct tickets. I was used to switching off when this happened as the loud announcements were always irritating. I realised that Konya was staring at me, alarmed. 'What is it?' I asked. She answered, 'Does the train go via London St Pancras?' I laughed. Konya's lack of geographical sense was now legendary. I began to explain with mock patience that Manchester was north-west and London was south-east. 'So why are we going via London? Do we need to change trains on the way?'

It hit me with a sick feeling in my stomach: I had gone on automatic pilot into the London – instead of the Manchester – train. I screamed and Konya stiffened. We struggled to get out before the train moved, scrambling books and phone leads together and staggering out onto the platform. Where was the Manchester train? By the time we found it, it was moving smoothly out of the station. I knew I had let down my child in her hour of need. We ran along the platform and up the steps to the main ticket office, to be told that the next train was in one hour, with no viable connecting train, and Konya would not get to the conservatoire until about one minute before her audition warm-up, *if* the train were on time. On top of this, I had to buy two more tickets, having already paid extra for the peak-time ones. But it was Konya's expression of despair which floored me. I had failed so completely.

We finally arrived at Oxford Road Station and stepped out into the cold Manchester air. There was no time for a steadying hot drink, so we began speed-walking up the road, firstly in the wrong direction, then in circles because the SatNav had no idea where we were. Once walking in the right direction, I knew I would eventually recognise the way, but we were now lost and we would soon be late. I sympathised with Konya's lifelong sense of disorientation, having lived with it for my life too, and I felt guilty that I couldn't lead her through. We found someone who pointed us on the right street and we raced off, arriving breathless and hot through the doors. At the desk, Konya was immediately taken off to warm up and I went up in the lift with her and sat in the corridor outside, ruffled and stressed. Somehow, the alacrity of the whole process seemed to focus Konya's attention and she came out of the audition smiling. It had gone well. We had the whole morning to wait until the names were posted on the noticeboards for the successful candidates who had won a second audition, so my next task was to feed Konya. We met Jess Gillam, who was a student there, and chatted with her, and watched the usual high tension in the faces of sixth-formers coming to audition. The day wore on. I saw Konya slide out of top gear and relax, marking time. Then the names were up. She walked over to the fraught space where the noticeboards were… and there was her name. I relaxed too. She was at the right standard. She had been given a second audition. We merely had to wait the long three hours for her turn to play again.

The Royal Northern canteen reminded me of the long afternoons at the Academy, when the early morning misery crept back and dragged me down. By the time the second audition came, Konya walked dreamily through the doors. It was late November and dark outside. I began to think of the weary train home in rush hour and the crowded platforms, when I should have been thinking of how Konya was performing behind those closed doors.

Konya came out of the room after the second audition, which was in front of the head and the leaders of the piano department. She forced a wavering smile and began to cry. She had blithely walked in, played under a mist of vague detachment and woke up to the cold realisation that it hadn't gone well. The smiles in the room were lukewarm. Before her, a confident boy had emerged with happy handshakes and promises of seeing each other again. She emerged with a cool 'thank you' and tempered indifference. She cried all the way home.

It was two weeks before her next audition, and the blazing girl who had been striding towards her possible future shrank into herself again. She couldn't play the piano with any conviction. I would tuck her into bed at night and her face, hair around it plaited tightly for bed, looked like a frozen mask. She stared over my shoulder as if looking at the wreck of her future, and it was astonishing to see my positive, warm daughter shut down. I didn't know how to reach in and warm her up again. I would lie next to her, rub her hands and speak hopeless words of wisdom above my panic. I whispered to Stuart, 'Have we tricked her into following a hopeless path? Is she simply in the wrong family?'

She went into Junior Academy on the following Saturday, and Sarah spoke to me after her lesson. Konya's playing had gone backwards and Sarah was apprehensive about the next two auditions. I felt my chest tighten.

Konya refused to check her online UCAS account to see if she had been given an offer from the Royal Northern. She knew a rejection would break her spirit so she simply moved on. By the following week, she had gritted her teeth, stood up straight and begun practising intensely again. She felt the rest of her life hinging on these auditions, and she practised late every night. She played in the Junior Academy Performance Platforms and continued to refuse to turn on her phone to check the Royal Northern response, choosing her own landscape of blind optimism in which to operate.

The day came for the Royal College audition. It was approaching mid-December and the air was freezing. We had to stay overnight in a budget hotel because that was cheaper than paying for the peak-time morning train to London. We had what we called a girls' evening – pizza and curling up in the double bed to watch Will Smith's *Karate Kid* on the television. It was incredibly inspiring. This beautiful boy beating all the odds and coming from a place of disadvantage to win the karate trophy through naked grit, determination and repetitive hard work felt like a reflection of Konya's journey. We soaked up the romanticism of it all, and the hope and sense of fate that it gave to Konya was huge.

The next morning, we walked into the bright, sunny cold day, full of a feeling of shining destiny. Konya walked into the Royal College early and eager and was given an earlier slot because the person before was late. The second audition was minutes after the first, and all was achieved in a lovely aura of joy and confidence. We loved the Royal College for its friendliness, its bright windows and the full scholarship that they offered Konya on the spot. She came out of the room, face shining with happiness, and we celebrated, arms in the air in a corridor with views into the London street, sparkling with winter daylight. Konya, from the lost girl, full of fear, who used to stoop to hide her height, had won a scholarship to one of the top conservatoires in London.

Stuart was returning that day from a business trip to New York for the Belmond company, so we all met at St Pancras. That early Friday afternoon, the windows and shiny shopfronts of St Pancras were bathed in a silver glow, and we loved London. Konya finally felt strong enough to check her status with the Royal Northern and found that she had been offered a place after all. After the flurry of text messages to everyone she could think of to tell the news – brothers and sisters first – Konya turned her thoughts to the following Tuesday and the looming Royal Academy audition. The Royal Academy, as the oldest conservatoire, was rival to the Royal College, and both competed for the best players, along with Guildhall. This felt like the ultimate moment of proof. Could she be capable of following the others to the Academy? Was she as good as them? Stuart and I discussed with her that maybe the College was the best choice anyway, asserting her individuality away from the Kanneh-Mason legacy, but we could see in her face that she had something to prove.

The day of the Royal Academy audition clashed with Sheku's album launch with Decca in London. I was torn two ways, longing to go to Sheku's celebration with the most important people in his musical life. He would perform some short cello pieces with Isata on piano, surrounded by friends, teachers (both from school and the Academy), mentors, fellow musicians, people who had inspired and supported him for years. And I couldn't be there. Konya needed me completely.

We caught the train with Vicky and Steve Manderson who, representing Trinity School, had a special invitation to Sheku's launch, and we watched them walk in another direction, excited about the evening ahead. We carried on along Euston and then Marylebone Road, heavy with nerves. The Academy was strangely hushed and shadowed when we arrived in the late-winter afternoon, and it seemed so different from the bright, busy Saturdays of Junior Academy. Current senior students in smart black shirts registered Konya and showed her where to wait for her warm-up. The air was hushed and solemn, and I was alert with fear.

Konya was eventually ushered into one of the practice rooms with thick wooden panelling and a grand piano by the dark window. While she warmed up playing scales, I looked at the heavy wooden door and the deep skirting boards and felt the confidence of an institution built on age, reputation and success. Why would it want our family, Black and new and from the outskirts of Empire? Even now, with three children studying full time with scholarships at the Academy, I had to wrestle with myself, the imposter.

It was time for Konya to enter the audition room. It was in Duke's Hall, the big concert hall, adorned with chandeliers and the stunning organ donated by Sir Elton John and Ray Cooper high above the stage. It was a long walk for Konya from the panel of professors to the stage with the Steinway grand piano mounted there. I thought of her, slim and tall with her Afro fanning out around her head, making that walk to the imposing concert platform. Perhaps that was part of the assessment. Could the candidate walk before an audience and own the stage? I waited in the canteen, ironically passing the framed photo – hung on the Academy wall – of Sheku standing proudly with his cello. I remembered when that photo had been taken. It was before Sheku had won BBC Young Musician and we had a spring-morning photograph session at Photo Nottingham, with Isata and Braimah. They had been photographed as a trio and individually with their instruments. Such was the talent of Stuart MacIntyre, the photographer, that this photo of Sheku, standing in a suit looking down at his standing cello, had gone round the world. Now it was my lovely middle child who I had left alone and at sea in that huge room where concerti had been played and great choirs sung. Now it was *her* turn.

I sat in the almost empty canteen for minute after minute. It was eerily still, just after the end of term, with some senior students, particularly pianists needing the pianos, coming and sitting for a while. Then Konya entered, smiling: 'I've got a second audition!' Relief spread over the whole room. I immediately texted Stuart, who was abroad, and Braimah, who was at the launch. We waited again. Konya went to the toilets and came back, covered in confusion. Another girl had been at the mirrors who had also had her piano audition. 'Oh, so you're waiting for your second audition?' Konya had happily asked her. It was uplifting for her to have someone to bond with. The other girl looked startled. 'Oh, is there a second audition?' Konya was mortified at her mistake, as kindness is so much a part of her. She immediately denied all knowledge of any possibility of a second audition and smiled her way out of the toilets and back to me.

The second audition seemed to last for hours. I sat in the low light of the evening canteen, empty of food and service and almost empty of students. Anxiety made the time drag with dread. Then suddenly she was in front of me. The space between me and her as she walked towards me seemed an age. She looked at me, stricken, and said, 'I got a scholarship!' and burst into tears. I ran to her and we hugged, and I laughed. She was still crying and I understood just how much she had wanted this, just how hard and unremittingly she had worked and what a mountain of self-doubt she had overcome.

I sent a message via the family Messenger, telling everyone

the good news. Sheku, Braimah and Isata came straight from the album launch and raced into the canteen, laughing and cheering. They were there, all four of them, and everyone was hugging and congratulating Konya, anticipating the next September when they would all be at the Royal Academy together. It was an extraordinary moment.

Now Konya walks tall, and when complimented by one of us for playing the piano well or looking good in an outfit, she breaks into a teasing dance of victory that is at once funny, cool and provocative. She knows that she can achieve anything, and since starting at the Royal Academy full time she has worked hard and intensively, developing an impressive regime of practice, structured with running and gym sessions to keep up her energy. Her social sense has made her a wonderfully collaborative musician and she seems to blaze with personality. With the help of Google Maps she travels to engagements and concerts around and outside London (a long journey from the young girl who didn't understand how her back garden linked to Vicky and Doug Black's house next door). I sometimes compare photos of her as a child – wilting and putting her head down shyly before the camera, sweetly unsure of herself – with the wide grin that radiates from photos now, arms flung behind her crowning Afro and meeting my stare straight on.

18

Falling Out of the Sky

MANAGING ANY BIG family is a hectic, full-time job. Overwhelmed by the mounting washing baskets, the serial cooking, the ever-growing piles of papers, clothes, books, forms to fill in, calendars to synchronise, errands to run, ironing, cleaning, school runs and everything else, there were many days when I just stood in the freezing cubby hole of the 'laundry room' and sobbed – and went to bed at midnight with the pre-dawn alarm set, unconscious before I hit the pillow.

If Stuart came home from work in London, I picked him up by car from the train station between 8 and 9 p.m. This was always difficult after a full day with the children. My body and mind ached from the intensive time I gave to each of them, and I was always completely drained. From Stuart's perspective, he was returning from a long day at work, with a wearying commute, and he needed gratitude, nurturing and attention as much as I did. Each of us wanted the other to be the hero, to listen to our list of anxieties and to pick us up. We inhabited two separate all-consuming worlds. Neither of us felt like taking on the other, having had no respite ourselves. It was like getting to the end of a back-breaking journey only to be faced with a mountain climb with another person on your back. In those moments we resented each other, and sometimes, both in despair, we collided with a sharp shock. It took all our individual strength to manage our side of the bargain, and it was sometimes difficult to remember the needs of the other person. Often, we were too wrung out to even consider *ourselves*.

Children who are gifted are often gifted in more than one direction, and these gifts have to be discovered and chosen. We were keenly aware of how responsible we were for giving our children access to who they needed to be. It's impossible to be too obsessive about one's children, but sometimes the wagon, driven too hard, threatens to overturn. With seven children, it was difficult to branch out and give each all that we thought they needed, but we certainly tried. At one time, when they were a lot younger, I was taking someone somewhere every evening, whether it was swimming lessons, karate, football practice, ballet lessons, gymnastics or cricket. The music grew in emphasis and clashes began to emerge. I couldn't be in three places at once. We began to pare down the regime, but instead we took up orchestra or chamber music rehearsals and concert opportunities.

As we became more and more frazzled, my mother shook her head and counselled, 'Kadie, you need to exercise more healthy neglect'. We took her advice. From a very early age, the children would spend time with the families of both Stuart and myself. My brother James's children, Lahai and Nyanje, would come and spend a whole week in the summer, going to the park with their cousins or out on day trips. At the homes of grandparents, aunties and uncles, our children would spend days camping in the Welsh hills, or touring the sights of London, or riding their bikes along village lanes. No instruments went with them, and they tumbled off their bikes, fell in streams and cow muck, went to the Tower of London and watched DVDs. They loved it, particularly when family came to visit *them*. Even now, a family Christmas is a slight disappointment if extra family are not here, or *we* are not there (a rare occurrence). When my Auntie Mini from Sierra Leone and a host of cousins came to stay, the children were delighted. We all went to London when Mariatu had just been born – had a Sierra Leone family party and danced all night, eating Saki Tomboi, Jola Bete and plantains. These moments are opportunities to take the lid off the steaming pot of family term-time life.

The pace has sometimes been too fast, and we have had to reassess what is possible. We sometimes went to events such as the Suffolk Festival of Performing Arts. That was a weekend of classical music competition, and the older children had entered several classes. After the Nottingham Music Festival closed down, we regularly entered them into the Derby and Grantham music festivals every spring and summer term, and the Birmingham Piano Festival in the early autumn. We were very conscious of how important it was for the children to be challenged with live performance, to experience playing in front of an audience, and to learn to manage nerves in the face of critical judgement.

The seven children, aged thirteen down to four months, fitted with us into our very old Ford Tourneo with far too many miles on the clock and a very loud diesel engine, but which was big enough for all of us. It still had its taxi sticker on the side window, but it was a big improvement on the summer of walking everywhere, baby strapped to my chest, because the eight-seater car had leaked its final drop of oil and broken down outside the house after a mad two-hundred-mile round trip to collect a baby-changing table at a good price.

We were travelling back after dark with a three-hour journey ahead of us, due to arrive in Nottingham at midnight, with work and school the next morning. Stuart and I had organised the weekend meticulously and the children had faced audiences for two days. I began driving but could feel the darkness on my face, the cats' eyes tracing a hypnotic line along the road, and the intermittent headlights blaring onto me from cars going in the opposite direction. My eyelids grew heavy.

We swapped and Stuart drove. I fell asleep and woke to see his eyes closing and face falling. We swapped again. I was soon falling asleep while driving. The steady breathing of seven sleeping children plus husband was dangerously beguiling and I knew I was sinking into dreams with them. We changed over again and Stuart got into the driving seat. I was asleep in seconds. A deafening, grinding noise woke me up with a start and Stuart was shouting, jolted awake just as we were about to smash into a telegraph pole. We swerved at high speed, the steering wheel wrenching Stuart's wrist, the car scraping through a hedge, into a ditch and into a tree. Branches crashed through the windscreen, close to my eyes, and Braimah, in the front seat between us, was blinking awake. Mariatu, her car seat upside down, was screaming. The car was lying on its side. Talking as though in a nightmare, I began asking Stuart to call the emergency services. He took out his phone and began looking at it with utter confusion. 'Dial 999', I shouted. He turned the phone over in his hand and vaguely tapped at it as though he had no idea what it was. Abandoning it, he began trying to clamber up out of the car, the door above his head. Several of the children were now calling as he made it out of the ditch and onto the dual carriageway. I realised that he was in a state of shock, grabbed the phone and called the police, who told me urgently to get Stuart out of the road. A passing car of helpful men drew up and peered, horrified, down into the sideways car full of yelling children. (I couldn't hear what they were saying because of Mariatu's crying and the police officer's voice in my ear.)

The police came and lifted us all out of the car and into a taxi almost identical to the one we had just written off. Stuart's wrist, responsible for saving us all, hurt for a long time, and our old car lay, two wheels in the air, with the log of a tree rammed through the front and into the steering wheel. (The instruments in the back of the car remained miraculously undamaged.)

We lay all together in one big bed, unable to go to school or work the following day. All we could hear was the sound of that grinding, roaring crash. It was there with us in the room and I couldn't get it out of my head. Stuart couldn't get up, crushed by the thought that he had nearly killed his whole family. I knew that actually he had just saved every one of us by his quick reactions and strength the moment he woke up. If I had been driving, we would have been dead. I thought of Braimah's eleven-year-old face waking up within inches of those branches breaking through the glass, and I moved closer to the children's warm bodies.

After this, traumatised and thankful, we re-examined our lives. We needed more time at home, lying in that big bed together, all of us sheltering from the noise of shattering metal and crunching wood. So we decided to draw inward.

We did continue with the Sunday football and the orchestra for a while, cutting the extra chamber music and some of the sport. Braimah had to relinquish the Saturday-morning cross-country running because of Junior Academy, and we had to stop travelling to the Suffolk Festival. The Derby and Grantham festivals were closer to Nottingham, so we remained committed to them. Organising these music competitions for five children at once was a feat in itself. I would have to time the length of each piece they were to play, decide which classes were suitable, think of balanced programmes, work out the class codes and prices on multiple pieces of paper, and spend hours photocopying music for the adjudicators who, due to copyright laws, had to destroy the copies straight after the class.

Then it was a question of organising journey times and car parking. For Suffolk, we had organised bed-and-breakfast accommodation and added those costs to the class prices. Along with petrol expenses, music festival entries for five children were pricey affairs, but we knew how important they were. We organised journey times and car parking, always an issue with our nine-seater car. (We had managed to buy another one with a loan, paid back every few months, from my mother. We couldn't buy one quite as cheap as the one we had lost, but we did buy another old Ford Tourneo ex-taxi.)

By the time I had packed suitable clothes and shoes for performing, organised each piece of sheet music, made sure the girls' hair was plaited, listened to all their practice performances, made sure that instruments, spike holders, bows, strings and rosin were packed and fingernails cut, wrapped up the sandwiches and changed the baby's final nappy, I was already exhausted. Stuart's role was to listen with me and give critical and enthusiastic responses to their practice performances. He would like to time the journey and was utterly emotionally involved in the competition and the children's playing.

When the children perform, I still become rigid with concentration, hanging on to every note and expression, suffering with every slip and every deviation from practice. I am often reassured by the first touch or bow of a note. I can gauge whether it will go well, whether they are relaxed and focused. The music festivals were wonderful opportunities to learn what could go wrong, and many things did. At Nottingham Music Festival, I put Isata, aged nine, in shoes that squealed and squeaked every time she pressed the pedal. It was excruciating, and I sat horrified with guilt as the sound of the music was drowned by the rubbery noise. (Afterwards, I saw the organisers on the floor underneath the piano stool, trying to work out what had gone wrong with the pedal.) On another occasion, at a recital in Bath, it was the piano stool screeching like a squeezed balloon every time Isata made a vigorous movement. On each occasion, Isata stood up and bowed, miraculously oblivious to the noise.

Braimah, aged eight, played an entire violin piece with piano accompaniment having forgotten to tighten his bow. He realised at the first husky note but was too polite to stop the pianist. Sheku, aged nine, played a cello sonata without music, with Isata on piano, and sailed off into the harmonically logical but wrong passage. Isata, with her impeccable ear, brought him back by playing chordal cues like breadcrumbs to bring him home.

I had insisted that they perform without music from the beginning. That leap of faith and memory was an important way for them to learn to trust themselves and enter the music entirely. It also demands depths of concentration that have to be tried and tested. Each of them lived through the scary moment on stage of having to feel their way back to a forgotten phrase, or key, perhaps tricked by a passage that echoed a previous or later moment, and were punished for allowing their minds to wander. Playing a stringed instrument, they've had to learn to pick up clues from the accompanist, and as the accompanist they've had to learn how to give the musical signposts needed to get back on track. As pianists, they have learned strategies of repetition or creative concealment, improvising musical ways back to the sanctioned text of the composer. Their sacred task as performing musicians is to keep the spell from breaking, to hold the audience safely in the magic of the music and not let them fall through the cracks. The bond between performer and audience is a contract that holds the musician responsible for that leap of faith made by the listener. Somehow, the mystery must be sustained.

As parents, we have to go through the agonies of watching the children learn these lessons in the glare of the public eye. These are lessons such as not to grimace if you make a mistake, and absolutely not to stop. Remembering your spike holder on stage so the cello doesn't skid into flight halfway through a dramatic run of notes. Learning to nod and bring in your accompanist rather than careering off on your own without them. Tune your stringed instrument before you play. Check where the pedals are under your feet at the piano so you don't press on the loud pedal when you were aiming for the soft. Adjust the stool height, lift the lid, put down the book stand. Go to the bathroom before you play, tie your hair back, wash and dry your hands. And don't trip while you're walking to or on the stage (Isata's hobby when younger).

Managing jeopardy on stage doesn't end with the early music festivals and competitions. Every candidate in the Category Final stage of BBC Young Musician knows the build-up and the strain this involves. The names are published in early January and the filming begins. Excitement coalesces around the Category Finalists and the pressure constantly mounts. In March 2016, we were all sitting in a row of family members. Isata, as Sheku's pianist, was backstage and the rest of us, with my sister, mother, her next-door neighbour and friends from Junior Academy were in the audience. Sheku was the second performer and I sat with every muscle locked. The television cameras were active around us and I was horribly aware of the panel of judges somewhere behind me.

Sheku's first piece was the unaccompanied 'Danza Finale' from the 'Suite for Cello' by Cassadó. This is a ferociously intense piece demanding fierce and sustained concentration, building from pared-down rhythms and plucked strings to a furious and whirling dance of deep bow strokes and chords. There are moments of lonely, sung notes and phrases swept into angry crescendos, revealing a range of solitary and communicated emotions. Sheku walked onto the stage and sat down. The piece begins with some short phrases and loud notes dug hard and low into the strings. Sheku put his whole body into them and there was a noise like a whip crack, then silence. Everyone was still and Sheku's face froze in shock. His C string had snapped and he couldn't continue. Breaking the heavy silence, Sheku stood up, bowed, smiled and walked off the stage. The audience clapped and broke into talking. Stuart and I, sitting next to Braimah, sat appalled with our heads in our hands. Mariatu started to cry. What if he couldn't find his spare strings? What if he couldn't regain his composure back on stage? Was this the end?

The same thing had happened at the Gregynog Young Musician Final in Mid Wales the year before. The G string had snapped in the warm-up just before Sheku was due to play. Each spare string cost around £85 and we couldn't keep up with these expenses. Unable to afford a spare set of strings, we had forged ahead in a kind of blind optimism and convinced ourselves that all would be well. We were indebted on that occasion to Richard Lewis, a double bass player in the audience, who drove home through dark country lanes to pick up a spare string for Sheku and even helped him to restring the cello. Sheku went on to win the competition.

On this occasion, with the stakes even higher – at the BBC Young Musician String Category Final 2016 – Sheku had to walk off stage and find Isata, dumbstruck in the wings, waiting to accompany him for his next two pieces. He appeared in front of her, stricken. Howard Ionascu, director of Junior Academy, rushed backstage to say some calming words, and Isata went with Sheku to his practice room. It seemed to be endless corridors and stairs away. Time marched inexorably on and Sheku was sweating. But he did have a spare. He removed the thick broken C string and meticulously wound on another, screwing the peg until it was fixed. He had to painstakingly tune it and run the bow across it until it settled into a workable, humming position with the other strings. Time ticked endlessly on and the audience sat waiting. Isata had to keep Sheku calm and in a mental zone of hope and determination when the evening seemed to be unravelling before him. They both hurried along the empty corridors and stairs until they were at the backstage doors at the side of the stage. They could hear the loud murmur of the audience members as they buzzed with curiosity and unsettled anticipation. Mariatu was still crying. Stuart was moving his head from side to side and shifting nervously in his seat. I was tense and still, talking with quiet agitation with Sarah and Zoë Perkins, a Brass Finalist, behind me. But I knew that Sheku was not alone. Isata was there, calm and solid. Isata was looking after him.

Sheku came back onstage, holding his cello before him like a bishop with his staff. He strode in front of the audience's rapturous welcome and planted his cello deep into the floor as though staking his claim. The first note, back again at the beginning of the piece, was a rallying cry, and I knew that he was rooted back into the music and into himself.

I winced every time he played a note. He wasn't holding back. He was playing even more powerfully than before and reacting to the crisis by even more attacking bow strokes. As he came to the heavy note that had snapped the string before, I thought he would release the pressure a little, but he drove the bow into the string with redoubled force, as though meeting fate head to head and *daring* it to beat him.

The day of the J.M. Barrie Awards, given by the charity Action for Children's Arts at the Prince of Wales Theatre in autumn 2018, all seven were going to give a performance together. Stuart and I were overwhelmed as we were being presented with the award, not quite believing we were joining such an illustrious list of recipients. I had to travel with the younger three by Tube, also bringing Konya's violin for her. I had been painstakingly counting instruments, children and rucksacks in and out of the train and up and down the escalators. I even had a written checklist for instruments, bags, clothes, shoes. In the Tube carriage Mariatu needed to sit down, so I took charge of her half-size cello and let go of Konya's violin. We all clambered clumsily off the Tube and onto the Underground platform, sweatily assembling all our luggage. The Tube doors shut and I watched the train move away with a sudden sick feeling. Konya's violin was still in the carriage!

I accosted an innocent man standing next to us, pleading with him, 'What do I do? What do I do?' and spent a panicked hour of running up and down the escalators, launching myself at one of the Underground staff and sobbing. I managed to phone Stuart to meet the girls while I ran off to the next Tube to trace the violin, having persuaded the sympathetic staff to phone ahead and get someone to remove it further down the line. (I am grateful, to this day, to the staff at Piccadilly Circus Underground and especially to the very patient staff member who allowed me to cry on her shoulder.) I arrived after a journey along the Tube line (by which time I was soaked with sweat), was buzzed into a locked office and saw the red violin case sitting on the table. At the theatre, I handed the violin to Konya, and all seven played beautifully. (My role with any family concert is to be the one chiding, scolding and herding the children into readiness. We have to be on time, they have to remember all their chamber or accompanists' music, instruments, concert clothes, accessories. I was assaulted with the radiant grins of seven children who, after all my years of remonstrating, revelled in the fact that it was *me* who had committed this most heinous of crimes.)

Travelling with instruments is a trial known well by classical musicians and their parents. Steven Isserlis, the cellist, tells famous stories of the horror of travel with classical instruments and the harrowing insouciance of the wider world. The fear of the precious violin being left on a train or bus, or the risk of an instrument being damaged in transit, is constant. We are all used to bracing ourselves to spring if a stranger, train guard or taxi driver makes a move to handle an instrument, whether to move it out of the way or to stow it somewhere. The practised care needed to carry a valuable instrument is almost innate in musicians and almost absent in the general public.

The train journey to and from London leaves us utterly vulnerable to the personality and mood of the train guard. Most are pleasant or indifferent, but there are some characters who either detest musicians or resent passengers. These we fear. The half-empty 6.12 a.m. Saturday train to St Pancras can be a drawn-out nightmare. The sight of a cello on a seat in an almost empty carriage can bring out the worst in an angry train guard who wants the cello removed. A cello cannot fit on any luggage rack and cannot be left vulnerable sliding alone around a bicycle rack, so each of us parents has had to spend several two-hour journeys standing by the door, leaning and slipping with a cello clutched against us, saving Sheku or Jeneba as children from hopeless fatigue and muscle strain before their day at Junior Academy has even begun. We know young cellists left stranded when there are cancelled trains and replacement bus services, because the cello is not allowed inside the bus.

Most airlines, except the budget companies, can cope with a violin or viola, but other passengers can find them a challenge. I remember opening my eyes on the flight to Los Angeles with Isata and finding someone taking out her viola from the overhead locker to balance it precariously on top of his suitcase. It inevitably fell out, caught in a panic by me. Also, the security area is an anxious place for musicians. The zealous security officer who wants the violin or cello out of its case so it can be pulled about or prodded by a machine is a danger. Furthermore, travelling with Sheku on aeroplanes is fascinating. He has to arrive early for every flight because most airline officials have no idea of what the procedure or policy is for a cello, no matter any phoning ahead or checking of guidelines. He has to have a seat bought for his cello and a ticket for it, because a valuable cello in check-in luggage would be an unaccountable risk. Often, at every stage, an official makes a determined attempt to take the cello away or to refuse to let it – and therefore Sheku – board. The bought ticket is often unrecognised because it does not reference an actual person for the seat, and, as Julian Lloyd Webber famously complained, it is not eligible for air miles despite the full seat cost. Once on board, Sheku is still often threatened with rejection, outright suspicion and utter resentment. The cello has to be strapped in with an extra child strap, eventually obtained by frequent requests. And yet, a cello is the ideal passenger. It cannot kick your seat from behind or suddenly collapse its seat onto your dinner.

The worst journey, however, was the apocalyptic trip on Eurostar. Sheku was happy and confident. The check-in had been easy, the cello had its bought seat and Sheku went through the barrier as normal, sitting in his seat and putting the cello in its assigned place. Suddenly another passenger claimed the cello's seat as hers. The train manager had to tell Sheku that his seat had been resold last minute because he hadn't scanned both tickets as he went through the final barrier. As standard class was now sold out, he would have to buy two business class seats at an unaffordable price. Sheku needed to get to Paris for a concerto with the Orchestre Philharmonique de Radio France and *had* to make the rehearsal. The manager came up with a solution: there was an office at the back of the train into which the cello could be safely locked for the journey, and he would unlock the office in Paris and return the cello. Sheku carried the cello and inspected the room, which was very safe and close to Sheku's seat. The cello was placed carefully inside and securely locked in.

On arrival in Paris, Sheku went straight to the office and waited. There was a small window through which he could see the precious cello. No train manager arrived. Sheku waited. He wouldn't leave his precious cello alone and was forced to stand and wait as all the passengers alighted. Still no train manager. The cleaner began cleaning and hoovering around him, unable to speak any English in response to his increasingly anxious questions. The train was still on the platform and not yet ready to make its return journey to London. Sheku had no choice. Already late for the rehearsal, he got off the Eurostar and walked the full length of the train to the front. No train manager was in sight. Asking increasingly desperate questions of everyone he could find, Sheku realised the train manager had left.

Finally, another person with a key to the office took the long walk with Sheku to the back of the train, but when they got there and looked through the window, the cello was gone. At that point, Sheku's world gave way. The cello is central to everything he does and one cello is not like another. It's a personal relationship forged over a long time. All the years of practice on the instrument...learning how to develop its sound, honing the depths of what it can do, moulding technique to achieve the tone he needs – *all* of this is irreplaceable. Insurance is vital because of the marketable value of the instrument, a cost raised by rarity, age, ancient skills and mature wood, but the cello could not be exchanged. And, to increase his terror, Sheku does not own the cello (it is part of the private collection of a wonderful individual). The emotional investment and the responsibility were nearly crushing Sheku. But all this, to the train staff, was incommunicable.

Sheku was pointed vaguely towards an office in the distance where luggage for international transit was taken and, damp with perspiration, he ran to it. With defiant indifference, someone eventually admitted that a cello had been seen, but he refused to show it. When the cello was reluctantly brought out from a back room, Sheku, nearly fainting with relief, still couldn't touch it. He had no international transit ticket, so the cello couldn't be his. No force on earth would now remove Sheku from that cello's side, and he staged a sit-in, refusing to move. The cello was handed over. Sheku, hollow with fear, immediately opened the case to check everything inside. Once he could see that cello and bows were safe, he raced to the rehearsal, nerves on edge and only twenty minutes of rehearsal time left.

This is, of course, a story with a happy (or at least relieved) ending. So many tales of instrument travel end badly. I've heard mournful tales from musicians of double basses in flight cases emerging from the hold in pieces, valuable instruments stolen (even from the luggage rack above the head on a train), valuable bows in bow cases left accidentally on train seats, instruments stolen while left by the musician's feet at a coffee stand. Jacqueline du Pré famously referred to travelling being a nuisance because of the 'wretched' cello. As a family, we have escaped the difficulties of travel with a harp, double bass or percussion instruments. Jeneba wanted to play the double bass as a child. The thought of trying to cram a double bass, beautiful as it is, into an already bulging nine-seater car was horrifying. She played the cello instead.

19

Of Guardians and Gifts

INSTRUMENTS ARE A problem, not just in terms of travel and security, but also cost. As the children grew out of the cheap 'student' violins and half-size cellos, needing instruments that could project and grow their sound and technique, there came a major problem: how could we afford the spiralling cost of those instruments? We discovered that the cost of a good bow began at two thousand pounds. A decent violin could be upwards of twenty thousand pounds and a grand piano could reach eighty thousand or more. We had bought a cheap upright piano for five thousand pounds, small and clear but with no depth and definition in the bass notes and sonorous weight in the keys. Isata won another upright in the Clements Nottinghamshire Pianist competition. But Isata was becoming a serious pianist and needed a decent grand piano with a bass that could be heard and balanced properly and a heavy force under the fingers. We bought a cheap Blüthner grand piano, too quickly and desperately, and very soon realised that we had made a mistake. It has rarely been played by the children and, when we consulted a piano workshop, we were told that we needed several thousand pounds more to make it a decent piano to play. We didn't have the money. Because all the children played, we couldn't have one good piano instead of three mediocre or bad pianos, and even so, the three together would not raise enough money for a decent grand piano. We eventually bought another mediocre upright piano to solve the quantity problem, but we still have no decent piano. Other households solve this problem with money, with inheritance, or with means-tested loans and bursaries. We had neither money nor inheritance, and we were not eligible for means-tested bursaries because Stuart had a decent job, and no one used the number of children as a criterion.

When the children started learning music, we did what parents have to do and did not project potential costs into the future. If we hadn't shut our eyes, we would have denied them the music learning and diverted them elsewhere. With their desire and talent came a heavy responsibility. We have lived through many stressful evenings wondering how we can get through the month, the week, the year with the music costs, feeling oppressively guilty about the opportunities we can't give, the quality instrument or bow we can't afford, or the music course we have to pull them out of. But then come the times when we are faced with such unexpected and extraordinary acts of kindness towards us that we are stopped in our tracks.

When Konya and Jeneba began piano lessons with Brenda May in Nottingham at the ages of five and seven, we were delighted to have found a brilliant teacher who demanded depth and rigour from their piano studies. She told us that she taught always with the goal that if her pupils wanted to become concert pianists, they would have the proper technique in place. At age five, Jeneba was so small that Brenda May would make her a stool out of leather-bound works of music piled at her feet. She was meticulous and kind, and we knew that the practice had to be done. The girls were completely dedicated and worked hard for the teacher they loved and respected. I would drive them to their lesson in Beeston and read to two-year-old Aminata in the car while they did their lessons, or if it was a time when Stuart was home, I would come and write notes during the lesson. When the girls were seven and nine, we knew that something had to stop as we couldn't afford all the music lessons we were giving the children. The older three were at Junior Academy and we simply couldn't afford to pay for piano lessons for the younger girls. This is a heartbreaking moment for any parent. We had to face the fact that, having set out to give them the music they loved, we now had to withdraw it. How could we fill the gap left by such a highly professional and gifted teacher? I decided that I had no choice but to try to teach them myself, limited and basic though my own skills were. It seemed incredible that something so sacred and desired as music could be taken away from a child through lack of money.

I had to quietly explain to Brenda May that this was the case and that, at the end of the term, the girls would no longer be able to come. My mouth was dry as I spoke. Then came an extraordinary moment: Brenda May looked at me and said that she would carry on teaching them for as long as I wanted, completely free of charge. 'You can call it a scholarship', she said. She taught Konya and Jeneba for over two years after that without accepting any payment, and now, when Stuart and I watch and listen to either of them play, both accomplished pianists who want this to be their profession, we still feel tearful with gratitude at the immeasurable gift she gave to them.

In 2018, Jeneba entered BBC Young Musician and, like Isata in 2014, reached the Keyboard Category Final, the final five pianists before the Grand Final. We were painfully aware that she couldn't practise properly on the upright pianos that we have. Playing Bartók and Chopin, for example, on pianos with less key tension and little bass depth was deeply frustrating, and she couldn't develop the colours and subtleties that she needed. I stoically turned my face away from the harsh reality of a world we couldn't afford. I realised that we had pushed Jeneba to reach for something desired above all else while failing to give her the financial means to get there. At Junior Academy on Saturdays she would rush to find a practice room with a Steinway Grand to work through her pieces, but that was only one day of the week. Then Neil Bennison stepped in with the offer to practise when possible on the Steinway at the Nottingham Royal Concert Hall. This was a major boost for Jeneba. He had allowed Sheku to come onto the empty stage there to feel what it was like to play out to a large concert-hall space in preparation for the Final at the Barbican. This had been an astonishing experience for Sheku who was totally unprepared for the reality of playing to an audience so far above and away from him. He had to adjust to a new way of communicating. For Jeneba, the chance, even sporadically, to develop her playing with the right instrument was crucial. She knew how to play with a tender intimacy that spoke with emotion from when she was very young. She was the kind of pianist who would make you halt your thoughts at the maturity of the feeling that flowed from her, even at age five. This wasn't a phenomenon we understood or even *tried* to understand. It just was and it spoke to us as a calling we had to guard. Now Jeneba needed to grow that sense of power onto a bigger scale.

Since then, Jackie Kendle has moved to Nottingham and made contact with us via the music department at Trinity. She has an amazing Steinway Grand, one that both Konya and Jeneba have tried and fallen in love with. Entirely out of generosity, she offered to let Jeneba practise on her piano in her home. Jeneba arrives once a week and practises for nearly three hours while Jackie simply gives her the space, time and piano to do so. This is a very special gift and one given so simply and undemonstrably, allowing Jeneba – and the older girls when home – to treat the instrument, while they play, as their own.

Generosity like this has made it possible for the children to continue learning and playing at key moments. When Sheku was desperate for a full-size cello, we began to despair for him. He was still playing on a 7/8-size cello that we had managed to buy for him at a good price, but it had taken all our funds, even though it was a very small fraction of the price of even a reasonable full-size cello. Sheku didn't grow tall at an early age. At twelve and thirteen, he was still a little boy with a high voice. But he outgrew what a small cello could do a long time before this, and we could see him struggling to produce the sound he wanted from a cello and bow that could never respond fully to his demands. Then he began to outgrow the cello in terms of his size and strength as well. At twelve, he won Nottingham Young Musician with a recital on the undersized cello, and at thirteen he performed an hour-long evening recital at Southwell Minster Great Hall. He played with a mature sound and technique, but we could see him trying to coax the cello to produce what was in his head. We knew that he *had* to be a cellist. The cello was his every mode of expression. How could we give him the voice he needed?

Then we met Frank White, a builder, plumber and carpenter, who in his retirement had made a full string quartet of instruments. It was an astonishing feat, achieved out of love of the wood and the music, and out of great skill. We met him with his wife, Elizabeth, at the celebration of their golden anniversary in Barnsley, Yorkshire. Sheku's and Jeneba's first cello teacher, Sarah Huson-Whyte, was playing there with her string quartet, Highly Strung, and they were playing Frank's two violins, viola and cello. They sounded beautiful. Sarah introduced us, and as the older four often played as a string quartet, they took over the instruments and played, Braimah and Konya on the violins, Isata on the viola and Sheku on the cello. It was extraordinary to see them all playing instruments that sounded so clear and strong, and Sheku on a full-size cello that allowed him to create the sound he wanted. At the end of the evening, Frank came to us with Elizabeth and announced that he wanted to let the children borrow them, take them home and play them free of charge. He wanted the instruments to stay together and for the children to make music with them. It was breathtaking generosity. He had made the instruments himself with all the time and intimate concentration that had taken, and we knew how much they meant to him. For the children it meant being able to play with instruments they loved – and Sheku gained the full-size cello he craved. Our relationship with Frank and Elizabeth has been a long-term friendship. They gave us a simple and powerful gift that, particularly for Sheku, meant that he could now develop at the pace he needed. They came to every concert in which the children played. The concert that Stuart and I always remember is Sheku at age thirteen, playing Haydn's 'Cello Concerto No. 1 in C' on Frank's cello, with the Djanogly Orchestra, his face alive in the music and the cello expressing his every thought. (When Sheku reached his full six feet, he still played Frank's cello and the sound seemed to grow with him.)

There have been gifts of *time* as well, given freely by other musicians and mentors. The world of classical music is full of musicians who are genuinely welcoming and want to encourage young talent. There are many financial and educational barriers, but these do not come from the musicians and teachers themselves, or from the audiences. The children have always had dedicated teachers who are passionate about the music and the young people they teach. Sheku could not have won BBC Young Musician, for example, without Ben Davies, of course, and also Patsy Toh and Krystyna Budzynska who gave advice and listened tirelessly to the duo playing of Isata and Sheku.

John Cooney analysed the score of the Shostakovich concerto with Sheku that he would play in the Final, and Tim Hugh, Desmond Neysmith, Guy Johnston and Julian Lloyd Webber listened to him and gave their time.

Leading up to the BBC Young Musician Final, we realised that Sheku needed a cello powerful enough to play a concerto at the Barbican. I keenly felt Sheku's disadvantage. He had the use of a lovely recital instrument, but without a cello that could dominate a vast concert hall, he would find it difficult to win. Florian Leonhard Fine Violins, with the help of Chi-chi Nwanoku, found him a beautiful Amati cello, which was more than four hundred years old, to play for the Final. Sheku loved it. (He was forced to say a painful goodbye to it afterwards, but they were reunited for his concerto with Chineke! Orchestra at the Royal Festival Hall the following September.) It went back to Florian's, and the Royal Academy wonderfully stepped in with an excellent cello for him to borrow and play. Sheku was already daily grateful to Ben Davies who was lending him a lovely Salchow bow, helping Sheku's cello voice to project with the warmth he needed.

A bow can be as important as the instrument itself. Playing with a weak or inferior bow can trap the sound a string player is trying to make, strangling all the projection and finesse at source. We were surrounded by support and kindness. Then Sheku got a phone call from Joe Stupple at Florian's to say that someone was willing to buy the Amati cello and let Sheku play it for life. I could not believe it. Did someone believe so deeply in Sheku that they would do that for him? And how could I adequately say thank you? (When I met the person who made it possible for Sheku to play this instrument, I couldn't stop the tears.)

Since then, there has been more extraordinary generosity with cello bows (via J&A Beare and Florian's) and cello strings (D'Addario and now Larsen), and acts of great generosity with expertise and time from other musicians. Steven Isserlis, for example, a busy concert cellist in huge demand, regularly gives time to coach Isata, Braimah and Sheku with their piano trio repertoire, and they love every minute.

Generosity comes in many forms. There are simple moments of recognition and interest that count for more than can be imagined: Vicky Manderson, head of music at Trinity School, and her husband Steve, for example, bringing us round to their back garden with their family to celebrate with all of us when Braimah and Sheku were accepted to Junior Academy, or travelling to London to see his prom and his album launch. Or family, friends, neighbours and former teachers making the effort to come to concerts or competition finals as moments of celebration or commiseration. This profound journey into classical music cannot be made alone.

It is impossible to thank all the people – all the teachers, musicians and benefactors – who help young musicians along the way, and who have personally helped *us*. This encouragement has been vital in making the children feel welcome and, crucially, good enough. Those years where we would look at the dark bedroom ceiling in that tired pit of self-doubt, worry and guilt, those days of keeping the heating turned off until the children came home from school and needed it to practise, the misery of seeing a child work so hard on an inadequate instrument – all were worth it.

20

Mind and Body

THE FAMILY HOME has evolved almost organically into a house of music. Our conversations are about music: listening, playing, concerts, practice. Most of the jokes and teasing insults are musical, and no day can be planned or imagined without first working out the logistics of each music commitment. Music encompasses a vast emotional and intellectual world, and spending the time to know it and to be its instrument is a great privilege. But the cost is high, and I often watch and listen to the children, knowing how exposed they have to be psychologically and emotionally. To become a professional classical musician is similar to training as an athlete. It demands intense physical discipline, being alert to injury and being mentally strong.

There have been times when this cost has been painfully apparent. As the practice hours and the pressure have increased, we've seen how vulnerable musicians are to the sheer physical strain of perfecting technique. The daily routine of practice starts early and involves a long warm-up. Scales and exercises move and condition the muscles needed to play. I often wake to hear the rapid and fluid drills up and down the keyboard from one or two or three of the pianos downstairs, or the slow intonation exercises on violins, rehearsing shifts up and down the fingerboard and blending notes into long, tuned chords. The low, insistent hum of cello passages breaks into the reverberating noise of the house as though an engine, crammed with competing functions, has been switched into life. I barely hear the clashing sounds in any conscious way. They are merely a sign that the house has woken up and the business of the day begun.

For years Stuart and I focused on the joy and self-confidence that the music gave to the children. It became a way of communicating with each other and connecting with the world outside the home. It provided structure and a discipline to their intelligence, allowing them to explore themselves and their possibilities in extraordinary ways. There were no limits to what they could say and where they could go in music. And it was rigorous. It demanded depths of thought and mental analysis that lit up their faces. To play the complexities of a sonata or concerto from memory, to perform a programme for an hour or two hours without reading from the score involved minds that had been stretched and exercised into taut efficiency. Playing chamber music enforced a level of deep concentration, not just on the music but on a community of shared responses and conversations both rehearsed and spontaneous.

We have become more aware of the toll taken by this exacting regime, and we have had to learn to be vigilant. The delicate balance between happy expression and frustration is always at risk. We have sat and applauded each of our children after they have played a glorious concerto in the foreground of an inspired orchestra, and the following week cradled them in our arms as they wept with the impossibility of it all. They have stood on stage and displayed mastery with an intricate piece that delighted an audience, yet hours before I may have been lifting them off the floor – prostrate with anguish in the face of having to play. The distinction between physical and psychological pain at these moments is often impossible to make.

Braimah faced his term of auditions for senior conservatoires in autumn 2015. He had just turned eighteen and was completely focused on studying violin full time. This audition term is tough for sixth-formers applying in the midst of their A-Level studies. The auditions are highly competitive and demand hours of intense practice at the same time that he needed to revise for mock A-Level exams in physics, English and music. He was quickly becoming more impressive, playing concerts with pieces like the big Brahms sonatas, and the precise and perfect Mozart concerti. He practised keeping the narrative of great sonatas in his head, expressing musical ideas that took the audience through powerful inner journeys that demanded unbroken concentration from the player. These performances demanded great brain and body stamina, built up through evenings of scales and studies, as well as fighting the pressures of self-doubt and anxiety. He longed to be accepted at the Royal Academy as a full-time student. To spend four years submerged in music, and join his sister, would be a dream come true.

He entered the Junior Academy John MacAslan Violin Prize, an important competition for Junior Academy violinists. Both Stuart and I went to hear him play, knowing how important this was to Braimah and seeing his performance as an indication as to whether or not he was ready for the auditions. His turn for the senior prize came after other advanced violinists had played, setting the standard very high. I was living every note that he bowed, knowing that his self-confidence was pinned to this. He played beautifully, holding us all in the world he created with such sincerity and love. I was overjoyed when he won the prize. All would be well.

The first audition, as with Konya two years later, was at the Royal Northern College of Music in Manchester. When Braimah emerged from his second audition, privately brimming with happiness, and told me that he had been offered an immediate scholarship, it felt as though all those hours of practice and worry had been worth it, and now he would be ready to face the other three audition days that we had paid for, carefully applied for, and for which we had bought expensive train tickets.

His audition day at Guildhall in London went well, and he faced the Royal Academy and the Royal College. A few days before his Academy audition, Braimah decided to put all his energies, with none spare, into the practice. He refused to go to bed and I, tired with six children in the house, warned him about the importance of rest and went to bed after midnight. He practised with the determination of the fanatic, focused only on his goal of gaining his place at the Academy. The next day, he couldn't move his arm. I instructed him to rest that day, but the following day he was still wincing and sore. The audition day was looming and, crying with anxiety, he had to postpone the audition to the end of their session. On the day, still hurting, he went with Stuart, Isata accompanying, and played through the wrenching muscles of his right shoulder and back, forcing his bow arm to move and getting through the two auditions thanks to sheer mental grit. The final audition faced a panel including the principal of the Academy and the head of Strings, and Braimah took his place on the platform and played through the pain. I was in the middle of Aminata's violin lesson with Jo Percival in Matlock, the phone on silent while I surreptitiously peeked at it for messages, desperate for news. When the celebratory message came, that not only did he have a place but also a big scholarship, I could not stop grinning.

What followed were months of the hardest time in Braimah's life. He was unable to play for more than a few minutes. The agony of lifting the bow to the violin made tears come, and he lay, fighting anxiety in a knot of contortion. I tried rubbing muscle-relieving creams into his back and shoulder, ibuprofen to help with inflammation. I took him to physiotherapists and specialists in muscle and back problems. I could see that the issues in his body were compounded by the tension and misery of his mind. He began to believe that his career was over when it had barely begun, that he would never be able to play again. As parents, we knew how anxiety can lead to an inability of the body to function, and I could see that a growing depression was increasing the pain and panic in his body. We tried to push him through this with positive words and breezy advice to let go of the negative fear and start again. He would accept concert dates and then be unable to face them, terrified to move his arm. We saw the darkness in his mind making him retreat to his room and his bed, and we worried that our job as parents was to push him out into the light again. We scooped him up and included him in family concerts in which he played small roles, tense and agonised.

We didn't know how to help him. We never relaxed our expectations that our children work hard and face challenges, ready to encourage commitment. We didn't know if a new strategy of indulgence would be the healthy one in the long run. Shouldn't Braimah face this tension and depression with blind courage?

Six months went by and it was getting close to Braimah taking up his place at the Academy. How could he do this if he couldn't play? Finally, helped by Junior Academy and a recommendation from Chi-chi Nwanoku, he saw two specialists on London's Harley Street. These specialists were used to treating musicians' injuries. We knew the horror stories and met some of the casualties of these injuries: Stuart's sister, Rhonda, having done a music degree at University of East Anglia and practising as a piano teacher, was working towards her teaching diploma in piano. She began suffering from an involuntary curling of her left forefinger, which would claw inwards towards her palm when she played. The doctor called it 'focal dystonia', impervious to acupuncture or physiotherapy. She could no longer play. Konya's piano teacher, Druvi de Saram, after unsuccessful surgery, was forced to give up his performance career because of a similar condition. We knew cellists, violinists and brass players who had months away from playing or had to end their careers because of these injuries. The stakes, and the psychological costs, were high.

The specialists prescribed exercises to release stress and a regime of building up the muscles to cope with the intensive and repetitive exercise that musicians endure. Braimah had hypermobility in his back and arm, and the right side of his body was over-developed in relation to the left side because of the muscle building required for bow work. He had to work on the fitness of his body like an athlete prepares himself to run. The attention from these doctors, who listened and touched where it hurt, along with the carefully prepared exercises, slowly brought Braimah back to performance.

We are now very serious about taking care of musicians' health. To play instruments at this level and for so many hours a day – between six and eight hours regularly – means that they all take a healthy diet, physical fitness and regular sleep (easy to sacrifice) as seriously as they can. I have spent years massaging arms and backs, prescribing rest and stretching, and talking through the psychological stress and strain of being a musician. Small adjustments to technique, the set-up of an instrument – the strings or the bridge – a change of bow or the height of a piano stool can lead to an escalation of pain. Effects from physical discomfort, such as Sheku sleeping awkwardly in the economy seat of an aeroplane or Jeneba accidentally lying on her hand in bed, resulted in near catastrophe. They all have to be very precious and particular about fingers, hands and arms, aware always of the condition of their bodies and attentive to unavoidable aggravation. Sheku had to battle through pain in a series of concerts where he wore an elasticated bandage to support his wrist, and had to be propped up with ibuprofen in a concert where his back was stricken from travel. Yet no one in the audience noticed a thing.

Isata, aged twelve, having got a lift home from school, got out of the car and shut the door on her thumb. I had finished cooking a big pot of West African stew with chicken, vegetables and pepper for tea, and the younger ones were eating – when suddenly there was a dull thud on the back door. Surprised, I opened it and a body fell onto the doorstep. Isata lay there, sweating with shock, her right thumb squashed and covered in blood. In that moment I faced the terror of a daughter injured and suffering, and the simultaneous horror that the one goal of her life, her overarching passion to play the piano, had been crushed. The agony of the injury hit her with full force when the embarrassment receded. She cried over how it hurt and looked.

For days, Isata was the breathless centre of a family disaster. Her thumb was blackened and distorted by the injury, and we wondered how it would heal. When we were optimistic that it would, we devised a plan of action: Isata's left hand, like with most right-handed pianists, was the weaker of the two. For the repertoire she needed to learn, that fact had to be addressed. She couldn't use her right hand, the thumb too damaged and tender to touch a key, but her left hand was still active. She spent weeks determinedly practising the left-hand parts of her pieces, doing left-hand exercises and putting her subservient left-hand thumb and fingers through concentrated studies. This had the effect of lighting up a part of her brain that previously had languished in the shade, her left hand trailing behind her conscious mind as she led with the right. From that time, I hear the left hand balancing perfectly with the right, the strength of her muscles aligned between the two hands, and when needed, the left hand can lead with ease and fluidity. I still wake at night to the imagined slam of that car door and the memory of how time stood still when Isata fell over the threshold – but what seemed like an end was in fact a new door opening. Similarly, I've watched the heightened awareness that Braimah has of *his* body and the increased care he takes to look after his health, entirely sparked by those months on the precipice of a lost career.

Isata's accident with the car door was a reminder that the body is as much an instrument as the precious violin, cello or piano that has to be cared for, tuned, maintained, restrung, polished and loved. Sheku, before the second round of BBC Young Musician 2014, refused to give up his beloved football. He loved the football pitch, the training and the matches, and not playing was like a prison sentence. We decided that pushing him to give up football was unfair as it was as much a part of his creative expression and his connection with life as the cello. He always played football and cello with total commitment and, aged fourteen, he flew into a swift tackle and landed on his wrist. The hairline fracture was enough to force him to stop practising for weeks, just before his BBC Young Musician category audition. I remember pleading passionately with the consultant, as though I could persuade him that a biological fact was simply a question of perspective. Sheku did not get through the second round that year.

The interdependence of body and mind is very much like the communion of player and instrument. The music cannot exist without both. One week before Jeneba was due to compete in the Keyboard Final of BBC Young Musician 2018, as one of the top five pianists, she began to tighten with tension. I would find her flat out on the floor after practising for three hours after school, sobbing. At the age of three, emotion would radiate from her as she played the A-minor scale. Now, at fifteen, it was as though that emotion was uncontainable, out of control. This had begun with puberty. As a four- and five-year-old, she could get up, stride across a room, adjust her piano stool in front of an audience and play with such iridescent abandonment that it would make us weep. It had been as though this small child had transformed into an agent of communication for something otherworldly and without words. How could this small girl play with such expression of loss, or joy, or pain?

Growing into a teenager tipped these emotions into overflow, and Jeneba had to struggle to contain and control feelings she couldn't articulate. These years can be difficult for musicians. That blind, simple giving-way to a performance suddenly turns self-conscious, as though someone switched on the lights and caught you naked. She woke at 5 a.m., a few days before the Keyboard Final, screaming. I rushed in and found her contorted on the bed, arm held at an odd angle. She couldn't move it or touch it. And she certainly couldn't play.

Stuart and I decided that the best thing to do would be to attack with optimism. Although drowning in panic, we decided to beam with complacency and, as the days went on, to be blithe and positive. Our strategy was to be kind and practical, calm in the face of her desperation, and basically to hope for the best. Stuart opted to be with her for the two days at Birmingham Conservatoire preparing for the Final and the BBC filming, and I arrived for the performance. Miraculously, Stuart had succeeded in returning Jeneba to a kind of absent-minded serenity, which told us that she had centred her focus again, and the pain was gone.

She played, full of inspiration and brimming over with expressiveness and musicality. She didn't win, losing to the impressive Lauren Zhang, but having watched her play I knew she would be fine in the future. She came out on stage, the cameras gliding up and down in front of her, and shone. When her fingers touched the keys it was with a conviction that felt like bliss, and she was free.

A few months later, in March 2019, she launched herself into Tchaikovsky's 'Piano Concerto No. 1' with the excellent Nottingham Youth Orchestra. The week leading up to the performance had involved intense concentration from me, from Stuart and from her siblings. She needed to draw unending support from us and we had to listen to her descriptions of physical suffering. We knew that these aches and pains were as much from the strain of keeping the extraordinary intellectual and emotional scope of the concerto in her mind. They were also effects of the physical demands of the concerto. It was as though it were too big for her slim body and she had to flex her muscles to contain it all. She practised relentlessly at Jackie Kendle's home, concentrating on gymnastic runs and detailed passages, for which her muscles had to be exercised into elastic fitness. She also had to look deep into the heart of the music and be taken over by its meaning.

When she walked on stage at the Royal Concert Hall, I was a knot of anticipation. The concerto is an incredible force of passion and grandeur, brimming with fluid runs and chords with an urgency that makes you sit up with wonder. The second movement, still and liquid, was almost unbearable, and the last movement flowed relentlessly into thrilling runs up and down the keyboard. During the first movement I sat stunned. How did this sixteen-year-old girl, prostrate just a few days ago under the weight of this music on her mind, huge in its concept, now command the stage? She was a beautiful instrument for a mystery none of us could understand.

The experience of the connection between body and mind helps me to understand the psychosomatic nature of playing music. I often see sweat on my children's faces when they perform, due to the brutal physical *and* emotional demands.

Classical music requires the player to engage deeply with a composer's work and channel that meaning through her or his own body, colouring it with vast emotional reserves and responses. It has allowed all the children the freedom to express untold and inarticulate feelings, and to let their intelligence expand into spaces without limit.

This balance of emotion, mind and body is delicate and often precarious. At age nine, Isata sat poised to play her Grade 5 exam pieces as a performance for Stuart and me. The exam was the following day, and she had her pieces ready from memory. This was to be the final day-before run-through for last-minute thoughts and general encouragement. We sat behind her as she prepared herself on the piano stool with the upright piano backed against the wall of the playroom. She began to play and we stared at each other. Instead of the perfect, clear notes, beautifully patterned and ordered, there was a torrent of inarticulate, increasingly meaningless, nonsense notes. She played the three pieces, one after the other, each one coalescing into a jumble of crashing, rushing sounds that formed no structure at all. We said nothing, and Isata turned to us with a face of complete calm, as though she had noticed nothing untoward. Stuart and I, in a pact of silence, congratulated her and told her she would be brilliant in the exam. We tucked her into bed, smiling, and sat together on the settee, our heads in our hands. What had happened? It was the equivalent of legs wobbling and collapsing under a runner at the end of a long race, but Isata was strangely unconnected from the event. The next day, still unaware of our alarm, she went into the exam, and we waited for the three weeks until the results came back. Unbelievably, she had performed so well in the exam that she gained the highest distinction we had seen.

Isata recently played a charged performance of the complete Chopin Preludes to a hushed audience in Cardiff. This is a deeply concentrated pianistic journey through twenty-four pieces and all the major and minor keys, without a break for audience communication or relaxation. The performer has to hold the entire conceptual weight of the work in the head and heart, with no back-up from orchestra or audience. The recognition comes at the end of a long and lonely forty-minute expedition through vast and changing emotional landscapes. After she had taken the rapturous applause, Isata walked to her dressing room and sobbed inconsolably.

If I think of the children's development – whenever there is a very rare quiet moment – I think about it through music. Their personalities are expressed through the music they play. The flowering of a sense of self, or crises of confidence, can all be traced through their relationship with music. Aminata's joyful violin playing in the ranks of Junior Chineke! Orchestra at age ten, eyes darting from side to side, lit up with the sheer passion of performance, had to take her into the very different experience of adolescence. When she grew tall and began to look much older than her age, it was like inhabiting a body that was bigger than she was. The violin became the thing that shouted her presence and made her conspicuous at a time when really she wanted to hide. I think of her walking onto the stage and somehow managing to shrink backwards out of view, almost reversing off the edge. Once, while being accompanied by Jeneba at St John's Smith Square, she retreated so much before she started her solo that Jeneba had to publicly call her forward. Once she began playing, the audience was lifted by the simple dancing energy of her sound. The cheers after she played the last rousing down-bow, full of a sense of triumphal laughter, met her standing mildly surprised and smiling shyly, as though she didn't think the applause could possibly be directed at *her*. Moving on from this, the mounting anxiety that preceded Aminata's performance of Mozart's 'Violin Concerto No. 3 in G' with the Orchestra of the Restoration in June 2019 melted away the moment she walked on stage and heard the full sound of the orchestra behind her. Leading the musical phrases, inclining her head and listening to the orchestra, declaiming everything she wanted to express. Particularly in the cadenza, the moment when the orchestra is quiet and the soloist stands alone, the sound of the unaccompanied violin the only focus in the hall, Aminata stood radiant. Afterwards, bright with excitement, she said she felt she had owned the stage. Yet the journey to that celebratory moment had meant living through lonely hours of agonised tears before sleep, and fear that made her sick to the stomach. As a parent, helping one's child through that internal battle is terrible and demands a rigidity of faith that the prize is worth it. It's not a simple route from adversity to triumph in any way. The concerts where things go well after traumatic days of self-doubt are equally balanced by performances that *don't* go well. All parents of performers, I imagine, have to see their child struggle on stage at some time or other, and we learn to concentrate on the brief, bright moments of joy.

21

When the Days Are Dark

W E HAD SOMEHOW learned to live under the constant stress of mounting debt, trying to afford the children's needs as the musical achievements grew. We felt that we couldn't let them down. How could we be responsible for taking away the resources they needed to keep playing and learning and practising? I would watch their faces as they played and I could see it was where they belonged. It was their common language, the world they came home for after school, to which they pitched all their stamina and determination.

Stuart would come home from work looking drained, and his body began to stoop and soften under the pressure. We would get to the middle of every month and run out of money. Then more bills would come in for replacement strings, or music lessons, or transport to London for the Academy or concerts. We had sheet music to buy, or concert dresses. Someone was always in need of an upgraded instrument, which we couldn't buy. On top of this treadmill of guilt and responsibility came the household bills that pile up with having seven children. The washing loads were endless, the cooking and shopping for food (restlessly trying to economise) were without pause. If all the children were in school, I would race round the house, carrying washing baskets, cleaning, organising, fixing, unblocking drains or trying to hook up fraying curtains. I would try not to think about the cold, which was making me shiver through the several layers I was wearing. I didn't put the heating on if the children were not in the house because the money was needed elsewhere. I became very good at strapping hot-water bottles around my stomach – but then had to be careful about the cost of boiling the kettle.

We hid all this from the children as much as possible and blamed the damp mould creeping through the walls and into the wardrobes on the age of the house. The old nine-seater car, violently red and loudly diesel, began to embarrass the older ones, but the cellos and the children fitted in, so I was happy. Once I drove to collect Isata from Purcell Music School when she was fourteen or fifteen. On my arrival, rumbling through the private gates into the grounds, a lively group of teenagers rushed up to get in. Isata, furious with humiliation, had to convince them this was not their taxi. Each service saw the mechanics disappear higher up under the car to cut off the rust and rebuild it from beneath, and it roared up the road with more outrageous insistence every day. Finally, due to the ubiquitous rust, it catastrophically failed its MOT and had to be scrapped, and the desperate search for another old nine-seater began.

Leading up to Christmas 2011, I noticed that Sheku, aged twelve and still small next to his cello, was thinner and paler. He arrived home from school, deathly tired, but he was still practising and playing football. The autumn term is always busy for footballers and musicians, and the colder, darker evenings are harder to tolerate. He started to break out in allergies. The children coated their damp skin with baby oil after a bath or shower, but I saw that Sheku's face looked ever tighter, dry and uncomfortable, and I realised that he had developed an allergy to the oil. His face was leaner, and the skin, itching from the allergy, made it difficult for him to smile.

His body became more ill at ease, as though it were reacting against him, and he started sleepwalking to the bathroom at night, sometimes not getting there in time. I tried to find alternatives to baby oil and gave him milder and more soothing creams. It was still as though he no longer lived easily in his body. He was alert and edgy when awake, but sluggish at night. The Christmas period is always full, loud and exciting, with everyone ready to play games together and look forward to the wonderful day itself. Christmas concerts begin to fill the calendar and there's no time to stop, consider or question.

January came with the bleak shock of going back to normal, of facing the new term of work with a determination I didn't have. I was tired because of having to wash extra sheets every day from the nighttime accidents. I began having to scrub the toilets and found that I was washing a sticky, syrupy substance from around the rim. We would be driving and Sheku would start moaning in a panic that he had to go to the toilet. (Once, Stuart screeched to a halt on the hard shoulder of a motorway.)

I was in denial. Perhaps Sheku had a urinary infection. My mother urged me to get him to a doctor. Just before the appointment was due, Stuart and I took Sheku to London for a masterclass with Jo Cole, head of Strings at the Royal Academy. The train home was packed with passengers and people were standing in the aisles. Sheku was desperately thirsty and kept begging for water, which meant battling through wedged crowds to get to the buffet car. As we got up to push through the crowds we noticed the parents of Madeleine McCann standing right next to us with their twins. Kate McCann was crying and stroking the blonde hair of her daughter, Amelie. She looked devastated, caught in the wilderness of a grief without bounds. I felt overwhelming sympathy and the thought of losing a child appeared like a spectre before me. Stuart quietly said some words of sympathy to her, and I stood choked in the presence of this desolation. I looked at Sheku, his tongue stuck to the roof of his mouth with thirst, his face puzzled, and knew he had to have an emergency appointment.

We waited for the end of the morning list to see the GP, Dr Mawji. I told him I thought Sheku probably had a urinary infection. The day was sunny and the doctor's face was mild and friendly. Sheku was sent to do a urine test and I saw the clear, syrupy fluid in the vial. 'It will be okay. There is a cure', I told myself and imagined the antibiotics I was going to persuade Sheku to swallow. The stick went into the fluid and the doctor cleared his throat. 'There's no infection', he said, 'but there *is* a lot of sugar'. I immediately knew what that meant and tears started flooding down my face. Sheku looked at me, concerned. 'The sugar level should be between 4 and 7', Dr Mawji continued, 'but it's 33. Get him to A&E – the emergency department at the hospital – now. And pack overnight bags. I'm convinced this is type 1 diabetes'.

At that moment, I was no help to Sheku. I tried to speak but couldn't. I knew that type 1 diabetes was incurable, that it was a life sentence and that it was a prison from which Sheku would never emerge. It came like a cloud in the sky and descended like a fog. There was no cure. There had been no prevention. And yet it came like a summary judgement on the head of a young boy who had done nothing wrong.

Outside in the gentle sun that whispered of an early spring, I was walking in unreal surroundings. On the phone, my Mum and sister immediately told me they were coming. Stuart's voice was loud and sharp, full of alarm, and he ran for the train back from London. I went home and quickly packed some overnight things for myself and Sheku. My sister, Isata, and Mum would be there to take over the school pick-up and after-school tea.

Sheku was quiet all the way to the hospital. He still had that puzzled look he'd had on the train, but it was deepening into a kind of slow grief.

At the hospital they already had Sheku's details from the GP, and he was whisked into a cubicle, given a blood test and straightaway his face was smothered beneath an oxygen mask. There was a lot of bustling around us and talking, but the fog persisted. I could see Sheku's eyes just outside the mask as though he were staring from a train that wouldn't stop. We were told that had we waited another couple of days, Sheku would have fallen into a coma. I said a silent prayer for the McCanns as though they had been a prescient vision, and I felt humbled in the shadow of their suffering.

Stuart arrived and laid his head down next to Sheku. Neither tried to speak. Sheku was injected with insulin at regular intervals and taken up to the ward. We were spoken to by the consultant, Dr Tabitha Randell, who was upbeat and practical. Sheku had to learn to inject himself. My head buzzed with all this paraphernalia of needles and injection pens and insulin cartridges. He had to stick the needle into his arm and press the insulin through it. The worst thing was the blood test. This had to be done several times a day and always before an injection and a meal. The sharp blade had to cut the tip of Sheku's finger to draw enough blood to test on the absorbent strip of the handheld blood-testing machine. It hurt and blood ran onto the white bed sheets. I wondered how he would play the cello with this regime? Each time he winced and the blood ran, I thought about how his fingertips would harden and become desensitised to the touch and vibration of the strings, or the subtle pressure and turn of the bow. Would he be forced away from his cello? He decided to prick only his right-hand bow fingers, which meant they were stabbed over and over again.

The insulin had to bring down sky-high sugar levels in

Sheku's blood. The effect over a short time was like someone pressing a lead weight on his small body. He sank into the bed and could barely lift his head. His face was a mask of misery and he had no energy at all. Stuart went home and brought Braimah, desperate to see his brother. Braimah lay on the bed next to him and I left them together, walking into the bathroom to compose myself. Sheku needed Braimah next to him, and he stayed for as long as he could. They shared a bedroom at home and occupied their own world together. It was difficult for Braimah to leave his brother, a lonely presence in his white bed, facing a future that stretched like a hard road in front of him, and I thought of the evening we had planned. It was Shrove Tuesday and Lent began the next day. Today should have been Pancake Day, with a kitchen full of shouting children waiting for the next pancake toss. They would have competed excitedly over the best toppings and the table would have been strewn with grated cheese and honey.

'Can I still play football?' Sheku asked. The answer was yes – if he had glucose tablets with him and tested his blood before and afterwards. Everything was still possible, and nothing denied, if he paid close attention to his body. Sheku's pancreas was being attacked by his own beta cells, which were destroying it in a catastrophic allergic reaction. It was an autoimmune condition with no reversal and simply came from within his own body. I couldn't have controlled it with a different diet or lifestyle. He was slim and fit and full of life, but it happened anyway and there was no going back and no blame.

During the night I was given a camp bed on the floor next to Sheku. But it seemed that, tired as we were, we were not expected to sleep. Alarms went off at regular intervals all around us from other children's beds and the nurses often let them carry on, regardless. There was continual rushing and shouting, and no one tried to talk quietly. Sheku was approached every couple of hours for another insulin injection and more blood tests. He was the site of an ongoing emergency with a paradoxical sense of permanence. He was an emergency with no escape and we were in a perpetual state of alert.

By the morning, we were exhausted and Sheku weak and low. He had plummeted from the sugar high that he had got used to over the past months and was left crawling under the weight of the day. Gravity seemed to have increased and he had to get through another day of needles and insulin and blood. There were young children in the ward with serious conditions or illnesses. Some were toddlers tied to their beds with drips and tubes, wires and alarms. Sheku had an intravenous line and looked worn out, but he would walk away from this institutional half-life. I was shocked to have been washed up on the shores of this terrible world where children clung to the edges of living, the alarm bells warning of imminent disaster minute by minute. I wanted to snatch Sheku away and take him home from the white sheets spotted with blood and the nurses accepting extremes.

He was allowed to leave at nightfall, his blood-sugar levels almost normal. We carried a bag of jumbled needles, injection pen and blood tester, and instructions on how to order more when needed. There was a complicated relationship between hospital and GP which I didn't yet understand and, though relieved to be out of the war zone, I felt panicked that we had been ejected to fend for ourselves. Stuart came to pick us up and we all sat in the three seats in front. Sheku cried. None of us could speak. When we arrived, all the children were awake and ushered him in, crowding around him with cries of love and welcome. My Mum and sister had cooked a pot of food and Sheku's siblings sat round him in a semicircle, all wanting to see him and touch him and comfort him. He had come home.

I looked around and couldn't see Stuart. Walking outside, I

found him in the back garden, sobbing. I put my arms around him as he shook.

Ryan Manderson, Sheku's neighbour and school friend of the same age, came over and joined the group of Sheku's brother and sisters, who wouldn't take their eyes off Sheku. Ryan came with presents and DVDs for Sheku to watch during the week he had to spend at home. Sheku couldn't smile and looked as though he had been slammed against a wall. I spent the night worrying that Sheku might become either hyperglycaemic (blood sugar too high) or hypoglycaemic (blood sugar too low), both of which would result in coma. We had suddenly been launched into life on a tightrope – and Sheku had been hyper-glycaemic for weeks without us knowing. During the day, he lay on the floor or on the settee, stunned in the wake of this loss of energy. Keeping his blood sugar between 4 and 7 meant keeping his spirits low and his body weak. He was desperate to go back to school and to be normal again.

The following Friday, the diabetes nurse came into Trinity School for a meeting with Sheku's form tutor, the teacher in charge of health issues, myself and Sheku. I knew the teachers from parents' evenings and school concerts. It felt strange to be here as a mother whose child had a lifelong condition that the school had to know about. The nurse talked about how Sheku had to eat regularly and could not go into lunch late. She talked about the signs of hypoglycaemia and how Sheku's friends needed to be informed. I had to bring a small box with 'hypo treatment' into the school – glucose tablets, juice, and crackers – in case he started feeling dizzy or confused. It seemed contra-dictory that a condition that would kill with spiralling sugar levels if left untreated also had to be *controlled* with sugar.

I tried to seem positive and business-like. I was the mother who would show Sheku that there were no limits. Life would go on as normal and there was nothing to hide or worry about.

But I was soon crying hopelessly. I was angry with myself to be doing this, embarrassingly in front of Sheku and all these professionals, but I could no longer hide the weight of this grief I was holding in. This was my son and he had to suffer. So many people, when I told them of Sheku's diagnosis, had asked why I hadn't given him a healthier diet or got him exercising. I had clearly fed him too much sugar. I knew it wasn't my fault, but yet I felt accused and found guilty. Sheku had been randomly selected by nature, but I shouldered the blame. No matter how the hospital staff reassured me, I still whispered to myself, 'Is it my fault?' The nurse announced that Sheku could not go back to school until the following week. Sheku spoke for the first time and insisted that he was going back before that. They suggested half days, but he wouldn't countenance it and wanted to get back to normal.

When he did return to school, his school friends made him feel instantly better. They drew him a huge card and each signed it. His best friend, Yago, had written, 'Can I have your chocolate, Sheku?' which made Sheku laugh for a long time, and having the right to go into lunch early with a friend made him very popular.

The following weeks were spent with Stuart and me in constant vigilance. The numbers on the blood-testing machine were like a game of chance. Sheku had to assess the insulin numbers on the injection pen in line with the amount of carbohydrate in his food. Everything was counted and submitted to science with the aid of books and calculations. Sheku is gifted with maths so there was no problem with the numbers and equations, and he immediately understood how to calculate what was needed to correct a hypo or to rebalance when the numbers were too high. But it was not an exact science. Whether he had played football, or practised hard, or got up early for Junior Academy on a Saturday and messed up his routine of mealtimes – everything had an impact on the numbers.

We lost a lot of sleep over the months. We would wake to hear Sheku stumbling or falling down the stairs in the middle of the night, his vision blurred and his mind lethargic, looking for carbohydrates. The hypos could be frightening or heartbreaking, and it could take a long time to bring him back. After the blood testing to see how low the numbers had got – sometimes 2, or 1, or critical – we would try to get the glucose tablets or juice into his mouth without choking him. Then we had to wait 20 minutes before testing again and feeding him toast or crackers. There was a lot of waiting in the middle of the night to see if sugar levels were rising or falling, and I would guiltily think about the alarm ringing at 5.40 a.m. for school and morning practice, or 4 a.m. for the Saturday London train.

When Sheku began growing again, the numbers would spike or plunge for no apparent reason. The doctors would look at the chart created by the patterns of highs and lows, which would be zigzagging across the screen. Some doctors would tell me to let Sheku learn to manage everything completely alone, and some would chide me for not being hands-on enough. These exhortations appeared to be entirely cultural and based on different views of parenting.

Sheku was so smart and responsible that I decided to let him be in charge for a while. Then, after a year of textbook vigilance, came the teenage rebellion they had warned me about. We went to the three-month hospital appointment to find that Sheku had just been missing out blood tests. While at school he wanted to forget that he was any different and would ignore the tests, rushing off to play football with Yago and Prentice, or having his dinner without all the bother of the finger-pricking beforehand. At night, he would fall into bed and take the nighttime insulin only if he felt like it. Type 1 was a trauma he was now bored with, frustrated by and angry against, and so he would refuse it. I had to change tactics: Stuart and I gave him nightly lectures on the dangers of not monitoring his condition. Nerve damage to his body, amputations, loss of vision, not being able to feel the cello – nothing got through. Stuart would get angry and take away Sheku's phone, which achieved compliance for short periods, but we were waging a battle against someone who was rebelling against his own body, which was rebelling against *him*.

When Sheku settled again into being more vigilant, helped by a new, less fiddly blood tester, he had to manage the short range between 4 and 7 like a gambler, guessing the future. Some of the hypos were now more dramatic, and as he grew into an older teenager I found them much more difficult to manage. One morning, I went to wake him for school and could not rouse him at all. Braimah and I shook him and lifted him and managed to get enough wakefulness for him to take a small amount of juice. He choked and spat out the glucose tablet, so we fed him small crumbs of it. He revived enough to enter a half-life of raging confusion. Suddenly he was roaring around the room, upturning chairs and completely out of control. The low sugar level meant he couldn't think or see, and he was shouting at the world from a deep, dark pit. The younger children were frightened by this unrestrained aggression, blind and undirected, full of anguish. Braimah, already late for his A-Level exam at this point, had to wrestle Sheku to the ground and, with sheer physical force, subdue him and slowly bring him round.

One school evening, Sheku wandered into the playroom where Aminata was practising the piano. He was obviously in a scrambled state and was grinning and speaking nonsense, knocking into the walls. This drunken-like state I knew was a hypo. We rushed and gave him sugar followed by carbohydrate, but this was a severe crisis and nothing was working. The twenty-minute intervals could not keep up with this headlong slide into unconsciousness. Sheku became increasingly distressed.

'I can't understand music anymore', he kept saying. He would try to sing something and then go to the piano, play a note and call out, shocked and upset, 'I've lost my perfect pitch'. The repeated sorrow in these statements, and the constant pacing back and forth in agitation, were terrible to watch. We were all surrounding him now, saying soothing words and trying to get his blood sugar to a higher level. He wanted to play the cello, but we wouldn't let him so he fretted and went back and forth to the piano, unable to pitch any note or thread together a tune that he could understand. It was as though the most precious thing in the world had been taken away from him and he was lost in a wilderness. We were all in tears around him and began to panic that his gift had gone for ever. Without his music, he no longer felt like a whole person.

When Sheku was eighteen, Stuart and I returned with him from a trip into Nottingham city centre. It was spring and Sheku was happy and excited with the concerts he was playing. We walked into the kitchen, delighted to have him home, and heard a weird scuffling sound on the floor. Looking back, Sheku was jerking on his back, struggling and thrashing, with froth coming out of his mouth. I screamed and we bent down to him, trying to hold him and bring him round. I had an emergency injection pen in the fridge that was supposed to deliver a shock to the liver to release sugar into the body. I panicked when I saw the pen was out of date, and Sheku was still thrashing and frothing. We dialled 999 and the ambulance appeared in minutes. The paramedics gave Sheku the injection he needed, and while he lay on the floor under a blanket, tired and confused, the woman held me as I cried. We spent the rest of the day in Accident and Emergency at the hospital, with Sheku getting more and more impatient at the waste of his day, completely unaware of what he had been like while unconscious.

Now, if I'm not there, I wait at the end of a phone before and after every concert Sheku plays, happier if someone is with him, or Isata or Braimah are playing a recital with him as a duo or trio. Sheku's concert schedule is incredibly busy and full of world travel, but he has never allowed the diabetes to dictate anything, and he gets better and better at recognising and knowing every sign. He is an ambassador for the Juvenile Diabetes Research Foundation, and he is genuinely surprised if anyone suggests that diabetes limits his life. It is now simply an aspect of him that is threaded throughout his day but impinges on nothing. Whenever we meet up in a restaurant or the Academy canteen, Sheku casually lifts up his top and injects his midriff with insulin without ceremony or notice. And he expects his body to take him into the heights of musical expression not despite, but because of, the condition he has.

22

Into the Sun

I T WAS EARLY in the new year of 2018. The school holidays
lingered on, but Isata, Braimah and Sheku travelled back
to London for chamber music rehearsals before the start of
term. The Christmas decorations were still up and I still stayed
up too late at night. After listening to *The Archers* on Radio 4
while I brushed my teeth, I decided to have a quick look at my
emails before collapsing into bed. It was my special time of day.
Up late with everyone asleep, I could think, uninterrupted.

An email from Kensington Palace appeared in the inbox,
addressed jointly to me and to Sheku. I knew he wouldn't have
read it because it came to an email address he didn't use anymore.
It came from 'The Household Office of The Duke and Duchess
of Cambridge and Prince Harry' and contained a confidential
enquiry about 'an upcoming engagement'. Given 'the sensi-
tivities' of this enquiry they required a signed non-disclosure
agreement (NDA) from Sheku and me before we could talk
further. I sat down in the old wicker chair in the crumbling
bathroom and looked at the broken tiles on the wall and the
horrible carpet – it seemed incongruous that Kensington Palace
was contacting us.

Following his win at BBC Young Musician there had been

an extraordinary concentration on Sheku in the media, and after one and a half years of this heightened scrutiny, I thought life would get back to normal. It hadn't yet. Sheku's face was in every major newspaper at what seemed like regular intervals. It was so important for Sheku to have someone he could go to for sound and caring advice, above the clamour that was rising around him. Julian Lloyd Webber became a valuable mentor for Sheku, always ready with calm words of guidance and caution. I remember one day when Julian had invited Sheku to the Royal Birmingham Conservatoire, where he is principal. He spoke very seriously to Sheku, saying, 'You are not just an important *Black* cellist, you are an important *cellist*. You must remember that and so must everyone else.'

Sheku's BBC String Category and Semi-Final win, televised in May 2016, just before the live Final, had brought an email into my inbox. Skim-reading, I saw it was from Decca Classics, part of Universal. Decca was the recording company whose label was on most of the CDs and old records we listened to as the children grew up, and Decca Classics had recorded many of those legendary stars of classical music the children loved. I squealed at Stuart, 'There's an email from Decca – to *me*!' We huddled over my phone like children meeting an idol. It was an email from Dominic Fyfe who said he had 'felt compelled to write to you after last night's semi-final'. He had watched the programme and wrote: 'Irrespective of the outcome of the Final, we would love to have a conversation with you'.

I look back at the DVD recording of the String Final that was sent to us by the BBC and I am incredibly moved by this sixteen-year-old boy, Afro lit up by the stage lights, playing with such emotion and intensity. Isata's intuitive piano accompaniment and the radiant seriousness on Sheku's young teenage face are extraordinary, and I understood why Dominic thought this was special. But I was bowled over by the thought that this huge recording company, having signed some of the biggest and brightest classical artists for many years, wanted to add this schoolboy to their list.

The day after the Final, I found another email addressed to me from one of the most respected managers in the UK, who managed some of the most important global artists and conductors, Kathryn Enticott. I couldn't believe this unsolicited interest in my son could come so suddenly. She wrote: 'I was watching the finals at home and was totally transfixed by his Shostakovich – which was not just technically assured but was so, so musical. It really touched me'. I was already in a state of unreality and thought how quickly Sheku had gone from a boy who loved his quarter-size cello to someone on the brink of signing with a manager and a record label. Sheku and I met her outside at a café on Marylebone High Street near the Royal Academy. It was sunny as we talked, then we were caught in a precipitous summer downpour which made us scramble madly for shelter. We loved Kathryn immediately. I liked her down-to-earth sense of humour and I knew instinctively that she would look after Sheku.

Dominic, who took the time to travel to Nottingham with Alex Buhr, the head of Decca Classics, was gentle and intelligent, listening carefully to Sheku. He and Alex were warm and sincere, and I knew how amazing it was having Decca and Enticott Music Management backing Sheku. Meanwhile, Sheku was continually featured in all the major national newspapers, headlining the arts and music sections and even simply the celebrity pages. I became accustomed to seeing him looking back at me in print, often with his precious Amati cello in hand, but I never lost the visceral excitement and flustered pride that always came with it.

That same first summer, I answered a phone call from Steve Manderson at Trinity to come to the school with Sheku one hot, bright day. We arrived, parked near the school and walked up to a sight that made my knees buckle: there was a double-decker bus whose entire back bore a giant image of Sheku with his cello. John Dexter, head teacher, and Steve Manderson, assistant head, stood grinning at our surprise. We walked towards this towering, full-colour image showing an intense moment in the Shostakovich concerto at the BBC Final. It was stunning. Sheku was sitting, mid bow stroke, head thrown back, mouth tight with passion, left hand mid vibrato. In huge letters were the words, 'Congratulations Sheku Kanneh-Mason. BBC Young Musician 2016'. Sheku's name was printed on the front of the bus with information about him on the walls inside. The 77 City bus also carried the schoolchildren from the town centre to Trinity every day, and we would regularly see the bus carrying passengers around Nottingham. It was an indescribable thrill on an ordinary day to suddenly see the bus ahead with the massive figure of Sheku and cello playing above the traffic. Sheku had to run every school morning, often in the nick of time, after the bus that blazed his image. Once, bleary with the effort of getting up for school after a London concert, he just missed the Sheku bus and had to watch it, with his huge poster, accelerate off without him, free bus pass in hand.

When Sheku's album was launched in Nottingham, every city bus had images of Sheku in bright colours covering their sides, and we would sometimes see three buses come past one after another with Sheku's face. For Black History Month, Sheku was one of the larger-than-life figures draped over the Council House in the middle of the city's Market Square, with people like Martin Luther King Jr and Bob Marley, and Nottingham celebrated Sheku with extraordinary warmth.

Bridget Boseley from Outline Productions came to see me in late May. I liked her straight away and knew this would be a relationship of complete understanding. She wanted to make a documentary about Sheku and his family, directed by Eddie

Hutton-Mills, with filming from June to September. There were to be no preconceptions or strictures on how we presented ourselves, just an honest depiction of who we were.

There had been no day off since Sheku had won BBC Young Musician. It felt as though every day lay in the glare of a camera or microphone. I couldn't keep up with the cleaning and tidying of the house, still filled with seven children as Isata was now home after the end of her term at the Royal Academy. I began taking piles of things cluttering up the downstairs space to our bedroom and shutting the door when cameras were due. These were often bags of things the children had dropped in the breakfast room that needed sorting through, or shoes, books, half-written essays, letters or abandoned clothes. I didn't have the time to deal with it all. When Bridget showed us the finished film, I realised that Sheku had decided to practise in our bedroom, lifting his cello over the bags and piles of stuff hidden in our room and begun playing, completely oblivious to the mess around him. Lovely Eddie plus camera had inevitably followed him in, and the chaos I had been trying to hide was now on show to the world. I was mortified. We began to be inured to the scrutiny, sometimes not even noticing the ubiquitous cameras. I would suddenly realise that I hadn't been at all on my best behaviour – even being caught on film sucking my fingers while eating a welcome chocolate brownie.

Poor Aminata, aged ten and still a little girl at primary school, had her Grade 5 exam on piano, her second instrument, during the filming. I had little time to practise with her as the family routine had gone crazy with trips to London for interviews and reporters entering the house at evenings and weekends. I did my best with her, cobbling together ad-hoc practice sessions, secretly horrified by how unprepared we were. By the time Eddie was filming us walking hand in hand into Trinity School where the exam was held, I was so tired I could barely speak.

The camera shows me, face collapsed, speaking as though from the depths of sleep. Amazingly, Aminata managed to get a high merit for the exam, but I still feel guilty in front of her very patient piano teacher, Vicky Manderson.

During the filming for *Young, Gifted and Classical: The Making of a Maestro*, we also hosted *The One Show* (BBC) who came to spend the day to make a mini documentary on Sheku and the family, where he thanked us for all our support. I remember a blindingly hot day in July in the summer term. We flung open every window and door of the house (a rare event as it's usually cold because of the single glazing and old wooden frames). The sun was pouring into every room and the children had to practise in the heatwave. It was a very relaxed day. We all simply carried on as we would have done without cameras. The children played their instruments and seemed to be pleasantly surprised when interrupted by an interview question.

We are so lucky to have these treasured documentaries. Their gentle concentration on the children's own point of view, moving with open interest into their private world, jokes and camaraderie, make them precious indeed.

We understood that this was a temporary turn of the headlights and that the spotlight would fade. Public attention, with its own temperamental moods and slants, feeding off escalating truths that are often internally generated, is a precarious friend. Everyone was used to this. During *Britain's Got Talent* we had been famous for a week, maybe even just three days, and had the experience of intense celebrity for that short time. Then, when Sheku became the BBC Young Musician, the media remembered us. We didn't take any of this seriously and thought about it as a fun, if tiring, interlude in our lives.

When Isata was seventeen, Sir Elton John visited the Junior Royal Academy, where he had once been a student himself. He asked to see their most talented piano student, and Isata was chosen. She met him on a day in early September at the Academy and was filmed chatting with him and playing for him in one of the grand-piano rooms there. This was a day of great excitement, before Isata was in the BBC Young Musician Keyboard Category Final and a year and a half before *Britain's Got Talent.*

It was like a dream day. She played gloriously well, her fingers flowing up and down the keyboard with the thrill of playing to an idol. Elton John asked her whether she would audition for full-time study at the Academy and announced that he would support her financially if she gained a place. This was a wonderful offer and a huge relief as we were panicking about the costs. What followed were weeks of camera scrutiny for an Elton John documentary. Isata and I were flown to the University of California for her to be filmed on stage performing with Elton John and talking with him afterwards. We had a fascinating time walking around the American campus in the hazy sunshine and watching the American football supporters at breakfast in the hotel. Isata met music students from the campus and we both marvelled at how different everything was: the heavy platefuls of food, the landscape with so much space and light – and the feeling of lonely anonymity. The campus and the parts of Los Angeles we saw were beautiful, but we didn't relate to that environment at all.

The cameras, with Marcus Haney, the American director, filmed us intensely at home. Mariatu was four and everyone else at school age. It was fun until I was spotted and filmed making a quick pasta with pesto for lunch. (I wanted to be thought of as a mother who always cooked complicated meals for her children, and I had surreptitiously slipped into the kitchen to make sure the children had something to fortify them.) To my consternation, as I was scraping a jar of green pesto into the newly boiled pasta and hastily stirring it up, the camera was trained steadily on me, and my effort at pretension evaporated at that moment. In addition to filming Isata's piano practice, they filmed her with Konya and my sister, Isata, at the Isle of Wight Festival, watching Elton John perform spectacularly and impressively in the open air. They've never forgotten the energy and commitment of his performance or the extraordinary experience of having their every move monitored.

The film was never completed and never shown, but Elton John remained true to his word and supported Isata with the Elton John Scholarship throughout her four years as an undergraduate at the Royal Academy. We learned to accept the vagaries of media interest and to focus on the important long-term goals, working hard and knowing that in such work was the *real* treasure. The rewards were in the music. The unfulfilled promise of all those hours of filming *paled* beside the bright fact of that personal meeting with Elton John.

The *One Show* mini documentary and *Young, Gifted and Classical* were shown in October and November 2016. We lived through a summer in the spotlight, with the excitement of full-colour spreads of Sheku in the press and cameras following us up the hills of Wales on holiday. Sheku played the Haydn 'Cello Concerto No. 1 in C' as the soloist with Chineke! Orchestra at the Royal Festival Hall in a concert that felt full of meaning and emotion. Chi-chi Nwanoku had asked Sheku to be soloist the morning after he had won BBC Young Musician, and he spent the summer working towards this moment. The diverse audience clapped between movements and broke the rules of the traditional classical listener. This made me feel joyous. It was evidence of a new audience unaccustomed to attending a classical concert and making the music their own. In the public spaces of the Southbank Centre they crowded around Sheku, wanting his photo and autograph in such a courteous and celebratory way that we all felt honoured. This was an occasion bigger than Sheku and bigger than our family.

The grand finale of *Young, Gifted and Classical* centred on the Chineke! Concert at the Royal Festival Hall, and *The Making of a Maestro* had its fitting and triumphant end. The film draws to a close with the virtuoso last movement of the concerto, the impassioned orchestra rising to the challenge set by the conductor, Kevin John Edusi, to play with all their heart and soul. Chi-chi Nwanoku, the orchestra's founder, is shown playing the double bass with all her charisma. Sheku, cello held to his body and swaying with it, lips pressed together in heightened concentration, and fingers moving in a blur with the bow's urgent crescendo, plays the last repeated down-bows with the final chords of the orchestra. While the audience members roar and jump to their feet, Sheku smiles, gently embraces the leader Ann-Estelle Médouze and, face sweating after the exertion and the emotion, hugs Kevin in a long, speechless moment.

Stuart's cousin, B.T. Lewis ('Uncle B.T.'), had flown in specially from Antigua, so proud to represent the Caribbean members of the family. Also present were Sheku's extended family, friends, teachers, Kathryn Enticott with her beautiful teenage daughters, and Dominic Fyfe. Sheku was doing what he had set out to do: to speak to everyone and welcome all to the music he played, no matter the background. And to do this in the company of Chineke! Orchestra, created with this mission in mind, was right and fitting.

This concert in September 2016 was the last night of filming *Young, Gifted and Classical.* We said an emotional goodbye to Eddie and left Braimah in London for the start of his student term at the Royal Academy, with Isata beginning her third year. Before the concert, Braimah had to travel to London so he could attend the week of rehearsals. There was no time for him to come back to Nottingham before the start of his first Academy term. He boarded the train at Nottingham station with just one small suitcase, refusing to bother with packing many clothes and belongings. (Isata, when she had gone two years earlier, had to be driven to London with a car full of several suitcases and boxes, and I had tried to spend a whole afternoon helping her to unpack until Stuart dragged me away.) Now here was Braimah, eighteen, tall and relaxed, jumping on the train with his one bag as though he were off on a day trip. I stood watching the train move as he smiled at me, and found I was crying. I was crying for both of us – him, alone and young and thrown into the future, and me, letting my son go.

I now had five children at home full time, and I could see how much Sheku missed his brother. He sat with his sisters much more than before and needed more affection and attention. He had been used to talking intently with Braimah about music and listening analytically with him to a new or old recording that one of them had discovered. They loved sharing jokes and speaking their secret language together (which I had banned during mealtimes). The house was just not the same.

Sheku's life grew busier. He next had to learn the Schumann concerto from scratch to perform in London six weeks after the win. The date had been decided the year before, but all learning of the concerto had been delayed due to the demands of the competition. Suddenly, he had to learn the whole thing in record time, understand it, know it without the music and make it his own. Between AS Levels and interviews, Sheku was in lessons with Ben Davies or in his room, concentrating manically on this piece, practising the fast passages slowly, thinking deeply over the slow moments and fiercely committing them to memory. He performed the concerto magnificently with the Angel Orchestra on one of those hot July days of 2016, the venue overflowing.

Sheku then caught a plane to Lourdes, France, to join his school friends on the famous pilgrimage. This was beautiful timing. Far from media attention, he focused on those who needed wheelchair help to get to the water and he worked hard in the heat. The spirituality of the sanctuary and being away with his school friends was a nice respite.

There were days when the children were small and I walked into town in Nottingham to buy their clothes from Primark or Peacocks, and I would stray to the part of the city where the old buildings seemed more on display. In this corner of the town centre where the shops look more like homes for the gentry is the beautiful Paul Smith shop. This is his home store, the place where he began as a local designer. Sometimes I would walk into the cool entrance where every item seemed to have been thought about individually and created like a work of art. With my jumble of cheap clothes (for which I was very grateful) in a bag, I would permit myself a few minutes to just look at what was not just useful but aesthetic. Stuart would, now and again, when it was a special birthday or a rare and spontaneous grand gesture, buy me one item (a dress, perhaps) or himself a pair of socks that seemed to last forever. I have one white dress, kept for about fifteen years, which is still a thing of perfection. That summer, Paul Smith invited Sheku and his family to visit him at his Covent Garden buildings. They have been friends ever since, recognising in each other a gentle modesty and sense of loyalty that matches the dedication they each have to their artistry.

Asked to play at the British Academy Film Awards (BAFTAs) for two years running, as well as concerts in the major halls (three appearances at the Proms – the Chineke! Prom, 2017, the BBC Young Musician Prom, 2018, and performing Elgar's 'Cello Concerto' with Mirga Gražinytė-Tyla conducting the City of Birmingham Symphony Orchestra in summer 2019), it was always Paul Smith who dressed Sheku.

These details in Sheku's life were singular and extraordinary for a classical musician. Increasingly, he seemed to walk the line between celebrity and classical artist, always choosing engagements with a sincerity and authenticity particular to him. He seemed to inhabit a newly invented space carved out with complete charm and nonchalance.

Sixth-form life was a desperate juggle between concerts and study. The teachers and head teacher, John Dexter, at Trinity School were superb. Sheku was able to practise in the school wherever and whenever he could – and try to cope with the tipping balance between school life and performing career. I would frequently collect him from Nottingham train station at 1 or 2 a.m. and then wake him for school at 6.30 a.m., face swollen from the short, deep sleep, and he would stumble for the Sheku bus, trying to get homework done on the ride to Trinity. He would come home for tea, facing an evening of practice and homework without Braimah to joke with over the meal.

I wondered how Braimah was managing with the new demands of conservatoire life and the rigours of increased practice hours. I knew what life in the first term was like – the shock of a new regime of teaching, where so much more was expected intellectually and physically. Then, an email arrived in my inbox just after Braimah had left to begin student life. It was from Grace Chatto, cellist in the chart-topping group Clean Bandit. The children had featured their song 'Rather Be' as part of the arrangement they played on *Britain's Got Talent* the year before. Incredibly, the band now wanted Braimah to join them on tour as a session violinist, and Braimah was soon travelling more than Sheku. He toured East Asia, the US and Europe, sending us photos of himself with Grace and the rest of the band in Japan, South Korea and New York. The other session violinist was Nicola Benedetti's sister, Stephanie, and she would joke with Braimah about how they were each a sibling of a famous classical musician. Parents at Junior Royal Academy began coming to me with requests for autographs from their teenage daughters, and when we went to Antigua it was Braimah that the girls wanted to be photographed with.

On Christmas Day, we all crowded in front of the television to watch Braimah, playing violin for the Clean Bandit number-one hit, 'Rockabye', on *Top of the Pops*. Braimah had recorded on this single, and every time we heard it we thought, with an eager jolt, *This is Braimah's violin playing!* He was featured with them on the Mobo Awards, on the Spanish and UK *X Factor* and in the big music festivals. He would come back from tour, race from Heathrow airport with jet lag and sit an academic exam or play Bach for a recital exam within minutes of entering the Academy building. He was eighteen and nineteen and relishing the movement between the two worlds, thoroughly enjoying his time with the band. But by the end of his first year, Braimah made the decision to put his studies first and step back from the band he loved.

The two-month gap between the last filming for *Young, Gifted and Classical* and the evening it was aired on television was a time when so much began to change. Braimah left home and joined Clean Bandit, Sheku started planning and fulfilling engagements with Kathryn Enticott and Decca, and we all felt our lives transform. The film became for us, watching on that dark November night, a breathtaking retrospective into a precious family world, still unsullied and whole. When Sheku, playing with all his young passion, let his flying fingers stamp out the final furious ending to the Haydn concerto, what had gone before felt like a glimpse into a glimmering landscape, steeped in the July sun, before our children stepped out into the world.

So in the new year of 2018, after the glorious hurly-burly of the family Christmas, everyone home and just as excited as ever, I sat all alone in the shabby family bathroom, staring at that Kensington Palace email and wondering about this 'confidential engagement'. I took very seriously the stricture of secrecy and mentioned it only to Stuart, whispering urgently with him, pillow to pillow. Sheku waited patiently to find out what this was about and I waited impatiently for another email. But it didn't come. I waited for the rest of the week and then sent a follow-up in case the first email I had sent hadn't arrived. Still nothing. Nearly a week had gone by and we were none the wiser, but of course we were agitatedly filling in the gaps ourselves: Prince Harry was marrying an African-American, Meghan Markle, in May that year. This was utterly extraordinary and celebratory news. For us, having Black representation right there in the heart of the monarchy was something we had thought impossible growing up in the UK. Could the interest in Sheku be somehow linked to this? Perhaps they were planning an ancillary, intimate, prior event or an after-party during which Sheku could play.

Sheku had met Prince Harry the summer before, at the Halo Foundation charity event in London, organised by the Governor-General of Antigua and Barbuda, Sir Rodney Williams, and his wife, Lady Sandra Williams. He had played privately for him there and liked him.

It was Monday of the following week when I got a response. The first step was the NDA. I talked with Sheku on the phone and we both got our copies signed and posted. We had looked at the date of the wedding – we just couldn't resist. It fell on 19th May 2018. Sheku would be in Los Angeles for his US debut with the Los Angeles Chamber Orchestra, a date that we had all been excited about and a very important occasion. I trembled at the clash but also thought I was running away with myself. A clash like this was the stuff of dreams. Once the NDAs had arrived at Kensington Palace, the office requested Sheku's personal mobile number and would not disclose anything at all. I phoned Sheku and he came out of a rehearsal to answer. I waited, pacing the house and trying to get on with something. Eventually, Sheku phoned me. 'Well?' I asked. He started teasing me, as I knew he would, beating about the bush and refusing to be pinned down. Then he said that Kensington Palace had phoned him and the person on the phone had said, 'Hello Sheku. There's someone in the office who would like to speak to you'. Then an American voice came on the phone. 'Hi, this is Meghan Markle. Want to play at my wedding?'

I shouted out loud and clapped my hand to my mouth. Sheku laughed. Meghan had said to him, 'I've been a fan of yours for ages and I didn't know you were British!' I said, 'What did you say?'

'Oh, I said no thanks', Sheku replied. I laughed, hoping this was one of his jokes, and I thought I'd leave off mentioning his US debut until the next phone call. Let him have his shining moment to himself for a while.

This was surreal. Sheku was going to play at the wedding of Prince Harry and Meghan Markle, and we were not allowed to tell *anyone*. I didn't even tell the girls, thinking that it was not fair to give them the burden of a secret they couldn't breathe at any point in school. I walked around with this private knowledge for so long that it seemed as though I occupied a different timeline from the rest of the world. We didn't tell family members or any friends, keeping completely silent until the news was announced less than a month before the wedding. Stuart and I waited for this day of revelation, having fever-pitch conversations after dark. A few minutes before the news was going to be announced by the media, Stuart finally allowed himself to ring his sister, Rhonda. She was shocked that she hadn't worked it out when Sheku's Los Angeles concert had been cancelled. We had old friends and Antiguan relatives with tickets for the US concert, and we could not tell them why Sheku had to withdraw. The management of the orchestra had been extremely gracious and very understanding, and immediately wanted to reschedule Sheku's visit to Los Angeles.

Before the wedding musicians were announced, Sheku met with Prince Harry and Meghan at St George's Chapel to discuss the music and the ceremony. Sheku was with Kathryn Enticott, and Harry and Meghan walked into the chapel. They each extended a hand and introduced themselves. This was a lovely show of manners as, of course, Sheku and Kathryn knew who they were, but at no time did they behave as anything other than extremely decent, polite and respectful people. They both asked to hear what Sheku would like to play on the day and they were eager to hear Sheku's ideas for the music. Put fully at his ease, Sheku told them the three pieces he would like to play, pieces he had discussed before with Kathryn and Stuart.

'Could you play them for us now, please?' Harry asked, and Meghan suggested they could walk around the chapel and listen to the sound. Sheku unbuckled the cello case and pulled out the Amati cello, calm and ready to play pieces he loved and knew well. Alone and without orchestral backing, he played as the couple quietly walked together around the empty church. He performed in full all three pieces he had chosen: 'Sicilienne' by Maria Von Paradis, 'Après un Rêve' by Fauré and 'Avé Maria' by Schubert. The chapel rang with the low, singing sound of the cello as Harry and Meghan, not interrupting, moved slowly around. When Sheku finished playing there was a hush and the couple walked towards him, taking his hand again. 'That was beautiful', Meghan said, 'and that's what we'd love for our wedding'.

In those months before the wedding day, Sheku received invitations to attend private occasions at Kensington Palace and Buckingham Palace. At Kensington Palace, he played his cello to the Duke and Duchess of Cambridge at a small, warm gathering. At Buckingham Palace, he was due to meet the Queen and the invitation from her was worded in the traditional manner, that she 'commanded his presence' that evening.

We knew this was archaic language but laughed that there was no leeway to excuse himself. The day arrived for his scheduled evening at Buckingham Palace and I hoped he had got his shirt ironed and his suit ready. As he was now a first-year student at the Royal Academy I could no longer fussily sort out his clothes and make sure he took his glucose tablets, although I still did when I saw him. In Nottingham, the phone rang. It was Kathryn. 'Have you heard anything from Sheku?' I said I'd heard nothing and asked if everything was okay. 'He's not answering his phone and we need to get the car to him to pick him up'. Worried – perhaps he was having a hypo and couldn't wake, or he had entered some student melee of disorganisation – I said I'd try. When I phoned, there was no answer. Then I phoned Stuart, but he also didn't know what had happened. We then phoned Isata and Braimah to try to track down their brother, and they found him in his room at the Hall of Residence, unable to get out of bed. 'I'm too ill', he told them weakly, 'I just can't go'. He was clearly struck down with something like flu and he could barely speak. Braimah and Isata made a quick assessment of the situation: Sheku was not expected to play the cello for the Queen and all he really had to do was nod, smile and assent, so there were no speeches required. All that mattered was for him to get dressed and stay upright.

They bought Sheku paracetamol and ibuprofen, made him drink lots of water, got him dressed and put him in the car. Looking at the media photos that night, Isata and Braimah had achieved the impossible. From being prostrate with illness, feverish and unable to get up, they managed to put Sheku on his feet, into a Paul Smith suit and got him to Buckingham Palace. He was photographed talking to the Queen, miraculously standing and smiling as though all were well.

Kathryn, having also signed an NDA, had to wait before she was permitted to tell the principal of the Royal Academy,

Jonathan Freeman-Attwood, and Sheku's teacher, Hannah Roberts, about the wedding. Sheku was delighted when he could break the silence because he was desperate to study the three pieces with Hannah and gain detailed guidance into the music. Deceptively simple, the pieces demanded great attention to phrasing, emotional expression and tone. He worked forensically with Hannah, both aware of the exposed quality of this playing where every note would matter and be heard. Hannah was able to guide Sheku to think ever more deeply about each piece, about what dynamics would be effective and the style needed. The occasion would be one of solemnity, joy, love and dreaming. It was formal but intimate, grand but private. The religious meaning had an incredibly personal tone. And it had to be carried by a nineteen-year-old.

Sheku met the director of music at St George's Chapel, James Vivian, a man he liked very much who discussed everything with him in a light-hearted manner. The orchestra, made up of musicians from the BBC National Orchestra of Wales, the English Chamber Orchestra and the Philharmonia were among the highest professionals in classical music, and the conductor, Christopher Warren-Green, conductor of the Charlotte Symphony, made everything straightforward. I knew Sheku was happy and relaxed. He felt free to play in exactly the way that felt right for him, with the support of everyone around him. He has been lucky to work with conductors and orchestras that respond to him and listen to the soloist as he listens to them. Sheku's love of chamber music, nurtured for so long with his siblings, makes him especially attuned to this conversation of understanding between musicians. This glorious moment in the chapel was chamber music at its personal and tender best.

My mother and her sister, my Auntie Gwyn, were coming to spend the weekend with us. My adored Auntie Gwyn, who would come to visit us when we were small African children new to Britain, with her fashionable hair and cigarette smoking, had flown over from Florida for the wedding. (She and my mother have grown more alike over the years and their voices are very similar. The cigarette smoking, no longer fashionable, has since disappeared.) Konya, Jeneba and Aminata had to travel to Junior Academy without me that day, Braimah was watching in London and Isata was travelling to Nottingham to play Rachmaninov's 'Piano Concerto No. 2' with Nottingham Trent University Orchestra at Nottingham's Albert Hall. Sheku was desperate to get to Nottingham to watch his sister play and was determined to travel straight after the wedding.

For us, waiting in front of the television with snacks and drinks laid out that I couldn't eat at all, it was nerve-wracking. Sheku would be playing live across the world (estimated as over two billion viewers globally) and I could not help trying to micromanage the day from Nottingham. I phoned him in the early morning. He had got up and was trying to grab some breakfast at the café over the road from his student hall of residence in London. 'Mum, I can't buy any breakfast because my card's run out'. I went into the bank accounts on my phone and quickly transferred some money into his account. 'You're late!' I shouted. 'It's fine', he said. 'I'll just eat quickly'. My heart was beating. 'Have you got the Amati cello, Ben's bow, the suit and your glucose tablets?' 'It's all cool', Sheku said, 'don't worry'. He sounded sleepy and hungry, and I began worrying about the traffic. What if he missed the wedding? Kathryn was in the car, travelled with him to Windsor, and was going to be with him all day. I waited for her texts and phone calls, which she sent and made whenever she could. I relaxed a lot more, reassured by how well she knew him and the fact that she was a mother of teenagers too. She sent us a report after they had got to the chapel. As we all sat in a fever of nerves, watching the commentator on the television building the scene for the day, I asked, 'How's Sheku? Is he getting nervous?' 'No', Kathryn said, laughing, 'he's taking a nap!'

Kathryn sent us photos of Sheku smiling with the priest, Michael Curry, and all the members of the Kingdom Choir. Everyone looked happy and relaxed in the May sunshine. It was a glorious day. I sat and felt a mixture of sickness and surrealism. It was a wonderful day, but Sheku was under so much scrutiny. All the pressure didn't seem to touch him. It was as though he were in a protected, sunny place, sealed off from the world outside. We watched the crowds gather and the excitement build. The guests began arriving, the hall glamorous with Hollywood and royalty. The commentator, Huw Edwards, reassuringly Welsh with a form of educated kindness that I hear in his voice, was telling the story. The most senior members of the Royal Family began arriving, with the Queen entering last. Prince Harry looked as nervous as I was, and Meghan, arriving in sleek white, looked beautiful. The ceremony was perfect, the priest brilliant and the Kingdom Choir amazing. We watched the couple leave with the senior Royal Family to sign the register, Prince Charles putting his arm out for Meghan's mother to hold. I realised I was identifying with her, as though I would also welcome that comforting arm because Sheku was about to play. The chapel was hushed and all eyes turned to Sheku who was there, sitting framed in the arch of flowers, wearing the Paul Smith suit and colourful socks, serious and focused. Huw Edwards told us that we were in for a treat, and I felt my controlled panic rise.

Sheku played the first soft, low bow of 'Sicilienne', leading in the chamber orchestra tucked behind the flowering arches. He was locked within the world of the music and focused entirely on the audience before him in the church. We gazed from outside this magical space, watching and listening, and nothing interrupted the perfect peace of this music. Sheku seemed able to bring his listeners into the secret, privileged unity of these invited guests while keeping the moment private. Each piece seemed to build on the emotion of the last, and when 'Avé Maria' began, we all sat, still holding our breath, fixated on the screen. When Sheku came to the end of his last singing bow, he sat, still inside the music, listening intently to the orchestra's last notes until the harpist's hands silenced the strings. All was silent.

We all smiled and uncurled. It had been perfect. I allowed myself a few minutes of relief and then turned my thoughts to Isata, who had a rehearsal to get to on time and a concerto to play. Her dress needed looking at and I needed to check the tickets. Stuart and Isata raced off to the rehearsal and he took a short video clip of her, in casual clothes, running through the concerto with the orchestra. It was clear to us, hearing from Kathryn that Sheku was being grabbed for interview after interview with television crews from around the world, that Sheku wouldn't be able to get back for Isata's concert. He kept texting in between interviews to ask how it was going and how she was playing. Stuart sent the video clip to him. We spent the evening at the concert, fielding questions from the audience about a wedding we hadn't attended but felt as though we had, and Isata was magnificent.

Sheku proudly posted the video clip on his Twitter page in between interviews as it dawned on him that he wouldn't be able to get away that evening. The tweet had three million views. Sheku's Twitter account went from 3,000 followers before the wedding music announcement to over 7,000 followers. After the wedding, it shot up to 110,000 followers, with his Instagram account up above 130,000 followers. Sheku remained calm, quiet and cool in the face of all this attention. He spoke to all the microphones held before him with complete diffidence. For him it had been a beautiful day where he had played for a couple that he sincerely liked at a special moment in their lives.

Meanwhile, our Kanneh-Mason Twitter account had gone crazy as well. We had to turn off our notifications because our phones were pinging constantly all through the night and our email inboxes filled. The responses were global. The US was fascinated by Sheku and our YouTube videos were also growing in viewers. When Sheku's short tweet with Isata rehearsing the Rachmaninov concerto hit three million views, we knew that Sheku had achieved something extraordinary.

It was strange to read the newspaper articles about this mystery teenage cellist at the wedding, and to be contacted by people who didn't know who Sheku was. In the world of British classical music, the BBC Young Musician competition is a big deal, but we were suddenly facing a world outside all of this. In February, three months before the wedding, Sheku's album was launched in Nottingham at the Royal Concert Hall, bringing crowds into the building to see the 'Homecoming' video made about his album recording in Birmingham Symphony and Nottingham Concert halls and about his return to Nottingham. It showed him arriving at Nottingham station, coming home from student life at the Royal Academy to eat chicken and see his siblings, visiting Trinity School and looking at the schoolyard and classrooms as a past landscape, even though he had left only half a year before. So much had happened. Sheku played on stage at the Concert Hall with Konya accompanying him on piano, and they also played at Loxley House, seat of Nottingham council, seeing his previous, beloved head teacher, John Dexter, again. Then it was into the city centre to perform at Paul Smith's store.

Sheku's album had gone straight to number one in the classical music charts and number eighteen in the main charts before the royal wedding. Afterwards it even went to number eleven in the main charts. It seemed that every time I turned on the radio Sheku was playing. I would always stop what I was doing and listen intently, breath held to the end, even though I had heard each piece many times and it was the same recording.

Walking to school and seeing Sheku's face on the buses that passed, and opening the local newspapers with full spreads on Sheku, became a strange kind of normality for us. Then, with the wedding, a new charge came into everything. Sheku entered the US Billboard charts at number one in the Classical Overall and Classical Traditional charts, but also incredibly number thirteen in the US Top Current Album chart and number one in the US iTunes Pop chart. He was number one on the Emerging Artists chart and he pushed US classical music sales to their biggest week for over a year. This was an extraordinary feat. He remained number one in the UK classical chart for week after week, and it became a secret Sunday night pleasure for Stuart and me to listen to the Classic FM Top 10 for months. Classic FM (John Suchet) voted Sheku the Best Classical Album of 2018, and Sheku was being hailed as the most exciting thing to happen in recent times.

Sheku began winning prizes. In 2016 he won the Royal Philharmonic Society Duet Prize. In 2017 he was given *The Times* Breakthrough Award at the Southbank Sky Arts Awards. In 2018 he won two Classic BRIT Awards for Critics' Choice and Male Artist of the Year, with a moving introduction by the legendary Nile Rodgers. He won the first BRIT-certified Breakthrough Award for his album sales, and The Hospital Club h100 Award. I placed all the awards in the room with the two pianos, along with other trophies and prizes that the children had won over the years, including the *Nottingham Post* Student of the Year Award that Sheku won in 2016.

The Times Breakthrough Southbank Award is an amazing trophy with a peep-hole where you see a magnified 3D painting of Sheku, with the iconic yellow cello case that he had at the bus launch, looking into a crater from which rises the giant scroll of a cello. It's an incredible work of art that stands next to the slim female statues of his BRIT awards. Next to the shining BBC Young Musician awards is a large photo of Sheku with Ben Davies, taken on the night of the Final. Teacher and student stand in a bond of achievement and celebration that makes the trophy and photo inseparable.

Isata was Sheku's pianist for all his recital concerts and loved watching him being surrounded after each performance by people wanting autographs and selfies. Completely gracious in these situations, it never occurred to her that it should be any different. She would efface herself so gracefully at times that we had to seek her out. She had no idea how beautifully she played, or how beautiful she was, thinking only of how to partner and enhance Sheku's music, giving him advice and exploring possibilities with him. He relied on her absolutely and they had a hypnotically spontaneous musical understanding, each being able to respond to, and augment, the other.

In autumn 2018, Decca Classics approached Isata with the idea of a new album of Clara Schumann's piano music. Isata was thrilled. She began reading about Clara Schumann and looking at her neglected music scores. Clara was the wife of Robert Schumann, the celebrated Romantic composer of the nineteenth century who is still widely played and loved. Clara Schumann was an extraordinarily gifted virtuoso pianist and composer in her own right, her life constantly overshadowed by her husband's overarching psychological needs, and the demands of being mother to eight children, one of whom didn't survive beyond childhood. Clara Schumann's music is astonishingly beautiful, bold, soulful and dramatic. Isata's CD included her 'Piano Sonata in G Minor', the 'Scherzo No. 2 in C Minor' and her 'Three Romances for Violin and Piano' where

Isata was accompanied by the violinist Elena Urioste. I was at the studio recording of Clara Schumann's extraordinary piano concerto with the Royal Liverpool Philharmonic in Liverpool, conducted by Holly Mathieson. It had been weeks of hard work for Isata: practising, reading scores, reading biographies, focusing deeply on her piano lessons with Carole Presland. In the studio, the piano, grand and furious in its virtuosity, backed by the orchestra, washed over me. The second movement is breathlessly tender, simply a duet between piano and cello, and astonishing in its sweetness. The final movement is almost impossibly demanding on the soloist, exacting a marathon of furious chords, arpeggios and pianistic drama that's thrilling to witness.

Isata phoned me a few months ago, quiet and uncertain. 'Mum, I think, though maybe I'm wrong because I can't believe it, but I think I've just been signed to Kathryn Enticott!' She sounded thrilled but disbelieving, afraid to rely on this extraordinary turn of events. Isata could not believe that Kathryn Enticott, as a major artist-manager, could possibly want to sign *her*, with Joseph Chadwick closely managing her development and promotion. 'Well, what did you say?' I asked. She replied, 'Well, I was very polite but I was afraid to sound too pleased in case I had misunderstood!' I laughed. This was typical Isata. She was so modest: she had supported Sheku so completely on his recital tours, playing duos with him as his pianist and never being any more than delighted at the spotlight *he* got. Her love for her brother had made her forget what an extraordinary pianist and musician she was in her own right. It took her a few days to fully trust that Kathryn really did want to sign her, and only when Enticott Management advertised it to the media did she really believe it.

The release of Isata's album, *Romance: The Piano Music of Clara Schumann*, came in July 2019 and shot to number one in the Classical chart. The newspapers, announcing the album release, carried photos of Isata looking gorgeous and young and exciting, with a new confidence I hadn't seen before. The performances that came from the album, in Germany and in Britain, were brimming with energy, and her playing remains full of passion and commitment.

23

In the Spotlight

I HAVE TO force myself to remember that certain occasions, bright with excitement, happened *before* the wedding. Sheku was playing to sold-out concert halls from May 2016, and concerts with the family were also crowded. The sense of responsibility to an audience increases exponentially in this situation. In the early years, the children had to work extra hard in order to prove that they were good enough to be heard. Now they had to work doubly hard to meet both the rising expectation and the consequent scepticism that came from being hailed in this way. Could Sheku and his siblings really be as good as all that, or was it simply a media sensation? Every time an audience rose to its feet at the end of a concert, I would sigh with relief and know that the stakes had risen again. I packed away the newspaper articles and reviews in bigger and bigger boxes, filing videos and commentary in whatever haphazard way I could, not having the time or the psychological space to dwell on any of it.

Stuart and I both felt the pressure to keep up with the pace, the growing depth and breadth of what was needed for the music, and the schedules crammed with concert dates and the competing needs of the children. Suddenly we couldn't go to every event. Concerts clashed and we had to draft in my sister, Isata, Stuart's sister, Rhonda, my mother and my niece, Kadie, to be the family support. Soon, Sheku's support would often be Kathryn, Joe, Sarah or Magda from Enticott Management, or Dominic, Alex or Rachel Tregenza from Decca, rather than one of us, as it was impossible to support the other six children and travel to all of Sheku's events. Due to the increasing demands for interviews, events, filming, media and social media, we also now have help from the impressive Janie Garnon. Stuart flew to New York to see Braimah play with Clean Bandit. We flew together to New Orleans to watch Sheku (along with Auntie Gwyn and Sheku's cousin, Megan, from Florida) play the Elgar concerto with the Louisiana Philharmonic. I flew to Italy and Paris to be with Jeneba while she played her recitals, and Isata, Braimah and Sheku played in Charleston, South Carolina, at the Colour of Music Festival (with my mother, Auntie Gwyn and cousin Megan present). My sister Isata would often be there to help when daughter Isata, Braimah, Sheku or Konya played in Wales, and sometimes in Newtown, Lampeter or Aberystwyth, and Rhonda was always there for London concerts, Isata and Rhonda both travelling to Cardiff to see Isata's piano recital at St David's Hall.

Konya and Braimah are increasingly playing recitals around the country, and both are involved in modelling shows, with Stuart attending as many as he can in London. The family concerts involve the same muddled logistics, with the added mania of siblings travelling from different places. We get together after the panicked jumble of travel itineraries and my crazed lists, and there is always the moment of joyful realisation that we're all together again, lending a fizz of excitement and childhood wildness to the whole event.

Sheku's appearance at the wedding led to other Royal occasions. He had already played at the BAFTAs twice, but now he was invited to play at the Royal Variety Performance, and meet Prince Harry and Meghan again. He was seated on stage with his cello, again in front of flowered arches, and played his second wedding piece, Fauré's 'Après un Rêve'. Prince Harry and Meghan could now see him play the piece directly in front of them, having only heard it before from the vestry where they were signing the wedding register. Sheku played the piece with all his passion, seemingly oblivious to what the occasion meant, and focused only on the intimate logic of the music. 'Après un Rêve' is a song of unfulfilled desire and a fading dream of love, and Sheku's ability to take his audience on an emotional journey, locked within the world that he inhabits while playing, is overwhelming. Later, he chatted with Prince Harry and Meghan in the Royal line-up. Meghan was now visibly pregnant. 'Hey, it's so good to see you again, Sheku', Meghan said. Then she told him something that he quietly treasured and only reported to us: 'We've been enjoying your music and I've been playing it to the baby'.

Since then, in 2019, all seven siblings were invited to play at the Royal Variety Performance, and they chose what they had really wanted to play that summer of *Britain's Got Talent* in 2015: they brought the piece they had worked on with such belief in what they were doing, the 'too classical' 'Czardas' by Monti, which they, under the diligent supervision of Braimah, had arranged themselves. This time, they wrote a part for Mariatu, now old enough at ten to be on the stage with them, not propped up on a cushion in the audience. I smiled at the irony. Part of the *Britain's Got Talent* prize is to play at the Royal Variety Performance and, by remaining true to the music they cared about, they had managed it anyway.

In November 2018, the Royal Albert Hall in London was hosting the Festival of Remembrance, filmed by the BBC. It was a hundred years since the end of the First World War, and

Sheku thought of the young men his age dying senselessly in battle. He was to play his cello as the soloist for a moment in the evening where the descendants of those families who had lost loved ones during that brutal war would walk into the centre of the auditorium holding photos of the men who had been killed.

Sheku came into the centre of the impressive and crowded hall, shrouded with ceiling-to-floor white veils on which were beamed the photos of young soldiers who had died in the trenches, faces from all over the world, pulled into the war by the reach of the British Empire. The bitterness of this sacrifice and the phantom nature of its meaning to us now was symbolised by those shifting, translucent veils from which came the lonely sound of Sheku's cello. He played Leonard Cohen's 'Hallelujah', from which the broken, separate sounds of that Hallelujah came across as a lament and a repeated question. The bewildered love in the song and the harsh reality of loss was communicated by the distance between solo cello and the gentle orchestral accompaniment. As the veils lifted, Sheku was circled by relatives of the dead, each holding for witness a photo of the young person who had died. The unbearable grief of this moment and the determined message it carried, with such respect, was so present in the music that we were all undone.

Preceding this, Braimah had been asked to play in another Remembrance concert in Nottingham's Royal Concert Hall. We met the relatives of Albert Ball, a decorated local member of the air force during that same war. He had been a violinist, a handsome young man who had been the same age as Braimah – just twenty – when he was killed in the war. He took his violin to the trenches, and his favourite piece to play was Dvořák's 'Humoresque'. After playing Vaughan Williams's 'Lark Ascending', Braimah was asked to play 'Humoresque' on Albert's violin, accompanied by Jeneba on the piano. When Braimah first held the violin in his hands and played the first warm notes in our house, it floored me. To know that the violin last had been played in public by a young man who had lost his life so young, and who'd had such talent, made me think deeply about Albert's mother. Like Braimah, he'd also had an elder sister who played the piano and a younger brother who played the cello, and they would also play together as a trio. When Braimah played in the big concert hall that day, the space seemed to get smaller and more private, and I thought about that mother whose beautiful son had been killed, and it was the music, curiously clear and naked, drawn so bitterly from the strings, that brought us face to face.

Since then, Sheku and Braimah have played the duet they arranged together, 'Prayer' by Bloch, for the Holocaust Memorial Day concert on BBC2 in January 2020. Bonded together in sadness for all acts of racism, genocide and hate, the brothers played that Jewish melody of sadness and appeal – and were able to express more than words ever could.

As we hurtled into Christmas 2019, driving through the mud to my sister, Isata's, house in Mid Wales, we were ready for time to stand still for a while. We unloaded the car full of presents, everyone shouting and laughing, and crowded into Isata's and Steven's house on top of a hill with views of fields and mountains and trees. The siblings all slept in the big barn together, with its hot wood stove, and opened their stockings crammed together on the mattresses in the roof space. Christmas dinner was served with all of us – cousins, grandparents, aunties, uncles – in a room full of Christmas tree, lights and noise, and loud board games continued into the night.

We returned to the announcement that Sheku would receive an MBE in the New Year's Honours List. We laughed with Sheku, and his brother and sister teased him, overflowing with pride. He worked constantly, committed utterly to the music, was dedicated to the children who looked up to him and to whom he gave so much time. Respectful of his teachers and mentors, Sheku had declared that autumn, lying on the lounge settee, 'I just want to be the best cellist I can be'. We knew how much this recognition meant to him.

The release of Sheku's second album, *Elgar*, brought him, in my mind, full circle to the little boy with the under-sized cello who mimicked Jacqueline du Pré's vibrato from the television screen and the internet. (The darkness in Elgar's cello concerto and Jacqueline du Pré's impassioned performance had been part of the inspiration of his childhood.) Sheku's current teacher, Hannah Roberts, has developed his technique and musical insight to ever greater depths. Extraordinarily inspirational, she was taught by William Pleeth, Jacqueline's teacher and her 'cello Daddy'.

Piers and Hilary du Pré, brother and sister to Jacqueline, contacted Sheku and asked to meet him. Later, they published this statement, which will always live with us and one that leads me again to dwell in reverence on the magic of time and how vital it is to dream:

> Jackie would often say, 'So many cellists can play techni-cally well, but can they make music?' Sheku makes music. He's the first cellist since Jackie who has that natural and vibrant abandonment when playing. A sheer delight. Jackie would have loved to meet him.

Such an extraordinary endorsement gave Sheku real joy, and it was followed by his visit to Berlin in early 2019 to meet the famous conductor Simon Rattle, and play football with him and his son – a great highlight – but mostly to play the Elgar cello concerto for him. Simon agreed to conduct Sheku with the London Symphony Orchestra for his recording of Elgar's concerto, and Sheku was so thrilled and happy about this that he phoned me on speaker as I drove in rush-hour traffic to take Mariatu to her cello lesson with Sarah Huson-Whyte. (The journey to Southwell in rush-hour can take fifty minutes, and Sheku is *not* verbose. He talked on the phone for the entire journey!)

The recording at Abbey Road was a big family celebration. The whole family crowded onto the gallery with Sheku's close friends from the Academy. Hannah, Ben, Kathryn and Dominic were all there, and Simon Rattle turned and welcomed 'Sheku's family' to the event. The night before the album, which hit number eight in the main Pop charts and number one in the Classical charts, was released, we went to see the screening of the concerto recording in a private cinema. We saw close up what we had first experienced on the day itself: Sheku deep in the emotion of the piece, in acute communion with Simon Rattle and the London Symphony Orchestra. I was so entranced by every expression on Sheku's face, and every nuance of each note, brought painfully to life in the film, that I felt exhausted afterwards.

As the profile of Sheku and his siblings has grown, they are often asked to reach out to children and young people who look to them for encouragement and inspiration. I have spoken to many parents who clearly remember the moment they saw a young Black girl playing the piano in the BBC Young Musician Keyboard Category Final in 2014. There had been a wonderful Black recorder player, Charlotte Barbour-Condini, in the BBC Final two years before, and now here was a pianist of African-Caribbean descent. As a member of a minority group within classical music, it is incredibly uplifting to see someone like you breaking into a world to which you hardly dare aspire. I know how seriously the children all take their position as young Black artists in classical music and what a responsibility it is to hold the door open for others. It is also significant for any young person, regardless of background, to see other young people playing with skill and passion, inhabiting without apology a world that can seem set apart. When they walked onto the stage of *Britain's Got Talent*, they were determined to bring the message that the power and depth of classical music can be accessed by everyone. Since then, they always rejoice when they see children and young people in the audience at their concerts, whether those people are learning to play or just enjoying listening.

Sheku receives wonderful letters written by children. One lovely young female cellist sent him a pair of colourful socks for Christmas, and a primary school class had a whole project on Sheku. The members of this 'Sheku Class' each sent him a beautiful letter of thanks for his inspiration. Another school started a 'Kanneh-Mason Class'. These letters and messages, some saying that they began playing the cello entirely because of Sheku, mean an immeasurable amount to us all.

Every year, all seven siblings travel to Antigua and Barbuda for 'Playing to Inspire', a project set up by the High Commissioner, Her Excellency Karen-Mae Hill, which aims to encourage local young people to learn and appreciate classical music. A new Antigua and Barbuda Youth Symphony Orchestra is being developed, and the Kanneh-Masons love meeting and mentoring these incredibly musical and receptive children. The enthusiasm that the Antiguan and Barbudan children have for the music and for hearing the siblings play is inspirational in return. One of the pieces that the seven played together for one of their Antigua concerts was the old calypso, 'Island in the Sun', adapted by them for strings and piano, and dedicated to their Antiguan grandfather, Arnold. Every year, young people on the islands overlap classical music with soca and calypso, playing Bach, Mozart or Chopin on the steel pans. These are jaw-dropping performances of great skill, playing the music with all the harmonies, developments, intricate counter-rhythms and delight that make of it something new. When I listen to those Caribbean children reinventing classical music, I feel again the energy and excitement I always felt when *my* children, still small, played together. They were approaching something new and making it theirs, letting the music live in the same space as their own playful, imaginative lives and filling it with love. I hear the same ability to respectfully play a piece of classical music, throwing the phrases from one to the other, bringing out an underlying harmony, lingering over a beautiful chord sequence and lighting up the playing with a musical conversation.

When over two billion people, already agog at an English prince marrying an African-American, tuned into the wedding and saw this teenage Black cellist framed between the flowering arches and playing with all the love and passion he knew, it was clear the world was going to change.

On Reflection

House of Music and Memories

RECENTLY, I WALKED around our untidy rooms. There's never yet been time to get on top of the chaos fundamental to the house. Years of new babies, new toddlers, growing children and lively personalities has created a jumble of all the things they have made, drawn, achieved, worn, worked on, read and handed down. We have souvenirs of concerts played, photos taken, shoes and clothes grown out of and waiting to be passed on to a younger one. We have sheet music, old instruments, toys they still want (or have forgotten about), board games they still play, art accessories, hair products, pots of Vaseline, hair grease and abandoned cosmetics. I trip over old diaries, boxes of music certificates and concert programmes. The windowsills are crammed with football trophies and ornaments the children made in school. Out of picture frames decorated with painted hearts or coloured tissue paper, I can see the primary school faces with front milk teeth lost and the eagerness of a child at Christmas, Easter or Mother's Day.

For me as a parent, the days now are a time suspended between past and present. Some of the children are stepping into adulthood in that in-between moment of student life and coming home. Some are still in school, waking up every day and returning to the place they have lived in since they were born. For them, the house is complete when their siblings are back, either for a concert, a rehearsal, a gap between terms or a break from London. This is still everyone's home.

But memories of a time that has gone keep growing. The older ones see their younger selves in the sisters who remain, going to the schools they used to attend and playing the music they loved. For the past few years I have had to give away baby clothes, toddler clothes, the little T-shirts or trousers that bodies, when small, shaped and faded. Shoes below a certain size can no longer be kept and toys can't be hoarded for a child younger than nine. I have boxes of books already read and discarded but from which I cannot part. Stories written or days recorded in pencil by children, in secret notebooks, lie packed away beneath the beds.

We lived together and had no time to notice change because there were no empty spaces or quiet days in which to reflect. Sometimes I have to launch a panicked hunt for something needed that cannot wait and, rummaging through a drawer or a forgotten box, I come across a photo, newspaper article or old programme that knocks me back across the years to an Isata, Braimah or Sheku whom I had not noticed then was so young. I wonder how I knew they were already people then, fully fledged, with intelligence as deep as mine, when here they are, gazing across the years at me, as little children.

Walking into my bedroom, I can still remember seeing all seven of them on the bed, six of them cradling Mariatu, a baby of a few weeks old, and singing her song. Isata is thirteen, Braimah is eleven, Sheku ten, Konya eight, Jeneba six and Aminata three. Mariatu is crying and they're soothing her with the song they made up together, for her, complete with harmonies and counter-tunes. Percussion is introduced, gently, on the bed's headboard, and Mariatu stops crying. I take the opportunity to grab Aminata for hair washing and plaiting, knowing that I have to seize every spare moment to get jobs done while the baby is occupied.

While I hurriedly plait Aminata's hair, oiling the damp scalp and using the Afro comb to draw straight lines and cubes of hair, I hear that the song has changed, reformed and developed into a full-fledged symphony. Different orchestral sections are mimicked in the voices and the music now has greater depth and breadth. There is not a sound from Mariatu who, like a baby queen, is being serenaded in the middle of a creative bond that is already a living thing. I don't contribute my poor voice – it would be an intrusion to their perfect circle – and when I release Aminata she bounds and clambers onto the bed to join the last chorus. I stand in the bedroom door and smile.

Walking to the next bedroom, I remember waking up at 3 a.m. to muffled crashes and barely stifled giggles. Opening the door there was mayhem. The laundry baskets that we used as toy boxes had been pulled out from under the beds and upended over the floor. Toys, games, craft materials and soft toys were spread over every inch of carpet, and the five children I then had were playing a wild and hilarious game in the midst of it all. I was horrified. What had happened to our careful plans? What had happened to the tight, nighttime rules that meant we were in control of this gang of children? They saw the structure we had put in place, tidying up after themselves and the correct order of bedtime, and they had decided, unilaterally, to subvert it all. I was speechless then, but now I was laughing.

In the bathroom next door I can still see the little pockmark holes in the linoleum floor, as though a lively woodpecker has been at work. Little, deep dents sit under bare feet like Braille leading the way to the toilet seat where Sheku would sit on the closed lid, skewer his cello into the floor and play for hours, loving the concert-hall sound that would echo from the bathroom walls. If someone lurked in the doorway to watch him he would lean further back, fix his eyes on whoever it was and play with all his heart, digging the cello deeper and harder into the floor. We had to curb the habit of bathroom playing because practice can't all be in a concert hall and string players must learn to project in less giving acoustics.

In the bath I can see Konya and Jeneba as toddlers, splashing and banging the water like drummers, manically creating such waves that no one could get past the doorway. Konya is in charge, the older of 'the girls', and I see myself and my sister, Isata, in them both. The games of dolls and soft toys, elaborate and covering their beds, side by side, are ruled over by Konya. I see them in that bath, having divested the fairy dresses and wings they were wearing, the shiny crowns and wands on the floor, continuing the intricate soap operas of their games with the bath toys.

The next room has been through different occupations, beginning as the twin bedroom that Isata and Braimah shared for a couple of years from ages five and three. It was the 'big ones' room then. Towers of Lego or Jenga would fill the middle of the floor, or jigsaws and toy cars in long lines and patterns. Braimah would go to sleep, brows furrowed and thumb in mouth, and Isata would still be talking, precise and bright, as I closed the door at night.

Later, when it became Aminata and Mariatu's bedroom, their painted pictures, mostly from school, began decorating the walls. Some are still there, reminding me of a time when their image of themselves was in those funny brown bodies and smiles that seem to bob and bounce with life on the paper.

Aminata still walks in and out of this room, usually with her violin in her hand but always with a dramatic pose and a funny caricature of someone preening, scorning, teasing. As a little one, she would flounce out of the room with a scene to enact with bravado, eyes gleaming with the scandalised laughter she would receive, then just as intensely flounce back in, wracked with inconsolable anxiety. She is still two people at once: the brilliant extrovert who makes us laugh out loud and who can fill a stage with personality, and the worried little girl in a body too tall for her confidence.

I think of all the mornings that I've walked in to wake up Mariatu for school. She's always the last one. I peel back the layers of duvet, teddies and fleecy blanket to push my face into the warm, soft sleeping face and neck. She smells of the sweetness of childhood and I wonder how long that will last. Her hot little arms will come easily around my neck and hold me there in the safe place between dreams and morning, like a little bird in her nest. She is still eager to please and ready for adventure, always polite and wanting to keep up. But she has a temper that suddenly flares and shocks us all, and she will unfailingly stick up for herself at home. But in school, her politeness and kindness make her vulnerable. The oddness of her life, always at classical music concerts at a time when music is being squeezed out of the city schools, push her a little to the edge, making her identity a separate thing. And she's so used to being loved.

The next room is the bigger, family bathroom, an old converted bedroom where some tiles are missing and the ceiling, where the old-fashioned wallpaper peeled off, remains undecorated. When we came back from Bahrain, the children would not get used to going outside to play, confused by this strange British habit, so we had given in and brought the trampoline – a small-child version – into the big bathroom. Sheku would use this as a method of escape, running and bouncing on it when he was meant to be brushing his teeth and evading capture by ingenious ducking and jumping that made his Grandma Enid pretend to be furious. Grandad Arnold, though, would unfailingly stick up for his beloved grandson and hear nothing against him.

The next, steeper set of stairs, where I remember flattening myself against the walls for the manic Easter-egg hunt, year after year, after the sunlit meditation of morning church, has the same carpet that covers all the stairs. Its bald patches have increased with time, the thumping of children's running feet and sliding bodies to blame, and I've thanked the splashed and mottled colours in the fading fabric for hiding the stains. There, on the bend in the stairs, is where Konya, at age three, decided in the midst of the hunting mayhem to completely change her clothing and sat methodically undressing while children roared and thundered past her. Her self-possession was admirable. Braimah, worried and thoughtful, stopped at another bend in the stairs to ask, face screwed to four-year-old concentration: 'What if I find an Easter egg but it's too high for me to reach? Do I ask an adult?' Meanwhile, rushing past him, came Isata and Sheku, baskets filled with the eggs that Braimah was not finding.

The first bedroom on the top floor, views across Nottingham with valleys to the horizon, became Braimah's bedroom when he moved to the sixth form. If family came to stay, he would move back in with Sheku next door, where all his clothes and most of his things remained. This was where he occupied the liminal space between childhood and adulthood at a time when all his future seemed in jeopardy, hanging in the pain of his shoulder, a pain which came into the lonely fragments of violin we would still hear. Now, Aminata likes to practise here, and when Braimah's home, he will enter and listen, full of interest and quiet kindness, and give her advice on sound, technique and posture.

The next room is Sheku's room, the windowsill still full of the boys' football memorabilia, with their football medals hanging in a bunch from a screw in the wall. A poster of Bob Marley is attached to the sloping ceiling and a guitar, one string broken, leans against the wall. It was here that I had to force Sheku – comically bleary-eyed and heavy from a late-night concert or the physical challenge of being a teenager – awake every morning for school or Junior Academy. Like Jeneba, his transition from sleep to wakefulness is drawn out and heavily reluctant, impervious to any sense of urgency under the weight of a sleep-sodden body.

The next room changed from box room and boiler room to attic bathroom with roof window. Open on hot days, little brown bits from the beech trees softly fall on the floor and in winter the snow or ice lie in layers on the glass.

Turning to the left is Isata's bedroom, created out of the hidden wall space when she was nine. We decorated it in lilac with a built-in window seat, but she wouldn't sleep in it for years, not wanting to be alone. The boys would sleep head to toe in one of their single beds and Isata would have the other bed, so they could talk and scheme before they fell asleep.

The boys' room, now Sheku's bedroom, was the place where the biggest projects would begin – the cardboard houses they built with intricate furniture and fabric wallpaper, the chess-boards, the shop and 'conkerland'. Braimah would write stories at the desk or they would record music mixes with their own songs and lyrics, and later the music videos and film-making began. This developed to involve all the siblings as they grew up, with acting scenes and improvised music scores. Braimah was the comic actor, brilliantly mimicking teachers or his father, or creating a character that dominated a scene with expertly observed mannerisms. The girls specialised in drama or mystery, and Sheku played, with uncanny aptitude, cleverly disruptive teenagers. Some of these videos are still stored on outdated phones and half-working iPads; some are lost for ever.

Downstairs in the 'breakfast room' I remember scenes of many birthdays. Candles blown out on cakes with a growing chorus of children surrounding the special child. There is a birthday almost every month and no one shares a birthday month. The months without birthdays are Valentines, Christmas and our wedding anniversary in October.

The 'playroom' is scene of endless train sets and toy cars underfoot, baby toys and board games on the floor over the years. The piano stands against the wall, piled with the scale and grade books, the sight-reading and aural practice of seven children, on top of which sit Chopin and Prokofiev, Bach and Beethoven. On the opposite wall, the shelves still heave with playdough, games and jigsaws, Monopoly, Boggle and Scrabble.

The first set of shelves was put up by Stuart when the children were little. Neither of us are any good at practical jobs in the home but, as young parents, we thought we ought to learn DIY as everyone else seemed to be able to do it. Stuart spent all day with drill, brackets and screws, and he very proudly showed me the red and blue shelves which he had immediately stacked with books. I was very impressed until, in the middle of the night, we heard a noise like an explosion and rubble crashing to the floor. Once we entered the playroom, every shelf had collapsed and the screws had pulled out chunks of plaster and dust everywhere. We laughed with relief. Not only had it happened with no vulnerable children around, but it also meant that Stuart needn't bother with practical home tasks again!

In the hallway I walk into our main performance space. Sitting on the stairs, Stuart and I have watched theatre productions, dance sequences, the boys' gymnastics and many 'family concerts' where the children would perform their solos, duets, trios, quartets or septets. Solo performances were, and are, always given to a rising gallery of family critics on the stairs, each with an exacting summary of what has just been heard to help the performer learn. These performances, usually held on Sundays, were events that they would all be nervous for and take very seriously, and which everyone tried to make as merciless and encouraging as possible.

The piano in the hallway, an upright against the wall, has suffered many years of the table-tennis table being wheeled out from its folded up position against the wall of the 'piano room' and clicked loudly and heavily open against the piano's side. Once opened out, no one can get either side of the table as it's tight against the walls, but obsessive and noisy games of increasingly fast table tennis have taken place here since they were small children. Family tournaments involving the cousins, aunties and uncles are favourite memories, along with the shuffleboard tournaments of family gatherings.

What was originally a dining room, before we moved in, became the 'piano room' with two pianos, some cellos and stacks of violins, instrument accessories and sheet music. Under the grand piano, which needs renovation, is dust now and the odd dead bee which seems to have got in through some crack in the woodwork. In days gone by a small child would be under there with a stray foam Frisbee or plastic lorry, singing to the sound of an older child playing the other piano. Sheku and Aminata would have their cello and violin lessons in here with Sarah Huson-Whyte and Siân Evans, and Braimah would practise his violin sonatas with Konya at the piano. Now the grand piano is crowded with trophies from the various competitions or awards received. Two Classical Brit statuettes stand next to the Southbank award. Nottingham Young Musician trophies jostle with BBC Young Musician glass and framed souvenirs, photos and Royal Philharmonic Society awards or young-musician prizes. A letter from Elton John to Isata and a thank-you letter from Prince Harry and Meghan to Sheku sit next to an invitation from the Queen, overlapping with a smiling photo of Sheku with Ben Davies after the BBC Young Musician Final.

Seen all together like this, it's easy to forget the hours of practice and tired wading through the work that needed to be done every evening after school: the frustrating sight-reading sessions or the wrestling with technical passages that one or more of the children just couldn't get right. There are memories here of coming back into the room the day after losing a competition or having a performance that went wrong, or a lesson that showed they needed to work much harder, and starting again with that first press of a piano key or opening of a violin or cello case. The prizes and successes all jostling for the same space belie the acres of time and work in between when each child had to get by on faith.

The family and our parenting are still day-to-day realities. Stuart gets up for work before dawn, travelling to London or abroad for a few days at a time. I also get up before dawn and prepare myself for the morning, waking the girls in time for last-minute school preparation and cello or piano practice. I don't have to wake a whole house of five heavily sleeping teenagers and two little ones, or impose order on seven shouting, giggling, bouncing children. But the phone still rings or pings with constant texts and emails from the older four with requests, needing advice, wanting to talk something through or asking if I'll be there at a concert. Sheku still turns up on a Saturday while I'm at Junior Academy, his face half asleep after alighting from another international flight with an apologetic suitcase of performance clothes and dirty laundry that he can't find time to wash and iron in between student classes and deadlines. Braimah, Isata and Konya will gather with Sheku and their younger sisters at the back of the canteen, sharing gossip and eager to know the latest plans or jokes.

I still travel across the UK with a concert dress in a bag, or an electric shaver that one of the boys has forgotten, or the pair of Paul Smith socks that Sheku left in his room and wants to wear while he sits to play. Stuart and I still worry about the future for all of them, while celebrating the joys of the present. We watch as many of the concerts and recitals as we can get to, seeing the professionalism and certainty that they have on stage. It's all under their control now and the choices belong to them. But we know the look we get when we appear in the audience and the change, a subtle ripple effect of attention, at our presence. I see it sharply when I let one of them know that Dad can, after all, make it to their performance. The face lights up with excitement and attention, and the occasion takes on a greater significance.

I know that things will change. Eventually, they may move further away or get married and have other families to prioritise. But for now, we still have our family holidays all together and the relationships between us are the same as ever. For Easter weekend, the weather glorious with sun spilling into the front of the house and brightness and warmth in the back garden, we were all home enjoying time with other family members and friends. (Steven, my elder brother, was missing as he is in New York with his wife, Cheryl, having recently suffered a stroke.) When everyone sat to eat – four pots of stew on the cooker, rice, sweet potatoes and fried plantains – the noise was deafening. Everyone was laughing and talking at the same time, excited to be repeating this family communion and re-establishing our importance to each other. (My sister's baby grandson, Amiri, joins five-year-old Aneurin, who loves to play football, as the next generation.)

The children grow taller, but the connections remain the same. I watched Lahai and Nyanje (the children of my brother,

James) running, giggling and playing wild games with everyone just like they all used to for a week every summer when they came to stay when they were younger. I watched Kadie and Idris (the children of my sister, Isata), both parents now, still wrapped with affection from the children who are no longer all children, and my mother, the eldest now on my side of the family, watching how the family has grown. I wondered if she thought about that long journey on the ship to Sierra Leone when she was twenty-two years old. She had lost all she had sailed so far for, but now there was all this – a garden and a house full of the future.

The day before, Stuart and I, along with our seven children, had a day's photo shoot with *Hello!* magazine. It was a beautiful day, and we enjoyed the company of the photographer, technical assistants, journalist, make-up artist and stylist. It was easy and fun because they simply asked that we be ourselves and be together. They walked around the house looking for places where we could be photographed, and I laughed at how the *Hello!* magazine team must be used to glamour and perfection. As it was, I had spent two days tidying and hoovering, and mostly moving piles of stuff to hide out of sight in our bedroom. I gave up trying to keep our door shut to keep back the sense of looming chaos. But still the house was cluttered, the music books stacked as best we could, the shoes filling the back-door entrance and books everywhere. We spent half an hour trying to create hanging space for the stylist and worked hard to get a table surface for the make-up artist. It was a lovely day because we were happy to be photographed where we all still belong, with nothing fundamental having changed. It was an excuse to all be together, with practice pushed aside and talking with people who were interesting and had other stories to tell. How funny that anyone would want to see this ordinary life where we all recognised each other so well! Doors flung open on that sunny day, we were at ease in the camera's gaze.

At the end of the next day, Easter Sunday, we found a moment to sit outside. We had finished the Easter-egg hunt, the same as it had always been, with shouts and intense excitement, everyone running up and down the stairs, rummaging through beds, table drawers and toy boxes, laundry baskets and clothes – in a frenzy of noise and joy. Now, children and their cousins were playing a very loud board game inside the house. The sun was gentle in late April and still warm on the garden. It was me, my mother, sister and brother, talking quietly at the end of the day. And everything was the same.

Redemption Song

The Year We Lost and Found

I LOOK BACK at January 2020 through a telescopic lens. It is a shimmering landscape where we stood, surveying the year ahead. The months to come were mapped and planned in a schedule thick with dates.

Upcoming was the MBE ceremony with royalty, an honorary doctorate; family concert tours to the Caribbean, Australia, Ghana; sitting in sold-out concert halls to witness my children play. The Royal Albert Hall, Carnegie Hall, the Wigmore Hall, tours throughout Europe, USA, Brazil... There were A Levels, residential music courses, music exams, graduations, Freshers' Week. The days were brimming with aeroplane flights, train journeys, early mornings and late nights. Beneath the detailed precision of check-in times, rehearsal duties, concert openings and media appearances was the exotic impossibility of far-flung places, spaces yet unseen and music yet unheard.

I was hurrying to be ready, barely afloat between performances I wanted to watch and the emotional needs of so many busy schedules. Sheku's Elgar album had peaked at number eight in the overall charts and remained number one in the classical chart for weeks. Isata had her Royal Albert Hall concerto debut in April and Braimah's Final Recital at the Royal Academy of Music was coming close. We had another year of recording, another year of travelling. The year, a fabled adventure, lay ahead in its own bright dawn.

One Saturday in February, after the usual pre-dawn train to London, I left Jeneba, Aminata and Mariatu at the Royal Academy. Even the weariness of the early journey and the grim exertion of hauling violin, cellos and sheet music along Euston and Marylebone Road didn't dim the glow of pleasure watching children and teenagers arriving with their instruments and music books at the grand entrance. The girls dispersed through the marble hall and up the wide staircase under the stained glass window, or down the steps to the cloakroom, and I waited by the doors for Isata. She arrived, cool cheeks and long, bright braids, and we swept out of the building for our morning of dress buying. We were also choosing clothes for Sheku's MBE ceremony, and for the concerts they would soon be playing in Antigua. The shops were full and the new clothing collections had come in. I chose a long dress that reminded me of the yellow daffodils my mum loved, and Isata picked out a sparkling jumpsuit that wrapped like a glove around her body. We met up with Braimah, Sheku, Konya and Ayla (Braimah's girlfriend and Isata's flatmate) in a café on Marylebone High Street. There we were, in the warm, steamy room with the promise of spring beginning in the cold white air.

It seemed to have begun in Italy. News stories since January had told of a sickness spreading gradually westwards from China, but we thought it would be halted, coming up short against borders of distance and time. The older ones had been telling me about incidents with Chinese students they knew being spat at in the streets, which filled us all with despair. It was a bubbling undercurrent, one that we hoped would drain below the surface again. In the news and rumours that swirl around every recession, war or disease run the threads of blame. It is always the fault of another group, a nation, an ethnicity.

Isata and Sheku went for their recital tour to Italy in the first half of March. They loved Florence, golden with cobbled streets that they strolled along after meals in the nearby cafés. Their apartment was clean and quiet, with pristine tiled floors. Writing their septet arrangement for music from *Fiddler on the Roof*, they huddled together over the Sibelius software in the open-plan living room, letting their imaginations meet in the precise notes on the stave. A theme floated between two violins, taken up by one cello, then another, and swelling into a chorus of three violins, three cellos and a piano while a new theme began tentatively, teasingly underneath. I listened as Isata described it to me over the phone and I loved their attention to personality and humour in the music. They had such excitement anticipating the rehearsals in which they'd finally be able to share what they had written.

They had been playing to full concert halls and suddenly the doors ahead of them were closing. The concert tour was shutting down around them and they had to cancel flights to Italian cities already in lockdown. Soon, the coronavirus was spreading out of control from north to south. Stranded, Isata and Sheku found themselves abruptly at leisure, with a pool of unrippled time to write music.

It was a crisis without a trajectory. None of us saw how it would knit itself into our lives for months to come. We largely ignored the growing fear and carried on following the plans we already had in place. Isata and Sheku flew back to the UK and continued working. The others forged ahead with their concerts and studying, and Stuart took the train to work in London in the early morning. Then the four elder children, who were living in London, began telling me on the phone about the general behaviour of people around them. A subtle cultural shift was taking place, with people edging away from each other in an atmosphere of suspicion that seemed to seep into every encounter.

Bemused, we carried on. I went to Tom Poster's piano recital at the Sunday Morning Piano Series at the Royal Concert Hall in Nottingham. The stalls were as full as ever and we all cheered and clapped, meeting for tea and cake with the audience all together on the upstairs level. Looking back at that day, mid-morning sunshine coming through the big windows as Jeneba and I talked with Tom, Elena Urioste and Neil Bennison, I realise it was the last time I went to a recital in a public venue that was untouched, unchanged.

The following Saturday we caught the bleak early train to London. Dawn broke as we sat in the cold carriage, inexplicably chilled with intense air conditioning and unceasing, booming announcements. Finally, we arrived at St Pancras International. Walking onto the strangely quiet platform, we looked for the usual crowds. The ticket barriers were wide open and, with the eerie feeling of being in a disaster film, I walked off the escalator at the bottom with Jeneba, Aminata and Mariatu to see an empty concourse. The Eurostar didn't have its usual passengers with suitcases, the customary jostling groups were nowhere to be seen. I could hear my footsteps as we walked out of the station. Sheku and Isata had been playing concerts during the week – Isata in Germany and Sheku in the UK. There had been a slight increase in empty seats in England at what had originally been sold-out concerts, but we thought the danger of Covid-19 was limited and temporary.

I decided that, as a treat, we should all get in a waiting taxi. I was tired with preparations and packing for Antigua the following week, with concerts that were almost every night leading up to our Thursday-morning flight. The taxi driver wouldn't let us in his cab. 'Where are you travelling from?' he asked in a voice so full of panic I wondered what we must look like. 'Nottingham,' we said. He let us in, still fretting, apparently terrified at his own decision. I wondered why he would wait in a taxi outside an international train station if he were so afraid. He spoke to us in short, ejected phrases from behind his glass screen and I was careful with all my responses. London looked different suddenly. At the Academy, the driver waited until we had lugged out the cellos, violin and bags, then took a huge bottle of disinfectant from the front of the cab and drenched the seats, floor and handles, afterwards washing himself. I felt desolate. At that moment, it was impossible not to take this personally. As though we were infections to be cleansed away, like rats carrying fleas or creatures that had crawled, blinking, from the sewers.

The feeling of love withdrawn stayed with me as we descended to the canteen. Acres of empty space seemed to have opened up and I could see the bare legs of the tables and the naked floor. The few parents who were there didn't draw together with laughs and hugs and touches of the arm. We had arrived from virgin territory, where the world remained unchanged, to this frontline of a war I didn't know had started. And the enemy was each other.

I sat at a table and someone joked about an 'elbow bump', which was the first I'd heard of it. How could we greet each other like that? When Konya, and then Braimah, Sheku and Isata, walked in, I ostentatiously drew them in and cuddled them, as always, trying to fill the cold hollow opening up inside. A friend of theirs I hadn't met came and joined us and

I reached out and shook his hand. In the polite awkwardness that followed I found myself apologising as though, by touching his skin, I had committed a crime of indecency. I couldn't wait to get away to Antigua in a few days, to feel the warmth of the welcome and to hug the children's grandparents. Mum would be with us, and amidst the energetic schedule there would be time to sit on the veranda and talk.

I looked at the messages on my phone with disbelief. Her Excellency Karen-Mae Hill, the High Commissioner, was dealing frantically with what was becoming a turbulent situation in Antigua and Barbuda. Growing concern over Covid-19 was threatening to close the hotels and flights. Without the hotels, some of the concert venues and a lot of the sponsorship would go. Without the flights, of course, we were not getting there at all. And without hotels, flights and visitors, Antigua and Barbuda's economy was in trouble, its people at risk. Sheku refused to believe it. He looked tired and said he needed to get to Antigua. They all saw the annual trip as an oasis in a relentless world, a place where they could step out of the shuddering routine of performance and practice, into one of connecting with young people who had so much to offer. They arrived as teachers and performers, but they never failed to learn something from the people they met on the island. It was an exchange that stimulated and informed their own relationship to music. They found themselves listening, having conversations, playing football, dancing, singing and hearing music that blurred the imposed barriers between classical and local, orchestra and street. And they learned new ways to celebrate and explore music they thought they already knew.

We were four days away from the concert tour, the orchestral tutoring, the performances around the island, interaction with schoolchildren and families, uniting with relatives, their grandparents and Auntie Rhonda, and fulfilling their role as cultural ambassadors for Antigua and Barbuda. Three UK concerts had to be performed before we boarded Thursday's flight, the last of which was due to take place in Grantham the night before our departure. And suddenly the trip was cancelled. Sheku played his final concert with Guy Johnston at Queen Elizabeth Hall in London the next day. I had not reserved a ticket, being happy for Stuart to go without me and regale me with every detail afterwards because I had anticipated a day of last-minute packing for Antigua. Instead, I waited in Nottingham with Aminata and Mariatu, looking with incomprehension at the half-closed suitcases and long dresses draped and ready to fold.

The next night's concert was cancelled. As I carefully took all the passports out of my bag and put them away, I felt dizzy, as though the firm earth beneath my feet had turned to slippery ice.

Instead of boarding a flight, instruments on their backs, in the early hours of 19th March, all four siblings who were in London came home on the evening before. I drove the nine-seater car to Nottingham train station to pick them up. It was an early spring day, and I was in the grip of a heavy migraine. In bed the night before, I woke repeatedly and found myself under an almost claustrophobic anxiety, so nebulous but all-invasive I couldn't crawl out.

They all stepped onto the platform from an otherwise empty carriage, looking tired and sad. My head hurt so oppressively I simply hugged each one and they put their big suitcases into the car. They could see me wringing my hands and all said, 'Don't worry, this will be over soon and then we'll be back playing our concerts.' But we were not in the clouds above the blue Atlantic Ocean, waiting to land on the island. We were in another universe.

At home, they ate the chicken and rice I had cooked and we waited for the younger ones to come home from school because

302 • HOUSE OF MUSIC

it was Stuart's birthday. As the Grantham concert and the rush to the airport had been scheduled for this day, we had planned a lovely birthday in Antigua. As it was, I could barely see through the pain in my head and I noticed that Sheku didn't eat much, while Braimah and Isata had no energy at all. Stuart had been to the supermarket to make sure we had enough to feed a family of nine, so we were self-sufficient for a while. They gave their dad his birthday presents and we celebrated as best we could. Konya, like the others, had brought her clothes home but left all her books, photos and pictures behind. The other three were in London accommodation that was rented through the summer, but Konya had to move in June. I thought about the huge London rents they were all paying, for which there would be no refund.

My headache lasted another two days and my anxiety grew as Aminata and then Jeneba and Mariatu were sent home from school. The week eventually ended, with school shuddering to a halt and the realisation that everyone was suddenly at home. As my headache began to recede on Saturday night, it was clear that we had to get Konya's belongings from London. Stuart and Konya set out in the car early on Sunday morning with the boot full of large suitcases, to begin the long drive to her student house. After they left, I noticed the older ones were not looking well. They were complaining of headaches, sickness, loss of strength and tight chests. We were all beaten down with stress and a kind of grief at opportunities lost. I knew we had to adapt.

Stuart and Konya came back later in the day with the car full of her things, all of which had to be crowded into the bedroom that she shared with Jeneba when she was home. The top-floor landing was full of suitcases, and we were soon tripping over piles of music and clothes that needed washing. Stuart began complaining of a horrible headache as I was rejoicing in the loosening of mine. The older three were obviously unwell and I could see it was more than the shock of life shunting onto a dead-end track. Sheku had been vomiting, and Braimah was sullen and cross, barely able to lift his arms. Isata just wanted to lie down, and Stuart was stretched out on the settee, moaning about his head. The next day, Boris Johnson announced the coming lockdown and we all thought about their fellow student, Plinio Fernandes, alone in the flat he shared with Braimah and Sheku, unable to meet anyone in an eerie, deserted city, thousands of miles away from his home in Brazil, in a London where people were fighting over food in the supermarkets and eggs had disappeared. Nottingham at this point was relatively calm and untouched, and we couldn't leave Plinio isolated and abandoned. He managed to get to us before the lockdown and Stuart and I cooked for a household of ten.

But soon we were all miserably unwell. My headache came back with redoubled force and Stuart began worrying about his 'tightness of chest' to the point where he was unable to sleep. We all had chest pain and difficulty taking full breaths, and for a few days we all suffered such dizziness we couldn't stand up. I thought of us all crammed into the house, sharing bedrooms, bathroom space and food, huddling together around the dining table, with the virus dense and thick between us, and decided it was a good thing. We had no time to be afraid of catching Covid because we already had, and we were so steeped in its fluctuating symptoms that it was simply an ongoing reality. We would manage to get out of bed in the morning, hopeful that we were getting better, and find ourselves supine with exhaustion before lunch. Aminata took to her bed with an intermittent high temperature, and Mariatu was completely well until the end of *Paddington 2*, when she began wailing with a sudden raging fever and had to go to bed with Calpol. After twenty-four hours she was fine, and we all envied the ability of ten-year-olds to sail through the virus. Then a few of us completely lost our sense of taste and smell.

For me, this was the most long-lasting and disturbing part of the illness. For four months I felt dissociated from the world around me. The blossom in the garden outside was copious that spring. We sat on the grass and looked at the beautiful colours that the frenzied bees so loved. But all I could do was remember the heady scents that should be filling the air. The food the children cooked as they experimented with spices and peppers left no aromas around me and no impact on my tongue. I didn't know if the house smelled musty with ten bodies always home, because I could smell nothing. I washed sheets, towels and clothes simply from the framework of time passing rather than the ability to tell that they were dirty.

But time didn't pass in the way it used to. We lived in a kind of circular universe, where days were superimposing themselves on similar days and where housework was part of that circular dance. No one could visit and we were in a separate world. We realised we had to create our own sense of time. I was surrounded by young people whose drive was temporarily crushed by coronavirus symptoms, but we would all recover, and they were young people who lived creatively and drew energy from self-expression. They had to communicate and reconnect with the performance life they had lost. Sheku wanted to give live performances on his Facebook channel, including his siblings and Plinio. They had so much music they had been developing, practising, preparing for their trip to Antigua and Barbuda, for Europe, the United States and the UK. There was so much they were missing and wanted to share. In the house, there were pianists to replace orchestras, chamber music companions, solo repertoire – all could still be shared. I worried about the strain of live performance without the ritual of the live stage in a concert venue. A concert was an event that had to be travelled to, with itineraries organised and concert clothes chosen. How could they garner the energy and emotion needed for live interaction if all they had were our substandard pianos and a tiny iPhone screen? It seemed as though a Facebook Live entailed inordinate stress and no psychological preparation in an unsuitable space. I would also have to make sure the rooms were tidy. They were perfectly happy to focus only on the music that was so intensely theirs, to see and hear only their own sounds and songs, ignoring any chaos around them. I fretted about our crowded, loud and ebullient lives, increasingly eccentric with in-jokes and burgeoning habits, recklessly flung out at the world.

Before the first Facebook Live, we were still reeling from the unimaginable uncertainty of this new and temporary life, a ship afloat on our very own sea, and most of us felt unwell. The strange excitement of connecting with an unseen audience was surreal and energising, and as the clock ticked to the appointed time, I realised my heart was beating too loudly, too fast. When I look at the date of the first Facebook Live, I can hardly believe it was on 20th March. The spring sunshine is coming through every window and the children seem to gain so much energy and happiness from each other that they look untouched. Locked inside my worry for them, I hadn't appreciated at the time just how much resistance and resolve their love of music gave them. Braimah took the phone from room to room, observing a Monopoly game, piano practice, scales, and Isata and Sheku playing Rachmaninov, which he quietly dedicated to those on their own during the pandemic. I'm sitting on the stairs, watching them play and trying to keep out of the camera's eye. Watching this first Facebook Live now is deeply moving as I remember how much their uncomplicated joy drove them to astonishing days of creativity when I was still buckled with confusion.

We began with two Facebook Lives every week for the first several weeks, on Wednesdays and Fridays. These entailed a mixture of talk and relaxed observation of the eight young people playing games together or practising, but they increasingly became simply concerts. The audience wanted music and the children were at their happiest playing it. We moved one Live to a Saturday, 18th April. This was still written in the diary as the day when Isata would be playing Beethoven's third piano concerto at the Royal Albert Hall. We had bought tickets for all the family, the extended family, friends and music teachers. I had booked hotel rooms so we could stay overnight in London with my mother, sister and niece. Isata had bought a shimmering new concert outfit and I had been counting down the months and weeks. It had taken me a while to accept that this concert was not going to take place and I was still unhappy. So Isata decided to play the first movement of the concerto anyway. Jeneba, on the second piano, Braimah and Aminata on violin, and Sheku on cello would play the orchestral parts. Our grand piano wasn't strong enough, so Isata played the solo part on the upright and Jeneba was on the grand piano.

The sense of occasion was extraordinary. They wore casual clothes and were close together in the 'piano room', the space where so much of their daily practice takes place. There were no chandeliers, no great stage with tiers rising into lavish royal boxes and rich hangings. There was no box office, no ushers, no stage lights and rustling programmes on red velvet seats. But the trembling hush when the phone clicked to 'live' transmission, and the intensity of their concentration – the seriousness of the moment – created all the atmosphere we needed. Isata played as though she wore layered tresses before a Steinway concert grand and she listened to her 'orchestra' in the same way as if there were a conductor in solemn white tie and tails. We were in the imaginary space of the Albert Hall and I was so enraptured by Isata's powerful command of the music in the terrific runs and end chords, bringing in Jeneba and the strings, that it was difficult for me to hold the phone. Reams of comments were rolling up the screen from an audience spread all over the world, and I realised their music had filled a space far greater than any concert hall. During the cadenza, I found tears streaming down my face with emotion. I couldn't stop or even wipe them away as I was holding the phone for the livestream. Looking back at this Live on Sheku's Facebook page, I can see him looking at me with concern, unable to come to me in the middle of the performance.

When the movement ended and they had said goodbye to their live audience, I sank to my knees and realised that Isata had faced the loss of her Albert Hall concerto debut, the wasted weeks of practice and preparation, with a courageous generosity and authenticity that was staggering. By the end of the week, the views numbered over a million.

The children approached the Facebook Lives as their connection with a shattered world. My mother, alone in her house in South Wales, waiting for each ticket reimbursement for concerts she had booked to see them play, tuned into every twice-weekly, then weekly performance. It gave meaning to the energy the children put into learning more music, arranging melodies, adapting concerti or songs. They played chamber music versions of Vivaldi's haunting 'Guitar Concerto in D' with Plinio, 'Chances Are' by Bob Marley, Rachmaninov, Bach, Chopin. They would spend the days leading up to the next Live thinking about, discussing and preparing the music that moved them most, then put all their adrenalin and emotion into playing it to a live audience. Afterwards, completely recovered from the virus, they would go in a lively group into the garden, the late-spring evenings lengthening into long midsummer days, and talk and laugh with the performer's mixture of relief and elation.

While spring was at its loveliest, and I couldn't smell the blossom bordering our path, Sheku turned twenty-one. It was 4th April, and their original plans still hung in the air. We were still at the point where we assumed we would be on our Australian concert tour by August, and the Musicworks chamber course would happen in July. We still inhabited the persistent illusion of living a temporary life, a short, wild step into an altered reality. While mourning the loss of the places, concert halls and study venues they missed, the children revelled in this shockingly beautiful spring together. Sheku had planned a meal and night out with his closest friends and London siblings, so we created a special day in the house and garden. The sun shone on us all as we played new, invented versions of group table tennis on the indoor table we had managed to squeeze and squeal onto the front lawn. We knew the blue, painted surface might begin to wrinkle and split as time went on but we were living in a novel continuous present, like a fairyland of childhood revived, and right here, the future didn't exist.

Sheku wanted his favourite meal: palm oil chicken with spinach in our biggest cooking pot, brimming with the red oil and onions and dominating our small gas hob. Our poor little kitchen, having endured nearly twenty years of a growing family and ravenous children without being renewed or decorated, was creaking at the seams trying to serve a nearly grown-up family of ten. We had replaced the oven two years earlier, but Konya, in the early days of lockdown, managed to set it alight with cheese on toast. Following the yells, I rushed in to see the small oven, which also served as a grill, consumed with flames licking freely up the cupboard surface above and destroying the oven seal. The four-slice toaster was working only for two slices and the kettle's leaks and drips were now causing lakes to appear on the surface with so many cups of tea on the go. I decided it was just as well to have stained tiles, grubby wallpaper, peeling plaster and an inefficient hob we now had to light with matches. The kitchen was in constant, heavy use from their ambitious cooking and abundant recipes. Stuart and I battled to move in what seemed a tiny space of loud, tall, shouting bodies, jostling elbows and different stages of creative food preparation. Chopping boards scattered in continuous use and the sound of vegetables sizzling, steaming or bubbling filled the space. I was used to the smell of onions and spicy food clinging to my hair, clothes and skin, which is why I held on to the habit of fraying home clothes. But now, I could smell nothing.

Today, Sheku's birthday, the old kitchen was my domain. In the 'breakfast room' next door, which is really our only dining-room/homework room/conversation room, they had reggae and hip-hop playing at full volume and the chairs had been kicked aside for dancing. I laughed as I chopped the vegetables and sliced plantains for the meal. Soon, they were outside again on the day-turned-holiday for Sheku. I thought of all the twenty-first and eighteenth parties cancelled or hopefully just postponed across the country this spring – but this one would be happy. First thing in the morning, Sheku's six siblings had rolled early out of bed to record their string and piano version of 'Happy Birthday' for him in the piano room; Isata on piano, Braimah, Konya and Aminata on violin, Jeneba and Mariatu on cello. Sheku, emerging later, was astonished to see their lively sextet on social media, filmed before he was even conscious.

After an afternoon of table tennis, everyone crowded into the breakfast room for the birthday meal, a raucous gathering, with Plinio adding another male voice to the chorus. When we chanted the years up to twenty-one, it was with an ecstatic gesture to a future still waiting for their energy and hard work. We were in our own, private world, a new, surprising daydream in its perfect sphere, one mote of pollen on the breeze. We imagined the landing would be sudden and dramatic, launching us all back into the larger world, spiralling away into separate journeys, converging only for brief, joyous moments. Now was the moment to revel in our own glade of borrowed time with lives and careers simply on hold for a while.

The schools had been forced to close so suddenly it felt like a rejection. Jeneba's A Levels, anticipated for so long, had given way to weeks devoid of the rites of passage endured and enjoyed by the older four. The Monday after-school ritual of walking next door for her extra maths lessons with Vicki Black; the piano recitals already performed and recorded for Music A Level, along with her chamber music compositions; the books read and notated for English; these were all swept aside in a day. The weeks of hectic exams; sixth-form Prom, post-A Level trip abroad with friends (full of the traditional sunny beaches, wild nights and inevitable quarrels), an intense and joyful music course, interspersed with concerts and tours – all was gone. Braimah and Isata, running at full tilt towards their Bachelors and Masters Final Recitals, found themselves uncertainly waiting for details of remote, recorded recitals. Stuart took up stressful residence on a corner of the lounge settee to work from home in a travel and tourism industry that had creaked to a halt, the settee sighing and sinking to such an extent that it finally broke and I had to prop it up with garden cushions. We needed goals and a structure encompassing more than loss management.

Our first family project was the *Come Dine With Me* enterprise. We thought of it as we ate together, ten of us shoulder-to-shoulder at the dining table. How about a cooking competition, which, like the television programme, would involve far more than that? The four teams had to prepare a three-course meal – starter, main course and dessert – plus entertainment, all of which would be judged alongside hosting and presentation. It was the perfect way to push against the sense of days repeating themselves in an ever-complacent round of mealtimes, bedtimes, practice and table tennis. It also provided the slow beginnings of a journey back to taste and smell, opening up a rediscovered reality with each new combination of herbs and spices, offered and received with such generosity of time and attention.

Everyone approached the challenge with great and concentrated excitement. The entertainment provided could not be a music performance but had to stretch the team's skill-set. Stuart and I went first, then Isata, Konya and Jeneba's team, then 'the boys' – Plinio, Braimah, Sheku – and finally the youngest – Aminata and Mariatu. Recipe books, long left dusty on the shelf, began littering the table, open at double-page spreads of colourful dishes. Sheku contacted the chef he knew in London, Ravinder Bhogal, who ran one of his favourite restaurants, Jikoni. The menus grew ever more ambitious. Stuart and I were under pressure facing the scariest part – the entertainment – what on earth would we do?

We all had to dress for dinner, mimicking a real night out at a restaurant open for business, and Stuart and I played gracious hosts to courses far more complicated and expensive than we'd ever tried before. Our menu was so pioneering we nearly didn't manage it but our nerves mounted further for the moment of our entertainment, which simply involved reciting a poem and a story. I realised, horribly, that we were performing to professional performers; it didn't matter that they were our own children. We were generously applauded but afterwards I felt nothing but laughing relief that our contribution was over.

Each time a team presented an evening, the stakes were even higher and the entertainment more elaborate. We had a quiz and treasure-hunt, a rap with dancing and a newly scripted play. Caught together in the small world of home, the space seemed to expand with these concentrated experiments in creativity and performance. We knew it was a collective survival technique, tinged with defiance, but it was also a celebration.

The next night, after we had completed the award ceremony and congratulated the boys on their deserved win, everyone danced ecstatically and re-enacted the theatre, singing, map-making, poetry, cooking, artistry and creative word-play of the last two weeks, all brimming over with the satisfaction of giving time beautifully for others. Then it was the moment for another Facebook Live and playing the music they loved.

I existed, caught up in this close crowd of young bodies, creative energy and noise into which I arrived, washing in from sleep every morning in a vague sea-change of consciousness. The early sun through the curtains brought the humming rhythm of piano scales into the room. High violin strings tuned into the low drone of cellos and strident sentences from yet another lounge conference call filled me with a sense of crisis management. As I stumbled from a bathroom wet underfoot from several morning showers, and wiped shaving hairs from the basin, finding the imprint of a leaning Afro on the mirror glass and damp towels with traces of white Noxzema face cream, I knew I was back in the centre of turbulent family life. Music books, rosin, discarded socks and manuscript paper began sifting into corners like blown leaves, and the pile of dirty crockery and cutlery in the kitchen grew as the dishwasher constantly churned. I took to walking downstairs with the hand-held hoover, chasing dust and Afro hairs from the skirting boards, sucking up crumbs and pencil rubbings from the breakfast room and trying in vain to keep the burgeoning spider-webs and dried wood-lice at bay. Life raved in two dimensions. The first dimension was filled with the rage and passion of music and ideas constantly in flow. The other consisted of the physical reality of ten people living together in lockdown for over five months. I remained detached, on one level, from the washing, cleaning and tidying between the continual motion and volume of bodies living together. The house was like a map spread out in a film or a video game, a visual conundrum to be solved. But the emotions were real. I bumped, tripped and fell against the tangible feelings and needs they carried with them, some murmured urgently to me, some heaved silently from room to room, or out into the still sunlight.

The news seemed to skim the surface, and we fretted over the hidden debris brushed out of sight. Beneath the one, thin narrative of coronavirus infections and deaths, the one-phrase or two-word propaganda mantras we heard from TV and radio, we knew a world of meaning teemed, connections blurred, stories untold. Like a war, we were kept protected, in line, locked down, simplified. Paranoia rose around us. Newspapers abounded with stories of whispering neighbours spying from windows at someone's second outlawed exercise trip of the day, or trolley spies calling out profligate supermarket shoppers. It was tiring and claustrophobic, and we mourned the shuttered concert halls and opera houses, the theatres and cinemas, the restaurants and meeting-places. We watched recorded ballets, plays and orchestras, marvelling at the breadth of expression allowed, the depth of meaning delivered, faces and bodies communicating expansively.

I contacted my mother, alone in her house, over FaceTime. In my restless, lively world, where nothing put down would stay there, and every empty space was immediately filled, Mum spoke from the lonely tranquillity of her living room. I wondered what it must be like to fear leaving the house, the virus a real threat, not just to personal opportunities, or work and career, but to life itself. For us, Covid threatened everything we had worked for, trained for, loved and planned for years. It layered uncertainty and panic into the stories we made of our lives and put a dead end where the horizon was meant to be. But, for Mum, it threatened her life. Whenever I spoke to her, I had to step into another lexicon of language. This framework of meaning used words like staying safe, and being careful. I soothed her worry about death tolls and ventilators and listened to the sound of isolation. I knew she had emotional resources vaster than mine, but I also knew she was soothing and reassuring me more than I was her. I told myself I was concerned with her loneliness but actually I was grieving my own separation from her. I was a child again, needing her hug, angry and anxious that she couldn't come to us. The children, out of school and home in a distorted non-vacation where they had to find new spaces to work, asked if we could go 'to Mama's house' for the summer. Caldicot, and Orchard Close, had always been the safe haven for their childhood nightmares, the place to which they would strive to escape when the zombies invaded, or people's faces turned bad around them. That this route might be barred was incomprehensible. I was surprised at the depth of my grief for a mother I couldn't reach. It was primeval and saw me taken over with crying when I least expected, all the more powerful because it lived in a place of habit and complacency. She had always been there.

We started an extended family quiz every Sunday as a temporary bridge between the missed Easter gathering we had planned, and a time when all the cousins could come together again like the year before. Every Sunday at 3 p.m. saw us crammed in front of the iPad screen on FaceTime with two questions each, seeing how many others we could answer. In order for all our faces to be seen, we put the iPad on a music stand and repeatedly swivelled it round to show the questioner, or to register applause, or witness a new hairstyle, a gesture, a work of art. Mum was in one box, my sister Isata and her partner Steven in another, my niece Kadie, her husband Glenn and their six-year-old son Aneurin in another. My nephew, Idris, and his partner, Tessa, joined once with little Amiri but, with a fifteen-month-old, it proved too challenging. The temporary family gathering is still ongoing as the fluctuating rules between England and Wales have meant we've not yet managed to reschedule the Easter family party, and now the summer and Christmas parties we never had. I can emotionally manage the quiz time well, enjoying the jokes and my niece Kadie almost always winning.

We gathered outside every Thursday for 'Clap for Carers', eager for a sense of togetherness and to see the faces of neighbours. Even two metres apart, it was reassuring to call across to other family groups or couples, the street warmed up with other people. Plinio was welcomed and it was a treat to talk about the world or other things outside the magic circle of our house and garden. Vicky Manderson, our neighbour and their former Head of Music, suggested playing Klezmer music on some of these dry, long, late-spring evenings, so the children dusted off their old Trinity Klezmer group music, dragging Plinio with them on guitar and Mariatu on percussion. Jeneba played accordion and Konya and Aminata sparred with each other on violin. Vicky stood two metres away on clarinet and they played wild and dancing Klezmer music while neighbours cheered and applauded on the street.

The older girls, cut off from the Royal Academy every day, and the younger ones, every Saturday, sorely missed the pianos there. They had to play their warm-up drills on uprights or a grand piano that offered less weight to their fingers and yielded less density and clarity of sound. Sheku and Braimah rehearsed and played the earlier Facebook Lives with piano accompaniment that didn't match the voices of their own instruments and we worried about the girls' muscle tone and training.

Then Janie Garnon had a conversation with Terence Lewis at Jaques Samuel Pianos in London, having been introduced by Erica Worth, editor of *Pianist* magazine. He, incredibly, offered us the free use of a Bechstein grand piano and two Bechstein upright pianos at our house during lockdown. The girls were ecstatic and I could hardly believe it was true. When the three pianos arrived, driven and carried in on their sides by two charming Hungarian piano movers as we watched from the top of the bannisters, I marvelled at how kindness shines so brightly in times most overcast. Here, cut off as they were from the hard-won privilege of the pianos they needed to play, this generous person had decided to provide them with first-class instruments in our family home. They took away our much cheaper pianos to be stored while the showroom remained closed, and we huddled first around the beautiful Bechstein grand that stood impossibly in the bay window of the piano room, like a new Ferrari replacing an old Morris Minor. When the keys were touched each one sang, resounding in the shaded afternoon light of the room like a great baritone in a church. All the pianos responded precisely and emphatically to touch, translating the smallest of movements into meaningful sound. The children were all inspired to play on or alongside these beautiful instruments and their interpretations soared to new heights. Knowing the pianos had to leave after lockdown gave an urgency to the music, a sense of a continuous and circular present to be lived in its entirety, full in the face and whole. The music, still seeping through the walls and floors as Stuart and I sank into sleep, seemed never to cease.

The humming, intense, unchanging present left the sense of a future just beyond their reach. We were all battling a restless anxiety about life. Plans unravelling inexorably blurred the road ahead and I existed cheek-to-cheek with so much pent-up youth and vitality that I felt both inspired and guilty. I knew I was becoming possessive of them. The loss of the artistic world in which they needed to grow and the careers for which they worked so hard, as well as the wide social landscapes that young people crave, made me want, paradoxically, to draw them even closer. On the one hand, I wanted them to have the chances and perils of voyages far away, and on the other, I feared the world outside and longed to keep them protected. Stuart battled daily against a working world demanding ever new forecasts and wells of determined optimism. I admired his ability to draw strength from crisis. I seemed capable only of soothing, talking, listening, managing the practicalities of a house full to the brim with personalities and imaginations too alive to remain cramped and confined for long.

Then the BBC asked if they could come and film a day of music performance and interviews at our home, rigging up remotely operated cameras as we were still in the eerie separation of lockdown. We approached this with a new sense of purpose. It was a day-long concert and our home was the concert hall and stage. It was the middle of a glorious May, as though the halting of our race through time and space had given rein to a burgeoning summer of birds, flowers and sweet, soft air. When I took down the dry clothes from the washing line after dusk, my feet sinking into cool grass, a badger loomed impossibly and massively out of the dark, the white stripes on its face coming far too close. I had never before seen a badger and we were both as frightened as each other, lurching away in opposite directions. Unable to travel anywhere, the busy sound of cars and roads receding, we gave way to a blooming awareness of the snuffling, rustling, encroaching noises of a world we habitually ignored. The green patch outside our door grew bigger, deeper and richer as each day lengthened, and part of the performances or the programme would be here, their new concert stage.

We had to linger outside as the cameras were wired downstairs in the house. The concert would take place the next day and we would be left to structure the music ourselves while a film crew watched on screens and computers in big vans and tents on the drive. It was an early start on that Saturday morning and we were all focused, prepared and happy. Over breakfast and in the meal breaks, we forgot the silent cameras were there, nestled in the corners and ceilings, and carried on joking, laughing, playing cards and chatting. The music was taken very seriously though because they had chosen to play what they felt most deeply at the time. The youngest three played the piano trio 'Valse Russe' by Frank Bridge, where each could sing their instrumental solos in expressive conversation with each other on piano, violin and cello. The oldest three played Samuel Coleridge-Taylor's 'Deep River', a song of slavery, freedom and longing. There was a Rachmaninov piano and cello sonata, Chopin and Bartók piano solos, 'Scarborough Fair' on cello and guitar in the grass under the trees. The concert moved from piano room to hallway, to garden and back again, windows flung open so neighbours could hear, and birdsong rose undimmed between the notes. At the end of the day, the sun only a month away from midsummer, all seven children played their version of music from *Fiddler on the Roof*, the composition that had begun in that apartment in Florence as Isata and Sheku's Italian tour had stalled. The musical had been a family favourite since they were very young, and Stuart and I had also watched it as children. Its melodies, encompassing Klezmer rhythms, the haunting minor keys I associated with Welsh music, humour, tragedy, loss, migration, change and love made its music vast and complex. As they played, wittily throwing lead melodies from one to the other and layering musical ideas and themes, I found myself invited to dance, laugh, sing, marvel and mourn. And when it came to 'Sunrise, Sunset', a song of parents at the wedding of their daughter, having to accept the end of childhood and the passing of the years, I was hopelessly in tears.

They loved making the programme, with music right at its centre. They were interviewed over Skype by Alan Yentob, about music and their relationship with it. Dominic Best, the producer, became a great friend in this strange time of stasis. The final scene, with the children playing the last moments of *Fiddler on the Roof*, was filmed by drone, taking a camera from outside the open windows and upwards above the house, street and neighbourhood. The music, seven instrumental voices in a single family room, floated to fill the sunlit air, bigger and more expansive than the greatest trees and highest chimney pots. Almost drowned in the looming sounds of our small summer garden, the meaning in the music filled the sky.

In many ways, physically cut off from the world outside, we lived more closely within it. Listening, watching; every sign and word carefully examined for meaning and portent, we waited for bad news. Our own uneasy recognition of oppressive newspeak, of stories hushed and hurried underneath the surface, was daily supported by the news coming from the USA. We felt akin to those left out by a new type of citizenship unfurling across the globe, suppressing dissension and the creative arts, approving, in a slick slippage of language, further dispossession and poverty. Locked within the house, we felt more connected than ever with a wider world of tension and struggle.

Then it happened. An old familiar story, framing the psyche of a people for generations. But its visual impertinence, the stark and brutal, unblinking stare of the video, the sound of voices raised in suffering and opposition, broke violently into our lives. Watching the slow and deliberate murder of George Floyd, his

neck crushed under the knee of Derek Chauvin, was a courageous act of bearing witness, of looking directly at what made
us sick with fear. We watched as a form of communion and
because it was a duty, but it was a descent into a grim and wild
grief we found hard to contain. For ten days we each retreated
into our separate corners of thought and music. The image of
the Black man who was our father, brother, cousin, calling in
anguish for his dead mother at the end of the world brought
us up against what we, in order to live, left under a veil. Sheku
had been silent for days when, facing the prospect of another
Facebook Live, he and his siblings could not lift their arms to
play without releasing the weight of their emotion. A sense of
bereavement, unexpressed, was crushing their ability to speak.

This was a moment for all ten of us to stand together, so we
decided that Stuart and I would open the Live standing side by
side in front of our seven children and Plinio, a Black Brazilian,
immersed in the same rage and grief. I talked about our sense
of shock and sorrow, our anger that the murder of Stephen
Lawrence in London twenty-seven years before, when Stuart
and I were young, was not part of an unthinkable past but
stalked and threatened our own children's lives today. I ended by
saying: 'Today's music is a tribute to those in our communities
who have suffered from racism and racist violence, either at the
hands of police or others. Music is a testament to suffering, to
hope and to love. Let it be a testament to change.'

Stuart and I were both shaking, and everyone's head was
bowed. We walked out of camera shot and the others lifted their
instruments, hands and faces as one, and played 'Hallelujah'
by Leonard Cohen. It was their own arrangement, developed
from that of Tom Hodge, using the strings, pianos and guitar
to form a chorus of voices. It began simply, quietly, and rose to
fill the room with blended sounds, the instruments humming,
questioning, mourning and welling up in a cry of strength and

pain. I sat, crying, next to Stuart and felt unspeakable pride, and despair that I couldn't protect them from this. Sheku ended the livestream, standing with his cello and looking straight at the camera. He said, firmly and with deep feeling: 'This has been a very emotional and personal Facebook Live for us as a family in what has been a very difficult time for us all. We want to bear collective witness to the violence that divides us, and stand together with those who want change. Racism is a global pandemic that has been going on far too long to stay silent. For us, music is our form of expression, protest and hope. Love to you all.'

When the news spread that Nottingham would host its own gathering and collective witness to the events in the USA and its echoes around the world, we all turned our attention to creating banners with artwork and words that spoke to our emotions. On Sunday 7th June, we walked out of the house and down the hill to Forest Recreation Ground. Along the way, the streets began filling with people like us, carrying slogans supporting Black Lives Matter, wearing masks and walking fast. We were all full of an energy that turned our sorrow into something bigger and broader. We wanted to shout, and sing and run. We wanted to gather together and make our silence into a roar. Music was playing from the speakers and we wanted to dance. It was almost joy.

From our sunken land of day succeeding day, we had been thrown into a harsh realisation of the world that still existed. It galvanised us and I tried to stay beyond the longing to keep a protective moat around my children and our borders close. The need to work, to have structure and to keep motivated had to be supported in more than one way. Very aware of our physical restrictions, we decided to work towards a Family Olympics. Plans got underway for an elaborate midsummer tournament spread over a couple of weeks. There was running, an obstacle course, Shuffleboard (like indoor bowls), an improvised shot-put as well as races of speed and strength so that all ages could compete. We began training and I even ran the three-kilometre course a couple of times. The competition had stoked all our interest. Then we heard from Decca that the family album would be recorded in August. They would play *Carnival of the Animals* by Saint-Saëns, with new verses by Michael Morpurgo, narrated by the author and by Olivia Colman. Morpurgo's book, *Grandpa Christmas*, would also be illustrated by their playing. The mood in the house turned from the excited sparring of the Olympics to intense collaboration for the album. There were duets with Sheku and Aminata, and Sheku and Mariatu, to illustrate the lovely children's story Michael Morpurgo had written. Solos, accompanied and unaccompanied, chosen by the children as tributes to the natural world – mosquitoes, bees, birds, the sea and the summer – all had to be practised until they fully lived in them. 'The Seal Lullaby' by Eric Whitacre, arranged for all seven by Simon Parkin, was delved into, pondered over, meticulously tuned and crafted with such attention to each other that every hour mattered. The wild and mischievous humour in the *Carnival of the Animals* demanded muscular technique and a deep understanding of all the emotions – longing, pride, loss and love – in Michael Morpurgo's poems. We were waking every morning to the string and piano sounds of untamed animals, dreamy aquarium life and busy aviaries.

But the music demanded sincerity and hard work. To craft music that could make children and adults dance, sing, think and feel, that could communicate laughter, tenderness, agitation and peace, and harmonies blended to the last semiquaver, took time. Summer daylight filtered through open windows, rosin dust and birdsong on the warm air, as the children spent their time inside with bows, strings, keyboard and sheet music. The Family Olympics slowly receded into the future, and snatched walks and runs outside in the long evenings, the trees along the streets taking on a fuller and deeper green, had to suffice.

Absorbed in the music of the album, the children still existed under a heavy weight. They could walk in the roads, clear of traffic, cross the dual carriageway to the park without waiting for traffic lights, the wood and fields ahead in full view, but none of them felt free. Sheku began listening again to Bob Marley's 'Redemption Song', experimenting with it on cello. Wordlessly, it became a piano trio with Jeneba and Mariatu, and in the long evenings after a day of working on the album, all seven came together to play this song of confinement, slavery and hope. I could almost hear the words in their music: 'We forward in this generation, triumphantly'. They felt it had to be a part of the album, a testament to who they were and what the album meant to them.

The four days of recording at Abbey Road exist in their own place in our minds. Days in Studio 2, where so much music had been recorded before us, held everyone in a bond of concentration and inspiration. They brought the intimacy of the piano room into the high walls and ceilings of the studio. Jonathan Allen, the producer they all, especially Sheku, knew very well, was lively and funny – and demanded unflinching rigour. They all loved him, especially when he bought the younger ones ice creams, delicious, sweet and cold, in the hot streets outside. For the first two days, they were joined by musicians they knew well by friendship, reputation and skill, needed to make up the instruments for *Carnival of the Animals* – extra violin (Ayla Sahin), flute (Adam Walker), clarinet (Mark Simpson), double bass (Toby Hughes), viola (Tim Ridout) and glass harmonica (Alasdair Malloy). It opened up their lives again to play with vibrant, professional musicians, and the excitement was tangible.

For the second two days, Michael Morpurgo and his wife, Clare, arrived, deep in conversation with Dominic Fyfe, and a firm bond grew between us all. It was as though we had known them both for years, and we were humbled before a person who, famous as he was, had so much love to share. When Mariatu read her narration with him, acting as Mia in *Grandpa Christmas* while he was Grandpa, it was moving to see the kindness he showed to her, the solemn eleven-year-old who had so carefully practised her words. He allowed the story to be hers, even in the pronunciation of Grandpa where he simply shed his Southern inflection and adopted her accent.

Those days of walking in and out of Abbey Road studios, the bright heat on our backs and instrument cases, using the zebra crossing and walking up the flight of outside steps to the door, white with summer sunshine, seemed to us to be a beginning and a return. I sensed, in the weeks ahead, the unlocking of doors and the promise of blood returning to cramped muscles, movement possible, borders crossed. But the hardest days were coming close.

Braimah flew to Amsterdam, cycling on flat roads for picnics with Ayla. Sheku spent a week in Devon with Guy Johnston and his wife, taking trips into the August countryside and playing cello duets in open-air concerts. Then we all came together in Llangollen, in the cottage we visit every year, whose owners, Lionel and Mary, are our good friends. We walked for hours in the hills, picking blackberries from the hedges and eating ice cream in the garden. The autumn diary was filling up again. Concerts in Europe, London, Bristol, Nottingham. Jeneba packed her suitcases for her first term at the Royal College of Music, ready to pick up a new life in the hall of residence and meet new friends. Konya and Sheku got ready for their third and fourth years at the Royal Academy, and Mariatu tried on her almost-new school uniform, with the same blazer used by all the girls before her. The national message was to 'Eat Out to Help Out', to go back to work and the office, to lay the path back to the world.

Isata and Sheku played their Prom recital together to an empty Royal Albert Hall, Konya turning the pages for Isata at the piano. We could only watch on television or listen on the radio, and yet the music they played seemed more intimate and powerful than I had heard before. The camera came close to their faces and caught the intensity of their bond with each other. I felt the crackling determination of their hope for the future burning between them, the mesmerising encounter of two people who shared, wordlessly, the emotions of that music, of that year. Rachmaninov's Sonata for Cello and Piano, powerful, passionate and heart-rending, ended the recital and stayed in my mind as though I had breathed the same air and sat in the front row. This was a beginning. If music could still be played like that, and felt like that, the audiences, ready to share and respond, would soon return.

But the concerts, booked with so much hope, turned red in the online diaries. 'Cancelled due to coronavirus' started appearing again on all the schedules. Jeneba, excited to meet fellow students, was isolated behind a mask, all social events forbidden. We left her in her room on the first day, clothes and piano music piled around her, and listened to her crying with loneliness on the phone as we drove back to Nottingham. When she finally managed to meet other students, positive Covid tests in the group dragged her into two weeks of quarantine in her one small room. Instead of waking to a house reverberating with the noise, music, shouts and instrumental warm-ups of busy family life, bumping into sisters in the bathroom and brothers over breakfast, she was suddenly and profoundly alone. Flights dropped out of the calendar, teaching engagements disappeared as music courses were cancelled, and soon the conservatoires restricted students' practice time.

Miraculously, Jeneba was able to play Florence Price's Piano Concerto with Chineke! Orchestra at the Royal Festival Hall in September. There was no ticketed audience but I was able to sit and watch her play the concerto she had practised, hour upon hour, on the keyboard organised for her by Vanessa Latarche, alone in her quarantined student room. For Jeneba, having online lessons with Vanessa, who structured her practice and nurtured her self-belief, and the invitation by Chi-chi Nwanoku to Jeneba to play the concerto, drove her through those two weeks of an isolation she was not used to and for which, in a family of seven siblings, she had no emotional preparation. The concerto opens with the pianist's virtuoso statement of presence, weighted chords and dramatic runs on the keyboard that assert a sense of mission and joy. I sat up in my seat, elated. The piece is bold and moving and allows strains of African-American music to rise and sing to the surface, with moments of jazz, spirituals and folk music blending into a classical concerto. Sitting, separate from other people, masked into silence, I felt such hope for what would come.

We were also able to perform a family concert at the Barbican in London, in October, to a reduced audience, streamed live so our extended family and friends could watch. Josie d'Arby presented the concert and the evening. With all the children on stage, listening to each other as though they were back in the piano room at home, or sitting on the stairs for a family concert, it felt as though we were knitting our lives in with the fabric of the world again.

A cold November arrived and England entered lockdown again. Mariatu was allowed inside the Royal Academy for her Saturday socially-distanced lessons, but I spent the day walking the freezing streets with a fellow parent, legally unable to enter anyone's home and facing locked shops and cafés. Aminata and Mariatu had alternate weeks at Primary and Junior Academy, moving between online lessons and days on site. The family concert booked at Nottingham's Royal Concert Hall was cancelled, along with more concerts for each of the children. Lockdown ended and all our hopes rose for Christmas. I would allow myself to believe in a streamed concert going ahead only as it happened. I found I was protecting myself from this onslaught of repeated cancellations by numbing myself to the possibility of change. We bobbed violently from drowning to breath and, becoming deliberately blind to the light, I found it better to stay still.

The Christmas we had believed in, buying presents for the family we hadn't seen for nearly a year, was abruptly forbidden. I didn't enjoy the rushed meeting at the motorway service-station to exchange Christmas presents because the promised family Christmas couldn't happen. Mum, Kadie, Isata and I stood back from each other as we placed labelled bags of presents in each other's car boots and shivered in the open air. Their faces behind masks looked more distant and further away than when seen whole and uncovered on screen. It hit me hard in the chest how much I missed them and I stood with tears running down into my mask, my mouth and cheeks soggy with saltwater. I ached with loneliness, ludicrous when I had spent most of the year jostling against the bodies of my stranded children and husband. Perhaps the definition of loneliness needs to expand away from 'aloneness' to encompass love lost, love missed, the touch of particular people – taken for granted – gone.

Before the Autumn, the older ones had drifted back to a changed London, the boys and Plinio moving back into the flat they shared. Christmas was now simply our family of nine, with London shunting into Level 4 lockdown and Nottingham in Level 3. The country felt splintered and disparate so we drew closer together; food, tinsel, Christmas lights, decorating the two

Christmas trees, family games, films, and watching everyone opening presents. Our warm, old house, with darkness outside and Christmas lights inside, was a happy refuge from the world; time to talk too loudly and all at once; time to get music performances ready for a new year of longer days and brighter evenings.

One minute to midnight, at the end of 2020, we opened the upstairs windows to watch the dying of the year. Faces warmed by each other's cheeks and breath, we formed the audience to a lurid drama, the flashes of fireworks lighting up the sky in great sheets of stark light. We were all shouting, joking and breathing in the generously cold night air that flooded in from our wide view over Nottingham. For a moment, the silence outside exploded into a clash of colours and sound, connecting everyone. As the clock struck, we phoned my mother, on her own in Caldicot, and she yelled from her doorstep, deafened by the fireworks around her, glad to be propelled into shouting distance of neighbours and friends she wasn't allowed to touch. From Antigua, still five hours away from the new year, Stuart's parents and sister, Rhonda, were sitting on a sunny veranda, laughing at our Happy New Year wishes. 2021 would be better, eventually, and we were calling out to a spring and summer of unseen journeys to unknown worlds, where I would hug my mother again.

The next morning, I opened the curtain to New Year's Day, my body half-awake and head half-asleep in the middle of a washed-grey winter morning, reluctant to begin. I stayed inside, listening to Braimah tuning chords on his violin and watching several games of chess conclude on the dining table as morning dulled into afternoon. The half-dawned day sank into darkness before I noticed the transition and I'd already drawn the curtains over the same draughty windows that were wide open the night before.

Lurking in the house, we had shunted violently from midnight 2020 to January 2021, the last streaks of light dimming into day, uncertain when the older five should travel back to their studies, rehearsals, online concerts – not knowing how many more brambles and swamps were creeping onto their paths, and wary of traps and dead ends. In Nottingham, school was due to be closed for two weeks into the term, with online lessons four days from the new year, when term began. We paused at the open door, not knowing if it would creak open or slam shut, paralysed with uncertainty.

The older five were planning their return to London. Sheku had been practising the Dvořák cello concerto all through the Christmas break, and Isata had been working hard on Beethoven's third piano concerto. Braimah was looking forward to playing Mozart's G Major violin concerto and everyone was practising for the family concerts in mid-February in Nottingham and Cardiff.

But, on 4th January 2021, the doors banged shut. When the evening television announcement came that another England lockdown was beginning, we all looked at each other, bewildered. The intensity of working under pressure for a goal, fixed mercilessly in time, is a challenge. But to be left standing, suddenly, with no path and no direction plunged us into panic. As the days went on, the seven carried on practising, playing music for the concerts that waited, mirage-like, in our diaries. I walked into the 'piano room', the main music room, to listen to all of them carefully tuning passages of 'The Seal Lullaby', or to hear Isata finessing the cadenza for her concerto, Beethoven's chords and runs crashing in waves of excitement around me. And, one by one, day by day, hour by hour, the engagements disappeared. Mid-chord in a concentrated passage of Dvořák, Sheku heard that both concerts over the next few days had gone. Isata, ready to pack for her weekend away, heard that the orchestras couldn't play, and as we were finalising the last details for the family concerts, their spectres vanished from the calendar. The first working week of January 2021 saw us all on that usual diving-board into the year, stripped to the waist, trembling and ready to dive, and realising, last minute, that there was no deep and promising pool beneath us.

The school bus passes I had bought for the next two terms, useless, were tucked back into blazer pockets, and return tickets to London torn up. We tripped over presents destined to languish in unpacked corners and tried to find laptops and iPads ready for online lessons. The Christmas trees, lights no longer plugged in, stood redundant in the hallway and lounge, past 6th January, because I couldn't summon the energy to detach the baubles and pack them away in the garage. After all, what future would replace them? Wasn't the next season, the next term, the next step frozen?

In the snow and ice of a January lockdown, the album was a shining moment in that year of so much loss. I still can't think about the mass of flowers, the raucous birds or the warm sun coming through every window without the images of closed concert halls and theatres, musicians and artists watching their calendars empty of performances for which they had worked so hard. Stuart, working in the travel and hotel industry, his pay severely cut and workload doubled; Kathryn, working all night to reschedule concerts that were repeatedly cancelled; all of us huddled together to make sure the money stretched and loneliness was banished; the children constantly on screens, talking to friends who were isolated; trying to carry on working for a future from which the whole world seemed to shrink. Sheku, in the tiny autumn window of hope, was at Heathrow to board a plane to Germany, cello on his back. He bumped into a violinist friend who was now driving vans at the airport as there was no work for performing musicians. We all glimpsed the wilderness ahead and realised, even more, the importance of staying connected, of listening and communicating.

The world, intent on islands, factions and divisions, is creating so much silence. With the muting of the performing arts comes a narrowness of vision and room only for the loudest, angriest and most monotonous of stories. All of us home, close to midsummer, managed to hear, underneath the loudspeaker of official news, the story of George Floyd, an individual crushed under the collective weight of a history and politics made unrelentingly personal. His was the local story of an unimportant man, crying desperately for his mother. In that long moment, broken under a policeman's knee, he came into direct focus, recognisable and known. He represented us all.

I turn, in my bleaker moments, when I keenly miss my mum and sister; or when we face another cancelled concert, tour or event; when the path ahead is closed and the future dim, to the memory of the recitals held in a Peckham multi-storey car park, where Sheku and Isata played to the open London skyline in the middle of that desolate summer. The sun set slowly over a city deprived of music, and yet, in the concrete walls and floors of a building meant for cars and shaking with the rush of a passing train, Sheku and Isata played, with no compromise and with all their hearts, to a joyous throng of young people, rapt with hope.

Acknowledgements

THIS BOOK IS devoted to kindness. Any pain or struggle mentioned in these pages is set against the astonishing generosity of many individuals. This is a book born of the impulse to say thank you and to recognise the sacrifice and thoughtfulness of others.

Kindness appears in many forms, sometimes in gifts of time and material things, sometimes in deeds or simply words. All have inexpressible value and I am mindful of my inability to do justice to all. This page gives me the opportunity to list at least some of the names I couldn't fit within the narrative. There are many more stories to be told, much that I have left out in the interests of brevity and lucidity.

My thanks go to: Martin Downey, Lionel and Mary Clarke, Kenneth Olumuyiwa Tharp, Floella Benjamin, Louise Kaye, David Kaye, Bruce Harris, Jonathan Mould, Joanna MacGregor, Clive Wilkinson, Turner Violins, Margaret Casely-Hayford, Vanessa Latarche, Nile Rodgers, Gill and David Johnston, Jessica Duchen, Len Brown, Catherine Manson, Celia Smith, the Nottingham Soroptimist Trust and the Nottingham Education Trust. Sincere thanks to Jaques Samuel Pianos and Bechstein for their generosity during the Covid-19 crisis. And I save very particular thanks to the warmest and most encouraging agent

I could have wished for. Without Clare Alexander there would have been no book. Thanks also to my wonderful editor, Sam Carter, whose patient and intelligent guidance allowed my words to speak more clearly.

Striving, loss and grief exist only because of our passion or sympathy for others. Hope for the future rests in how we raise our children and how we listen to each other. Creativity, self-expression and communication help us all to live, and every story can be told again in many ways.

This is a tale of music, and, above all, this is a book about love.

Index

© Jake Turney

Kadiatu Kanneh-Mason is a former lecturer at Birmingham University and the mother of seven children. The third eldest, Sheku Kanneh-Mason, was Young Musician of the Year in 2016 and performed at the wedding of Prince Harry and Meghan Markle. The siblings have performed at the 2018 BAFTA Ceremony, *Britain's Got Talent* and concert halls across the country.